CHAKRAS, DRUGS AND EVOLUTION
A Map of Transformative States

By the same author:

Ashtanga Yoga: Practice and Philosophy
Ashtanga Yoga: The Intermediate Series
Pranayama: The Breath of Yoga
Yoga Meditation: Through Mantra, Chakras and Kundalini to Spiritual Freedom
Samadhi: The Great Freedom
How To Find Your Life's Divine Purpose

CHAKRAS, DRUGS AND EVOLUTION
A Map of Transformative States
Gregor Maehle

Kaivalya Publications

Published by Kaivalya Publications PO Box 181 Crabbes Creek NSW 2483 Australia

© Gregor Maehle 2021

This book is copyright. Besides any fair dealing for the purposes of private study, research, criticism or review, as permitted under the Copyright Act, no part may be reproduced by any process without written permission of the author.

First published 2021

Cover Design by Mandana Juon

 A catalogue record for this book is available from the National Library of Australia

Creator: Maehle, Gregor, author

Title: Chakras, Drugs and Evolution/Gregor Maehle.

ISBN Paperback: 978-0-6488932-3-3

ISBN EPUB: 978-0-6488932-4-0

Dedication

To all those who described their mystical experiences via language and attempted to turn them into a coherent system of thought, although knowing that ultimately, we always must fail.

Acknowledgements

To my wife, Monica Gauci, for editing the manuscript, and giving advice on political correctness. To the worldwide community of our students for continued support during the COVID pandemic. To Mandana Juon for cover design and graphics. To Barak Ben-Ezer for advice on Hebrew.

Contents

Dedication v

Acknowledgements vii

Preface xi

Introduction 1

Chapter 1: The Base Chakra And The Opiates 25

Chapter 2: The Sacral Chakra And Alcohol 41

Chapter 3: The Navel Chakra And Cocaine 69

Chapter 4: The Heart Chakra And …Ecstasy? 99

Chapter 5: The Throat Chakra And The Plant
 Hallucinogens 129

Chapter 6: The Third-Eye Chakra And Lsd 191

Chapter 7: The Crown Chakra And Mega-Doses
 Of Lsd 241

Chapter 8: A Map Of Transformative States 265

Chapter 9: The Evolutionary Pyramid And Maslow's
 Hierarchy Of Needs 293

Chapter 10: Horizontal Yoga And The Menorah 301

Chapter 11: The Spiritual Crisis And How We Went Wrong 309

Chapter 12: The Importance Of Spirituality, Yoga And The
  Chakras For The Future Of Humanity 327

Epilogue..335
Bibliography 339
Author Information 345

Preface

This book deals with the influence that LSD, DMT, Ayahuasca, psilocybin, marijuana, heroin, cocaine, ecstasy, coffee, alcohol and other drugs have on our mind, chakras and spirituality. The Yoga Sutra, the ancient defining text on yoga, says in stanza IV.1 about the relationship between empowerment and drugs:

JANMA-OSHADHI-MANTRA-TAPAH-SAMADHIJAH-SIDDHAYAH

This translates to, "Empowerment comes through previous births, drugs, mantras, austerity or revelation". The term empowerment named in this stanza has seven levels referring to the seven main chakras, which are only evolutionary stages. Each chakra can be activated via five avenues. The five avenues, being previous births, drugs, mantras, austerity or revelation, are listed in the order of difficulty of their integration. The last avenue on the list, revelation (samadhi), represents little difficulties of integration as the practitioner has performed long-term concerted practices to bring about the effect. A capability brought about through effort conducted in previous births (the first avenue on the list), is very difficult to integrate because a gifted person usually cannot remember what actions they have performed in previous lifetimes to bring about their capabilities. This book explores empowerment brought on through the second avenue mentioned in above sutra, using drugs. It looks at what empowerment on the seven chakra levels means, what difficulties of integration we may encounter, and what alternative ways besides drugs are available. The book also attempts to create a deeper understanding of the chakras and their connection to the natural evolution of life. Finally, it engenders an awareness of the different types of mystical experiences and their varying purposes for human life.

Introduction

FOR WHOM THIS BOOK IS WRITTEN

This is a book about the effects of drug use on our spirituality. This effect is linked to the psychology of drug use, but other books have been written on that subject, and as a yoga practitioner of 40 years, the spiritual side interests me most. The most frequently occurring question asked in my yoga events is whether higher yoga and spiritual evolution can be supplemented with psychedelics like Ayahuasca, Psilocybin or DMT, or whether these substances could constitute a shortcut. I cannot remember a single workshop where this question was not asked and this book will attempt to give a comprehensive answer.

I originally conceived the idea to write this book when I was contacted by a mother whose son developed schizophrenia after repeatedly using LSD. She was looking for an understanding of what was continuing to happen to her son. Family members of people who are harmed or changed by drug use often struggle with the perceived change. A map of such changes, of such transformative states, would offer them a way to understand what is happening.

As a yoga teacher, I also came across many people who had been recreational drug users and were still trying to integrate and understand these border experiences in their lives. Many were also trying to heal past hurts or overcome phobias, psychoses and anxieties, lingering on after episodes of drug use. Often recreational chemicals or plant agents were used to overcome, or come to terms with, earlier traumas.

A third possible audience for this book are users of recreational chemicals and plant agents, who are ready to listen to a critical examination of what is possible and impossible with drugs, including risks and aftereffects. I will also show there is a risk-free, safe, legal and natural alternative to drugs, i.e. the process of yoga and meditation. However, this alternative does require a fair amount of work, which is often where the problem starts.

Drug use can result from a spiritual alienation (particularly with alcohol, heroin, cocaine, ice and related drugs), but it can also have profound spiritual effects (with psychedelics), both exulted and negative. The idea that at the core of drug use lies a spiritual void, was once fringe, but today is becoming more accepted. But established yogis and meditators, without resorting to drugs, can come to a deeper understanding of what is possible through these disciplines by reading this book. The simple understanding of the effects that drug use can bring about, and how it relates to the map of our mind, can provide the basis from to embark on spiritual evolution. Far from following the latest psychedelic hype, I will also point out its spiritual and psychological dangers and the possible work ahead when attempting to rectify the arising pranic disturbances and restoration of pranic conduits.

The most important audience for this book, though, I see is all those who are concerned about the direction in which humanity is heading. It is becoming more and more apparent that our consumerist way of life is irreconcilable with the larger well-being of our planet. If our evolution is to continue, we need to learn to live in harmony with all nature. Our trajectory leads to extinction through climate change, destruction of biodiversity, exhaustion of energy resources, warfare and a pandemic of mental illnesses.

Many people accept that we have to change but which way are we to head? The yogic chakras offer a way to map our evolution up to the present and point towards a clear path for our future. They show a way to explain the evolution of life on Earth, integrating all knowledge that science has given us, with the truths we inherited from the world's religions and indigenous cultures. As in my earlier books, I explain a view of the chakras that is based on the natural evolution of life on Earth and our potential future spiritual evolution, rather than the worn-out new-age platitudes of the base chakra being responsible for "grounding" just because it's the lowest one, the sacral chakra as the sex chakra just because it's close to the gonads, or the throat chakra facilitating communication just because it's close to the voice box.

From early life forms such as amoebas to reptiles over mammals to more modern species such as primates and humans, the chakras show us a clear trajectory of evolution. The problem with science is that it cannot tell us how to continue our evolution, it can only describe what has happened up to this point. The yogic chakra model, however, also explains the possible future evolution of life. This evolution was seen by mystics, shamans and spiritual leaders down the ages, but no comprehensive map could put all their experiences into context and combine it with the evolutionary theory of science. The chakra model can do all of that. It explains all our past and shows the gateway to what is possible for us in the future. If the ramifications of this teaching are understood, the threat to our global civilization can be overcome and we can move into the future.

A MAP OF TRANSFORMATIVE STATES

Have you ever wondered how the feeling of pure love for another is connected to divine love? Have you ever wondered how the experience of pure consciousness is connected to that of an indigenous shaman?

Have you ever been confused by the fact that the spiritual experiences of a Buddha, a Jesus, a Krishna or a Moses led to such different expressions and traditions? Or that although they all admit the sacredness of live, their followers still often fall short in being compassionate towards those of different beliefs? Do you wonder why the spirituality of the above-mentioned religious leaders seems so different from the Earth-based spirituality of indigenous people? Why is it that neither religion nor Western Science seem to have much to offer towards our current ecological, ecocidal and omnicidal crisis, which more often appears to be the love child of both?

In this book I will offer a map that attempts to answer all these questions. This map will not only describe all major forms of spirituality that humans have developed, but it will also connect them to states experienced while under the influence of LSD, DMT, Ayahuasca, psilocybin, marijuana, heroin, cocaine, ecstasy, alcohol, coffee and others. The book will also show a way forward towards an integrated spirituality that avoids many associated pitfalls. I call this map a map of transformative states but will often use the synonymous term mystical states. Transformative or mystical states are technically speaking states during which we undergo an expansion of our sense of self.

INTRODUCTION

This book maps this expansion through what are commonly called chakras, a term that is shorthand for evolutionary brain circuitry.

There is great confusion in the general understanding of the chakras. There is no need to "balance" chakras and their activation is only the activation of evolutionary brain circuitry. Activation in this context means that the evolutionary function of each respective chakra becomes available to us, we thus become capable of reliably experiencing states associated with the respective chakra. An easy way to look at the chakras is to see them as seven steps on the way to cosmic consciousness. This book outlines the states of consciousness we assume when activating the respective evolutionary brain circuits, and which drug, plant agent or stimulant could typically stimulate it, including associated risks and setbacks.

A BRIEF BIOGRAPHICAL SKETCH AND HOW I CAME TO EXPERIMENT WITH DRUGS

The descriptions I am giving here are not mere theory but are born out of sustained consumption of mega-doses of psychedelics 40 years ago, during the late 1970s and early 1980s. In all my previous books, I have endeavoured to talk about myself as little as possible, partially because I'm a very private person but also because the teaching rather than the personage of the teacher should stand in the foreground. With the subject of this book, however, I have to give you some form of introduction to how I came to take the avenue described in these pages.

I seemed to have had a very odd childhood and youth. Until I was about 28, I was considered learning disabled, but later I found out this was only due to my having no interest in what was asked of me. Already during my childhood, my main interest was to seek mystical experiences. As soon as I could read, I grabbed the largest copy of the Bible I could find and read it repeatedly. I was fascinated by the descriptions of the prophets of the Old Testament because they seemed such misfits.

The first proper mystical experience I had was around the time when I was 7 years old. I was already struggling in the education system. I had difficulties communicating to my peers and family because I had nothing to say of import and a lot of what was being said did not reflect my interests. I was most happy when I was alone by myself in nature. Luckily, my family lived at the forest edge in a rural area and I usually could roam freely.

On this day, I was running alone through the cornfields. Suddenly I was overcome by an expansive feeling of happiness, which was different from my typical glum mood. I was running faster and faster, and for the first time, felt happy being embodied. Up to that point, I experienced being in my body more akin to imprisonment. The ecstatic feeling increased until I couldn't but let myself fall to the ground, where I laid spread-eagled and looked in abandon up into the sky. Like never before I became distinctly aware of the smells of this Indian-summer afternoon and of the sounds made by the birds and bugs in the air. I also have a clear memory of the balmy feeling of the air on my skin so untypical for my usual numbness at that age.

I looked up into the sky with an expansive feeling of great happiness. While I was so looking, I felt the presence of something, somebody else, a second entity, looking out of my eyes. I cannot help but resort to sophisticated metaphor when explaining this weird feeling I had, but I would not have put it into these words at the time. A big part of my subsequent life was about coming to terms, placing into context, and integrating what happened next.

When looking up into the sky, it felt like a second being looked up into the sky using the same set of eyes. There was the 7-year-old, clumsy boy of limited intellect and chubby physique familiar to me. But then there was another entity, as yet unknown that was looking past me, and out of the same eyes, up to the sky. Because I had never consciously perceived this entity within me, I briefly considered the option of being possessed by a poltergeist or demon. But this second entity was neither malevolent nor even actively influencing me in any way, so I reneged from this consideration.

As I continued watching this entity within me, its stance towards me seemed benevolent and accepting, even loving. This entity was somehow behind, or deeper than, my familiar surface self. I briefly mourned my inability to turn my eyes back into my skull to observe and see what was behind them. Eventually, I took a leap of faith, closed my eyes and let myself fall backwards into this entity, which felt like a newfound but yet somehow old friend. As I let myself drop into it, it felt like a drop falling into an ocean, losing its identity and then dissolving. I felt completely home, accepted and loved. In many ways, it felt as if for the first time in my life, I was accepted unjudgingly. For the first time, my many and obvious shortcomings seemed to be no issue at all. When curiously falling and feeling into this entity, I could sense it was infinite and eternal, that is it stretched endlessly in time and space. There was an incredible sense of freedom and expansion, dare I say oceanic ecstasy, in this. I had felt restrained, restricted, bound, hemmed in, contracted and limited my entire conscious life. Here for the first time, I felt free.

I must have been in this state of expansion for quite some time and was only finally pulled out of it when noticing the late afternoon breeze on my skin was getting cooler, hence the evening approaching. I knew that I had to get home to not run into trouble. But the greatest surprise was yet to come and awaited me on my way out of this state of expansion. I realized then this entity in which I had been absorbed was not a stranger, not somebody else, not some guardian angel, benevolent protector, or teacher, but that it was part of me. It was a yet undiscovered, deeper layer of my own psyche, my deep self.

I have to admit that it took me a long time to integrate this experience to the extent that I could use it to change my surface personality or get a reliable sense of happiness deriving from it. Contrary to common belief, these things do not just come automatically, simply from having an experience. What I learned that afternoon, was that I was not who I thought I was. I had no idea, however, what the experience meant, how I could repeat it, and how it related to my surface-self, my day-to-day identity and personality. But a lifelong curiosity was kindled. I now knew that theoretically, I could have such experiences and there was a layer to my psyche, although hidden most of the time, in which total peace, happiness and contentment was present.

Many years later, I learned that what I had seen was a typical experience of what the Upanishads (an Indian collection of sacred texts) call *atman* – the self, or *purusha* – the consciousness. It is an entity within us that is eternally free and uncreated, it is passively observing the world but not judging it. It is eternal in that regard that it neither starts or ends with the body, and

INTRODUCTION

it is infinite in that regard that it is the same consciousness, the same self, that is aware in all beings. That's why we all feel interconnected and that's why empathy comes naturally to us. But I am getting ahead of myself. I understood neither of all these things back then, but I knew that I had to find out, I had to learn. While this motivation existed already before this experience, a lot of additional fuel had just been poured on this fire.

The next mystical experience took place in an entirely different setting. It may have been a year later, I was about 8 and, as I was born into a Catholic family, I was prepared for the Eucharist. Being the person I was and being brought up in a setting of pre-critical belief, I took the proceedings quite seriously. At one point, I was sitting alone in our rather pompous village church, when I felt a presence. I look up and beheld in front of the altar a fully-fledged, crystal-clear vision of the Holy Mother Mary. She was clearly not a human and not made from matter but from light and incredibly radiating. She did not speak but from her heart went a beam of light to my heart, which resulted in me having an experience of pure love and beauty so intense that it was difficult to contain and sit through it (I was actually kneeling on a pew what made it somewhat easier).

You must be getting worried by now this book will descend into exercising religious indoctrination. It is not! What followed after the experience led to my split with the Catholic church, and instead adopting, at least for the next couple of years, atheism. The vision or divine revelation left me so excited that I ran to our village priest. That was a mistake! For mystics of all ages, the most important lesson was always to learn to shut up. The village priest would have none of it. He gave me a long and stern lecture that he himself wasn't experiencing any divine revelations, the bishop wasn't having any either, nor was likely the cardinal. The Pope maybe and Jesus Christ certainly, but low lives such as I weren't entitled to any, and therefore, I couldn't have had one.

Even at age 8, I could see in a flash what was going on. The guy in front of me never had had a divine vision and the only way for him to maintain his power over me was to talk me out of having mine. It took me not long after that to learn that in its long history, the Catholic church has burned at the stake most of its mystics as heretics. In other cases, mystics simply disavowed their statements and learned to shut up. It became very clear that the Catholic church and I should go separate ways and that henceforth I should become a freelancing mystic.

Before going on, please note how little congruency the two mystical experiences, discussed so far, possess. One is an impersonal experience of consciousness, which we would find in some schools of Buddhism and particularly in the Hindu school of Advaita Vedanta. In yoga, we call this a jnana (knowledge) experience. The second experience is a devotional, theistic experience typical of the Abrahamic religions, but also found in India in the cult of Krishna. In yoga, we call this a bhakti (devotional) experience. It would take me a few decades to find in the 19th-century Indian mystic Ramakrishna a voice of reason, who declared these experiences can indeed stand side-by-side, be different and still be one. It took me another ten years to find in the 14th century Belgian Benedictine mystic St. John Rijsbroek, a European voice of reason, who stated the same.

But back to the freelancing child-mystic Gregor, who was about to become a complete failure in mainstream education. I first delved into the study of Islam at around age 9, which was made possible because my dad had a multi-volume edition of the history of Islam in his library. By 12, I turned to Buddhism, and at 15, I studied the Upanishads and yoga. My early interest in comparative religion may sound progressive now, but believe me, I made up for it by being no good at anything else. I was a complete failure at school, I had to repeat three high school years, and by the time I completed secondary education, my classmates called me 'the ancient one'. Rather than due to my wisdom, this was due to my being the oldest person to ever graduate from this educational institution. I also had developed a reputation as an absolute weirdo. People would give me books nobody else could be bothered to read. That's how I ended up with my first copies of the Pali canon (Buddhist texts), the Upanishads and the Yoga Sutras. The two latter mystical Hindu texts remained my guiding lights ever since.

Although I intuitively understood what the Upanishads described, I wanted to experience it for myself. That's when I experimented with practices that could bring about these mystical states. Being 15 I started a simple formal meditation- and yoga practice, augmented soon by temporary isolation and fasting. I also spent as much time as possible alone out in nature, preferably in dense forests. Despite putting considerable time and energy into my practices, I felt I was not getting anywhere. Looking back, I realize this was only due to my young age and impatience. There were also very few people around, who understood what I was doing, and even fewer who could offer me advice or support. There were no mystics, sages or yogis present in Germany in the late 70s, or at least I hadn't heard or met any of them. I knew that you could find them in India but was not yet of the required age to travel to India. Postponing my spiritual freedom for several years seemed torturous. Something had to happen!

Then an older friend explained that the methods I was using, were outdated and there was a new, presumably faster and more efficient way of achieving what the ancient yogis experienced. This way was called 'psychedelics'. The terms psychedelics (revealing the psyche), hallucinogens (bringing about hallucinations) or entheogens (God-inducing) are all three tendentious. I will therefore use them alternatingly. In hindsight, there was little chance I could have escaped the lure of "faster and more efficient". The lure of "faster" easily attracts males at that age.

My friend introduced me to the books of John Lilly, Terrence McKenna, Robert Anton Wilson, Stanislav Grof, and Timothy Leary. Leary was a former celebrated Harvard psychologist who conducted a legal study about LSD (lysergic acid diethylamide) for the US government. After extensive study, Leary enthusiastically recommended LSD, but the US government had decided to make it illegal. Leary did not back down and continued his very liberal administering of LSD and other psychedelics to 'research subjects' for which he was eventually fired from Harvard. Leary then turned populist and under the epithet 'LSD prophet' or 'high priest' became one of the counterculture heroes of the late 1960s. Years later, I would twice meet Leary, and my impression was one of a person who was simply swept away by Zeitgeist. He seemed to impersonate an urge of society to break out from convention, without himself being aware where he was going, and by extension, where he was leading people. Although Leary's hippie audience believed him to be a spiritually advanced being, when I conversed with Leary, he did not seem to have had any true mystical experiences, besides being dazzled by psychedelics. This also becomes apparent in a video, which features the late Ram Dass (Leary's erstwhile colleague at Harvard, then still called Richard Alpert) and a terminally ill Leary. Here Leary expresses confusion that he never, under the influence of LSD, experienced anything he could have labelled a higher being. It is left to Ram Dass to point out to Leary that neither of them stopped long enough to seriously enquire into that option because the exciting 60s roared past so quickly. At this point, one can see from the confused and seeking glance with which Leary looks at Ram Dass, that the younger man has now become the older man's mentor.

What Leary essentially promised back in those days was that you could access any yogic state through using the appropriate drug and thus, he became the pied piper I was looking for. Leary stated in *Politics of Ecstasy*, that he practised a yoga of two LSD trips per week. Being short of any other fast-tracking alternative, I gave Leary's method a go. I experimented with psychedelics, chiefly psilocybin and LSD, over a few years regularly, of which I spent 18 months almost permanently under their influence. Completing that period, I concluded that I was not able to sustain the achieved states without drug use. I also found they made me less functioning in society and had other side effects, which I will describe when covering the various drugs related to chakras.

Because psychedelics were so-called schedule-1 drugs, they were lumped into the same category as stimulants and narcotics, like cocaine and heroin. Since the contacts from which I sourced psychedelics sold narcotics as well, I had very brief episodes with these substances, too. I quickly abandoned them because they seemed to actually contract my sense of self, rather than expanding it. However, they gave me an understanding into their psychology and the function of the lower three chakras.

Eventually, I stopped using drugs, from one day to the next, pretty much out of boredom, and because the experiences became repetitive. I then entered a phase of intense *sadhana* (spiritual practice) during which I often meditated many hours per day using various techniques. And no, I was not living on a trust, inheritance or unemployment benefits. I was simply happy to be poor, to own nothing, and do odd jobs on the side to fulfil my meagre needs.

During that period of my life, I had two powerful mystical experiences, which although it took me decades to properly integrate them, shaped my life and philosophy. Both came about accidentally and unplanned, rather than being provoked by formal meditation practice, but that doesn't really matter. Spiritual practice may not be the immediate trigger, but it still realigns our subconscious to make us ready to receive whenever the opening occurs. The first of the two experiences was caused by an accident. It was a near-death experience while being involved in a high-speed motorcycle crash. I have described the experience elsewhere in more detail and will only briefly sketch it here. While travelling on my motorcycle at over 100km/h I was suddenly hit by a semi-trailer, which changed lanes without indicating. The time from realizing that I would be hit by the truck, to it actually taking place, being flung into the air, and then hitting the ground, would only have taken split seconds, but in my mind, time stopped. While flying through the air, I had seemingly eons of time to peruse my whole life, still shot by still shot. My life floated past in slow motion while my supposed death played out, with me looking on like a distant spectator.

Similar to the experience in the cornfields some 12 years earlier, I found within myself a place that was timeless and infinite. From this point, I could watch my whole life like watching a movie. Interestingly enough, this time around, there was within me an evaluating entity that judged all actions I had ever committed with the same piercing glance I had previously judged others. And I came up short in most. I came across as an insensitive, uncaring, egotistical bully. Hurtling towards my likely death, I thought, "What a shame that I didn't know before what I know now, that life is not about me but about service to others". At the same time, there was again this deeper entity I had seen in the cornfield experience. I could clearly feel this entity had not changed, had not aged in the 12-years that had passed, and it looked at my impending death with the same uninvolved presence it looked at all the other still-shots representing my life to date.

Then the impact came, I unexpectedly survived, and was given another chance. I have to admit that it would take me another ten years to implement some of the changes this experience called for, and 20 years for the lesson to be fully integrated. I am a slow learner. Already here it becomes obvious that the overarching theme of my mystical experiences is that experience and its integration, the embodiment of the experience, are two different things. Often the two are decades apart and it would be common in human experience that the latter never comes to pass and the chance is missed. As I learned, this is even more common when experiences don't come about through our own sweat but are triggered by drugs.

The theme of delayed integration is even more obvious in the next experience, which took place a year or two later. I think it took me 30 years to integrate this latest experience and I'm probably still working on its embodiment. The experience took place after an intense period of meditation and fasting, which ultimately didn't get me the Nirvana I had wished for.

I remember feeling dejected because everything I was doing did not result in success. For the first time in my life, I felt that, possibly, I wasn't up to the task. It was a late-summer night in the forest, and I had just arrived on a clearing. I lay down on the forest floor and looked up into the starry sky. Despite my then professed atheism, I looked up at the sky, thinking, "I can't do this by myself. I need help." Then a giant presence pulled a curtain or veil from the sky, giving me the ability to look into deep reality. It felt as if a giant hand pulled a zipper across the sky, enabling me to see what truly is. I'm purposely saying "as if" because I remember noticing that my brain anthropomorphized the sensation as a giant hand, while telling me this was only a metaphor, used to better compute what was going on.

What I saw once the curtain or veil was gone, was an infinite presence or consciousness bringing forth, projecting forth, creating or exhaling an infinite number of universes and beings at any given time, while reabsorbing, annihilating or inhaling another infinity of universes and beings. My brain produced all sort of terminologies, trying to explain what I was seeing, without truly succeeding. I obviously was one of these beings, breathed out, projected forth and in turn reabsorbed. I remember there was an extended period during which I was in total awe of what I saw. At some point, then I was desperately trying to cast into words and understand this vision. Still later, I believed to have found a linguistic formula for what was going on and I raced home to my writing pad. Once I got there, all words and understanding were gone.

Twenty-four hours after the experience, I felt I had lost its essence and did not know at all what to make of it. For obvious reasons, the vision collided with my atheistic-Buddhist belief system. I was interested in nirvana or *shunyata* (emptiness) at best, and not in God. For the first few years thereafter, I found this experience disorienting, and didn't know what to make of it. Only years later formally studying yogic philosophy, and the higher limbs of yoga, that all came together and made sense. Again, the point is that an experience itself and its integration are two different things. The second realization I'd like you to take out of this passage is there is no one-size fits all mystical experience. The four experiences described point into amazingly differing directions. We must not yield to explanations that reduce all mystical experiences to one simple category. There are different types of revelations, and different strategies for life must be derived from them. But for now, I lived again in some sort of spiritual desert and realized I needed help, so at least I thought. Seeing I wasn't ready for some form of divine intervention, human help for now had to do. I was 20 years old; I was off mind-altering substances and ready to encounter my next drug, gurus. I packed my few belongings, bought a plane ticket to India and hit the guru trail.

The next 15 years I spent travelling back and forth between my native Germany (where during the night I worked in factories and drove taxis and during daytime studied subjects such as history, comparative religion and philosophy at various universities), and India, where I spent the northern-hemisphere-winters engaged in researching the various spiritual cults available. My favourite cult (I'm saying that with the cynicism one applies when looking back at one's errors committed due to the naivety of youth) was the one of the scandal-prone Osho Rajneesh, of Wild Country- fame (an exhilarating Netflix documentary). I spent considerable time at his Poona ashram but could not get myself to visit his Oregon/USA community because I was so fixated on India. I also travelled to India far and wide, visiting ashrams of Swami Vishnu Devananda, Satya Sai Baba and many other well-known teachers and cult leaders. And I spent time with lesser-known Indian ascetics and sadhus in places like Hampi, Almora, Varanasi and Pushkar. I took detours into two Buddhist sects, the Nyingmapa and the Kagyudpa school of Tibetan Buddhism, which left their mark on me.

Eventually, I became disappointed by all the occurrences in guru- and cult-land. The whole concept of guru worship is based on the idea that the personage of the guru itself is the path, and that service and surrender to the guru is what transfers mystical benefit to the student. In all cases of gurus known to me, this placed such great strain on their personalities that they couldn't escape the temptation to have sexual interactions with many of their students, although gurus usually claimed to have no desires. Many gurus also became adept at manipulating their students. When one guru received complaints from a female student because she did not want to have sex with him, the guru's reply was, "If you do not completely surrender to the guru and let go of your ego, the precious guru will disappear, and you will spend seven incarnations wallowing in ignorance before precious guru will appear again." I suppose the implication here is that occasional sex with your guru is way better than seven incarnations wallowing in ignorance.

Two caveats here: It looks as if I'm singling out Indian gurus, but spiritual authorities from all faiths and denominations worldwide have been found to manipulate their followers into having sex with them or exploiting them in other ways. It is not a hallmark of Indian spirituality but of religion worldwide. It is not just a hallmark of authority structures in religion, but the same mechanism is found in political, business, education, entertainment and military hierarchies. It is an altogether universal human problem, and I was at the pointy end of its spiritual manifestation, simply because it was the culture in which I moved.

I have also met Indian teachers who did not fall for this problem. Interestingly, they all had one thing is common: they refused to take the mantle of the guru. They were all teachers who did not place any import on their personage and its supposed mystical qualities. Instead of that, they stressed that the only important thing about them was their ability to teach techniques that the student could practice in their absence and still be successful. All these people were connected by the adage, "It is not the teacher but the teaching that is important".

Frustrated through my guru-disappointments, at the end of the 80s decade, I again washed up in the hippie-mecca Goa. Meanwhile, the hippies there had discovered ecstasy, ketamine, DMT and Ayahuasca, and I conducted another series of experiments to supplement my spiritual practices with these "new" substances. This time I had learned and most of my research projects (except for ecstasy) involved only one or two doses. Nothing I saw was sustainable in the long-term, and again integration was the key problem. While everybody talked with great respect of traditional methods of spirituality, few actually devoted themselves to disciplined daily practices. In January 1990, in the aftermath of a Goa party, I was introduced to the Ashtanga Vinyasa method of yoga. I decided to practice it exclusively to purge myself from any latent damage to my nervous system from drug use. I consider this took about 10 years of daily multi-hour asana practice. When you spend a lot of time practicing yoga, you get a good feeling about what you are up against. Most of the damage that my body sustained was from the party drug ecstasy, which I gladly took only about two dozen times. But it was serious work to repair my body.

I spent several seasons with K. Pattabhi Jois in Mysuru and the two Iyengars (BNS and BKS). Eventually, I added to my daily asana practice an intense kriya and pranayama practice and again some years later a scientific approach to chakra and Kundalini meditation. Additionally, I spent many years studying yogic treatises, some in the original Sanskrit. Again, several years later, I added the systematic practices of the eight samadhis that the Yoga Sutras and other texts describe. I have described all these practices in great detail in the first five volumes I have written. As I am writing this, I am looking back on 40 years of yoga practice, of which roughly three years were interspersed with psychedelics and recreational drugs.

THE STRUCTURE OF THIS BOOK

In this book, I have explained all psychedelic and recreational drug states as they apply to the cardinal seven chakras of yoga. You will find one chapter on each of the seven chakras, explaining in great detail the significance of each chakra for the natural and spiritual evolution of life on Earth, complete with the drugs related to the respective chakra. This includes the drug's potential as chakra activators and possible dangers such as psychosis, megalomania, and schizophrenia. When I was young, people who had no understanding about drugs gave a blanket statement akin to, "they are all bad and dangerous and shouldn't be taken at all'. Of course, few young, intrepid, independent-minded and inquisitive people will take to such simplistic advice. Today the pendulum has again swung back and everybody from psychologists, neuroscientists to tech billionaires have rekindled a Leary-esque drug enthusiasm, with the dangers and dark sides again downplayed, if not at all ignored. But our materialistic-reductionist culture is just beginning to question the progress-at-all-price bandwagon. Many individuals long ago have been bucked off this bandwagon, who are already self-medicating to deal with trauma incurred by racial, sexual, emotional, mental and physical abuse. As a result, recreational drug use, although largely illegal, is today ubiquitous. The WHO estimates that 50% of humanity have used, or are using, illegal drugs. The current war on drugs is an abject failure and is simply a war on people who need support, rather than being further pushed to the margins of society.

This book will describe the spiritual and psychological risks one takes when experimenting with recreational drugs and psychedelics. I will also not withhold any possible benefits and then provide a risk/benefit assessment against the backdrop of my personal experiences. Although the whole experiment had in my case a somewhat benevolent ending, I have seen many, who fared much worse. But the devilish picture, that the conservative mainstream paints of psychedelic drugs, is simply not true. Young people often feel that. When I was young, I could not accept warnings of people who had no true experience themselves. It is hypocritical to say that drugs are dangerous and cause addiction, and then consume drugs that cause addiction, but happen to be legal, such as alcohol, nicotine and coffee.

Through the experiences I had because of my yoga practices, I have concluded that the chakras are only a map of evolutionary brain circuitry, describing our development up to this point and further into the future. By awakening or activating the chakras, each individual can be a motor for the evolution of humanity.

Such evolution is urgently required since, as a whole, humanity is in constant strife and is now also increasingly endangering the planet. It is my firm belief, backed up through my experiences, that activating the chakras through yoga can give us:

- Inner peace by going beyond conflict with ourselves. This will manifest in our life as the end of conflict with others. Others conflict with us as a reflection of the conflict we fight with ourselves.
- An end of global and environmental destruction by realizing this entire planet, and the entire universe, is only the crystallized body of God. This makes every place, that we ever place foot on, a sacred site.
- An end of materialism and competing for limited resources, by realizing that we are living in the midst of abundance and there is enough for all of us, as long as we don't succumb to exaggerated needs.

For each chakra, I will explain what happens if it is activated in an order other than the natural one; and for each chakra, I have shown the resulting detriment, if one leaves it out and goes straight to the next one. This is what often happens when hallucinogenic drugs are taken. For example, the opening of the highest two chakras, without the previous opening the middle two chakras, can easily lead to paranoia or schizophrenia. Another typical problem arising from drug use occurs when higher chakras are blocked by using recreational drugs, such as opiates, alcohol, amphetamine or cocaine. These have been explained for each chakra and associated stimulant/narcotic. This section makes up the first seven chapters, each devoted to one chakra and the associated drugs.

INTRODUCTION

In chapters 8 – 10, I will amalgamate the findings of the first seven chapters into a cohesive map of transformative states, that explains our natural and spiritual evolution and relates to them the varieties of mystical experiences typically had by prophets of the Abrahamic religions, seers and sages of the far-eastern religions and indigenous shamans. I have also juxtaposed and placed into context my findings with authors who have previously worked on this subject, namely Aldous Huxley's Perennial Philosophy, Abraham Maslow's Hierarchy of Needs, and Sri Aurobindo's concept of horizontal versus vertical yoga.

In Chapter 11 I will explain that the multiple converging crises currently besetting humanity, cannot be solved individually (such as the tackling of CO_2 emissions independently from all the other problems), but is the results of a constantly intensifying spiritual crisis in which the whole of humanity finds itself. In the final chapter then I will present a condensed but comprehensive summary of the path of yoga as a safe and drug-free alternative to supercharge our spiritual evolution, on the way to escaping our crises and downfall.

Chapter 1.
THE BASE CHAKRA AND THE OPIATES

THE BASE CHAKRA

I have generally named the chakras by their locations (such as navel chakra), rather than their function (such as power chakra). The functions of the chakras are so complex they usually cannot be adequately summarized in a single term. This first chakra is called the base chakra, which describes its location at the base of the spine, near the coccyx (tailbone). Its main function is survival, with its modes of attack, flight and freeze. It represents reptilian brain circuitry, which is mainly in the brainstem. When I'm saying, "is representative," I do not wish to state that the chakra "is" the brainstem. The chakra is an evolutionary blueprint from which functions can be downloaded and brain structures can be formed. According to yoga, such blueprints (*dharmins*) exist independently from whether they are manifested or not. There is an infinite number of such blueprints and they are responsible, for example, for matter to know how to form hydrogen- or helium atoms, black holes or Higgs-Boson particles.

The same takes place in genetics. Look, for example, at dogs. A canine blueprint will use whatever genetic material available to form a doglike creature because it is a successful and workable design. In Australia, we used to have thylacines

(Tasmanian Tigers), before white colonialists, unfortunately, made this magnificent creature extinct. Thylacines are dog- or wolf-like creatures although they have no genetic relationship with canines or placental mammals whatsoever. Thylacines are descendants of kangaroos and are genetically almost identical with them. But genetically, thylacines differ greatly from wolves, although they are almost the same in looks and function. Nature took Kangaroo-genes and formed them into a wolf-like creature, according to an existing functional canine blueprint. In a similar fashion, the base or survival chakra forms reptilian brain circuitry and from that the brainstem. Humans (and mammals, too) share the brainstem with reptiles, with the difference that we have additional brain structures built on top of the brainstem.

To understand the function of the chakra and brainstem in humans we need to look at reptile behaviour. We could call reptile behaviour one-dimensional in that regard, that the reptile brain will analyse every situation according to whether it will aid or impair survival. If a reptile identifies an object in front of it is as food, the reptile will attack. In case of saltwater crocodiles, the female is identified by the male as food for 363 days a year, and only as mate-able for two days a year. The only other functions the survival brain has are flight, fight and freeze. If an object is considered too powerful to overwhelm, if the reptile is likely to be eaten, then the flight/fight reflex is activated. If the attacking predator is identified as faster and stronger, and flight or fight therefore as futile, the freeze reflex is activated, that is, the reptile will act as if it is dead. Since the survival brain acts predominantly on fast movement, playing dead is surprisingly efficient and often, the attacker will simply move on.

CHAPTER 1.

In the human and in mammals, too, in great danger, the more modern, higher brain centres are short-circuited, and all energy is wired into the survival brain, which can then act faster and with greater power. It is surprising with how much speed and accuracy reptiles can move when attacking or when threatened. The same is the case for mammals and primates, when in survival mode and therefore under the sway of the survival brain. For us humans, this is a two-sided blade. In survival mode nerve signals are not wired for ethical consideration through the neocortex. Without the neocortex slowing us down with complicated ethical inquiries we may perform acts of great bravery and "heroism". When later investigated by a war-crimes tribunal, the very same acts may then be labelled as war crimes. I'm not saying here there is something wrong with acts of bravery or war crimes tribunals. What I am saying is that to succeed on the battlefield, we train our armed forces to not engage in long inquiries about the right or wrong of a particular tactical operation. Otherwise, they would be at a significant disadvantage compared to an adversary not engaging in such inquiry. However, the war crimes tribunal will rightly engage the neocortex (the part of the brain conducting rational and ethical inquiry) in their considerations into the rights and wrongs of a situation at hand. While the tribunal may take months to conclude, defense personnel have to decide in a split second.

All available energy will be wired straight to the survival brain in a life-threatening situation, so any higher brain circuitry for the time may be suspended. After the danger has passed the higher brain circuits and centres will again activate. A person in which these centres scarcely or never activate in common parlance is called a psychopath. If we consider that although human, a psychopath is primarily guided by the base chakra and thus reptilian brain circuitry, we are not surprised to find human psychopathic behaviour to be similar to that of reptiles. Psychopaths have a high tolerance of stress and danger, a lack of empathy, guilt and shame, they have high self-confidence, are very assertive and have poor impulse control. Their underutilized mammalian brain circuitry makes it difficult for them to develop deep, rewarding and lasting personal relationships. They look down on the usual import given to such relationships and as a result often come across as mean, calculating and cruel. When dealing with them, one may interpret their gaze as cold, reptile-like and their behaviour as manipulative and conniving. Psychopathy has sometimes been associated with injuries to the prefrontal cortex (the most recently developed part of the brain) that processes moral judgement.

While the base chakra is obviously key to our survival, its activation is caused by fear. The more fear we experience in our life, and especially during childhood, the more we will be under the sway of the survival brain, that is our decisions will be affected by it. We need to consider this when thinking about cultures in which people grew up in permanent warfare, never knowing peace. If you lived your whole life in permanent warfare, you are wired for fear and its viable response strategy, attack. Many areas of the world, including parts of Africa and the Middle East have, because of colonialism, during our lifetimes never known peace. We may tire of reports of renewed barbarities from these areas, but if its inhabitants have been drafted into, or closely witnessed, acts of war from as early as four years of age, then we can commit ourselves to an ongoing effort to return these areas back to peace. Also understand that sometimes these countries are kept in permanent warfare to aid resource extraction, which helps to maintain the extravagant lifestyle of the Western middle class. This is an important issue to develop further, but it is beyond the scope of this book. However, as spiritual practitioners, whether utilizing drugs or not, we must ask ourselves to what extent are we complicit in keeping significant swathes of humanity (and other species) under the sway of the survival brain.

We need to also inquire into the role of the base chakra and the survival brain for politics. Ultra-right-wing populist leaders often have an uncanny instinct to manipulate the survival brain of their electorate for their own benefit, a strategy that could come straight out of the psychopath scrapbook. Although the template for this strategy was provided by nobody else but Adolf Hitler, since his days it has been copied over and over again. Hitler was the democratically elected chancellor of Germany, but initially, his powers were still kept in check by the parliament. Hitler had his own thugs set fire to the Reichstag (the building that housed the German parliament), but then claimed that foreign terrorists performed the attack. He said that German society was under constant attack from all sides and would descend into chaos and anarchy unless he was given sweeping powers. Being frightened and in a state of fear, Germany installed Hitler with sweeping powers to become its saviour. From that day onwards the "Führer" led by presidential decree, and without parliamentary supervision, and it was him and not foreign terrorists, who lead the country to its downfall. This episode is not confined to history but repeats itself with astonishing regularity around the world. We need to learn history's lessons, so they do not need to repeat themselves over and over again. Being reduced to fear, the function of the base chakra, we are open to manipulation, not just as individuals but also as a society.

For the yogi, the base chakra is important for the function it confers, survival, and because it is the seat of the Kundalini, the divine creative force. Think of the chakra as a potential and the Kundalini as the fuel that powers its function. The function is only then permanently available if the Kundalini is lifted to that particular chakra; hence fuel for the engine of the chakra is provided. Every time we lift the Kundalini to a next higher chakra, our sense of self will expand. For example, at the base chakra, our sense of self includes our body only, whereas at the next chakra, the sacral chakra (which powers mammalian brain circuitry), our sense of self expands to include our greater family. So reptiles may eat their mates and progeny, whereas mammals may readily die defending them.

But tragedies and certain drugs can contract and reduce our sense of self back to the base chakra. These themes will be explored in upcoming sections and chapters. An important factor in preventing the spiritual evolution of our civilization are cultural memes, such as social Darwinism and the selfish-gene theory. According to these memes we are here to maximize our self-interest and are to act egotistically if we want to survive. Whether Charles Darwin and Richard Dawkins intended this is not discussed here, but these teachings deeply entered into, and transformed our culture. If you watch reality TV today or any sports program, you notice that young people believe that they need to act selfishly and competitively to get ahead. This is, however, a learned behaviour induced by the belief that our purpose here is simply to compete to survive. In stark contrast to this pattern is worldwide indigenous culture, which until a few millennia ago populated the entire planet and there are still over 300 million indigenous people on Earth right now. Indigenous people generally act in the interest of the social and natural framework around them, and selfish behaviour is discouraged. That is why their cultures have survived so long and have protected the natural world around them, instead of exploiting it like modern humanity.

Unfortunately, large parts of our education system are still based on promoting competition between children instead of cooperation, which reduces them to the level of the base chakra. The base chakra is necessary for our survival, but to become truly humane and a fully integrated human being we need to go beyond it.

Reptiles, being ectotherms (cold-blooded), do not enjoy closeness with each other and cannot warm each other, as mammals, primates and humans do. Reptiles do not experience emotions in the way mammals and humans do. Emotions are created through closeness and physical contact. And humans have aesthetic, cognitive and transcendental needs (as Abraham Maslow pointed out) and to place too much emphasis on our oldest brain structure and its associated survival needs has unfortunately created a culture in which behaviours associated with survival (such as psychopathy in business, politics and entertainment) are normalized.

THE BASE CHAKRA DRUG: OPIATES

The stimulants for the base chakra are the opiates, such as opium, morphine, heroin and the synthetic opioids. Those under the influence of heroin often merely act from the survival instinct. The particularly damaging effect of the opiates is not that they close the first chakra (although this may happen after prolonged addiction) but more that they draw all available energy towards survival and often effectively close the upper chakras. The opiates do this so effectively that they cut off and burn your spiritual antennae and make it very difficult for you to have any meaningful and fulfilling meditation and spiritual experiences. They also make it difficult to have fulfilling relationships with others (directed by the 2nd chakra), be a leader or succeed in society (operated through the third chakra) or the functions powered by the even higher chakras. I'm saying 'difficult'. What I'm not saying is 'impossible'. As with all drugs, so also here, strong-willed individuals can overcome the inherent tendencies of these drugs, become long-term users still be functional. The stronger a mission in life a person has, the more likely they are to overcome the inherent tendency of a drug.

The opiates draw you furthest away from the Divine and make it the hardest of all drugs to connect to the Divine within you. While this may sound terrifying if you are an opiate addict, fortunately, you can manage it once you understand this mechanism. Understand that when recovering from an opiate habit it will take longer for you to reclaim spiritual experiences. If you use meditation or prayer as part of a program to get over your addiction, factor in that spiritual practices initially will not reveal to you as much as you hoped for. They will eventually, but the time delay is longer than with other drugs.

Families-ties are strained to the max when opiate addicts steal from other family members, which I have often seen. Through such tendencies, opiate addicts often destroy their support network and vital relationships. This is a typical effect of heroin's ability to close all but the lowest chakra and close the second chakra responsible for family relationships. Supportive family members need to see that coming, and rather than

CHAPTER 1.

judging addicts, pre-empt the situation by getting money out of their reach. If you grant an addict access to your money, you are provoking this behaviour, rather than helping them.

It is quite challenging for me to write about this, but there was a time when I used myself as a guinea pig for a heroin trial. At the time (early 80s) a popular theory claimed that one would be vulnerable only to opiate addiction when the bonding with one's mother was disturbed via trauma in early childhood or even intrauterine. Because the infant connects to the mother primarily via feeding through the oral orifice, Sigmund Freud used the term oral phase for the period during which the infant is primarily imprinted upon by the mother. However, the breastfeeding is just a symbol of the unconditional love, support, affirmation and appreciation a mother ideally gives the infant. This affirmation makes the infant grow up with the basic concept it is good, wanted and that the world is supporting it. During this phase, the infant depends heavily on its need for sustenance. When there is no complete bonding between mother and infant during that period, the theory goes, the infant remains unfulfilled, and relives hankering for oral and sensory satisfaction during their entire life.

It would be unfair to lay responsibility for the downfall of their children at their mother's feet. It is senseless to blame individual mothers for incomplete bonding with their children, when our entire civilization does not encourage mothers to do so and does not give them the support either. How could you give your children the support if you are a single mum and even with a father at your side, your children will still spend too much time away from their family. If you watch tribal and indigenous cultures of the world dealing with their infants, you will see we have bought industrial, technical and scientific progress at a high price. The ruling scientific paradigm we live in a neutral, meaningless, purposeless, cold universe that doesn't care about us, makes it hard to then turn around and love our children to bits.

In the days of my youth, the going theory regarding heroin was, that if during the oral phase the bonding with the mother was not completed through ample body contact, nursing, breastfeeding, affirmation, etc., then the child would acquire an oral defect. Thus it later became open to addictions, particular to opiates. Heroin especially constructs a chemical cocoon around you that, in its intensity, reminds you of the time in your mother's womb. If in your early infant years you did not experience a similar feeling of being carried, protected and supported through close contact with your mother, you may then long so much for the original safety of the womb, that you may try to emulate it through the only thing that can give you a similar strong cocoon feeling, heroin, or similar opiates.

But so the theory said, a person that did experience a complete bonding with their mother during the first few years of their life, was in no danger of becoming addicted to heroin. I did consider myself lucky enough to have had experienced such an early childhood and tested the theory with myself as a test specimen. From all that I ever heard about the experience that heroin provides, I have to add that I was not in the slightest bit interested in it. I scheduled a trial of daily consumption for two weeks (so addiction could set in) and smoked the opiate as I found injections unhygienic. I used so-called brown sugar during those two weeks, a somewhat dirty derivative of heroin not considered fit for injecting. As expected, the actual drug experience was anything from fascinating or endearing. Instead of the psychic expansion and feeling of limitlessness that some

CHAPTER 1.

psychedelic drugs produce, the opiate made me contract into an almost embryo-like state. It wasn't really a pleasant state as I'm used to interacting with my environment freely. I spent a fair amount of time on my bed curled up in an embryo-like position and showed little interest in what was going on outside of me. My self-awareness was most of the time restricted to what was going on under my skin and I was identified with my body. The state reminded me clearly of the concept of the body as the 'soft machine' in the writings of William S Burroughs or the drawings of so-called 'bio-mechanoids' of the painter HR Giger. Both of those artists were outspoken opiate users.

It was a state, which I did not fancy to continue any longer than necessary. My initial theory was proven valid in so far as I got off the drug at the set date, and since then have never in the slightest bit desired a repetition of the experience. In hindsight, what I did was a stupid experiment, but I came out lucky. I seem to be a relatively strong-willed person and do not develop addictions. I have on several occasions fasted for several weeks and the withholding of sensory stimuli has been almost a sport for me. I also have a strong affinity for Hindu asceticism, and self-abnegation is a natural tendency for me. Maybe I was simply lucky. Now, almost 40 years later, the craziness of my actions back then is apparent.

There were some physical withdrawal symptoms present, but they did not present an unsurmountable obstacle. What I had not factored in, however, was that my spiritual lucidity had become vastly reduced and remained so for over a year. I had no inspired meditation experiences, and I did sometimes ask myself whether this would ever change or whether I had permanently damaged myself. I had a very clear image that the opiate had burned off my spiritual antennae and while I dimly sensed that the quality of the world had not essentially changed and the love of the Divine was still somewhere there in theory, I just could not feel it relating to me anymore. This state was quite agonizing and painful and during the next year my thoughts circled between nihilism, existentialism, cynicism, agnosticism and rationalism. The feeling of being in love with life was gone.

Fortunately, my spiritual antennae eventually regrew, and my meditation took off again but not before more than a year had passed. Life was empty and strangely unfulfilling. Spiritual antennae sounds strange, I know. But this is exactly how it felt. For most of my life and even from early childhood on I felt strangely connected to the world. I always felt as if all living things and even all inert matter was communicating with me, as if one common intelligence was speaking through everything. After the heroin experiment, this was gone. For over a year, I walked more or less alone and cut off through a dark, bleak world, that was out to get me. Other people were at best competitors for limited resources, and at worst, a threat. I also found it difficult to make any satisfactory emotional contact with others. I felt about as cut-off from anybody else as I was from nature. Looking back, this gave me an understanding into the workings of the base chakra, reptilian psychology and those who were or are under the sway of opiates, but I wouldn't say it was quite worth the risk.

Another mechanism that can activate the base chakra is extreme fear. Usually, the next chakra, the mammalian chakra, ensures that, for example, a mother will protect her children even if she risks her own life. Similarly, a male will usually protect his female and his children and even risk losing his own life doing so. Extreme fear can short circuit all other chakras and keep only the base chakra active. The most extreme situation to trigger the base chakra is war. The situation becomes even more toxic if we combine war with opiate consumption. One of the most notorious morphine users of history was Hermann Göring, 2nd in charge of the Nazi hierarchy and architect of the holocaust. Part of the Nazi doctrine was that it reduced humans to bodies and discounted that a human is an eternal spiritual being, a reflection of God's consciousness. Having reduced people to bodies, it becomes easy to judge them merely by their physical appearance or make-up and then we are not far off from wanting to breed people like cattle.

I believe that his opiate addiction made it easier for Göring to ignore his feelings about what he was doing. Now I'm not saying you will turn into a holocaust architect from using heroin. What I am saying is this substance has strong spiritual repercussions that people do not factor in. When you recover from addiction, you need to consider that and give yourself time to heal. People drawn to opiates are usually so because they find the pain of being unbearable. They also often feel separated from the affirming principle, the mother principle within us. This often is a lack of self-love.

The only exception to take opiates would be if you are in extreme pain, for example, from a terminal disease, such as cancer. In this case, don't hesitate, as there is no glory in being eaten alive. When terminally ill, we can preserve or regain our spirituality even under the influence of opiates by disassociating from the body. There is a fascinating report of that in Anita Murjani's book, *Dying To Be Me*. I would not suggest this experience with opiates can easily be transferred to situations when not terminally ill. I found that out personally when wrongly diagnosed with AIDS and will report on it later in these pages.

Gabor Maté, in his excellent book *In the Realm of Hungry Ghosts*, argues that opiate addiction is a way of managing one's emotional pain. As the statistics show, addicts often in their early childhood experienced sexual abuse, domestic violence and other forms of trauma. The more ACE's (adverse childhood experiences) you had during your childhood, the higher the statistical likelihood you become an addict. At the time of writing this book, the understanding that drug addiction is not a legal issue, but a mental health issue, is only slowly percolating through society. The so-called war on drugs is really a war on people, and as Dr Maté says, we are only traumatizing even further the already most vulnerable people in society.

To inoculate people against opiate addiction, therapy must fill the spiritual void and emptiness that leads people into the clutches of these drugs. In Carl Jung's words, therapy must restore a person's spirituality. For that to happen, we must stop indoctrinating people with the dogma that life is a purposeless and meaningless accident. Another important point would be, that whenever we are refusing a community the resources, they need to create a loving environment for their young, we are creating a new generation of addicts. A mum and a dad alone cannot prevent that. In our society, communities are destroyed via urban displacement. This creates social disruption and more addiction.

I want to complete this article on heroin and opiate use by summarizing the views of an author who are completely contrary to mine. Dr Carl Hart is a Professor of Psychology at the Columbia University and a neuroscientist. In his book *Drug Use For Grown Ups- Chasing Liberty In The Land of Fear*, Dr Hart describes not only his own recreational heroin, cocaine and ecstasy use but also the view he is a better person for it, more caring and more empathetic. Hart quotes studies that show that less than one-tenth of all opioid users will become addicts. He also shows that each year in the US 40,000 people die due to cars, guns and alcohol, respectively, but nobody suggests making these illegal. Only 15,000 people per year die due to heroin and most of these deaths, says Hart, are due to impurities in the drug, which could be avoided if heroin was legal and obtainable through pharmacies. Hart skilfully points out many hypocrisies of the so-called war on drugs, such as the fact that while most users and dealers are white, in the US, 85% of those incarcerated are black. While Dr Hart appears to be a very caring and sincere person, I nevertheless found his book a hard read. Some people just seem to have a strong constitution and psyche and drugs seem to do them little harm. Carl Hart seems one of them and so was I in my younger days. But I saw many people dying from drugs and the drugs seemed simply stronger than them. If you read Hart's *Drug Use For Grown Ups*, I recommend reading it back-to-back with Gabor Mate's, *In the Realm of Hungry Ghosts*. This gives you a view of the problem from two angles.

Chapter 2.

THE SACRAL CHAKRA AND ALCOHOL

THE SACRAL CHAKRA

The name of this chakra is derived from the sacrum bone, to which it is adjacent. In common parlance this chakra is called the sex chakra, and although that is part of its function, this term does not do justice to its complexity. Some anthropologists have hypothesized that complex human emotions occurred because changes in the human pelvis allowed the human female to turn around during sexual intercourse and look the human male in the eye. A close emotional bond between both partners was formed through this new intimacy, further enhancing their commitment to their offspring. We will return to this subject later when talking about harnessing the power of sexual intercourse for spiritual evolution.

The sacral chakra is the blueprint for mammalian brain circuitry, which anatomically expresses itself as the limbic brain. Amongst other things this chakra gives us the ability to closely care for and raise our children, something that reptiles spend little time on. Reptiles may lay huge clutches of eggs, but because their offspring are left to fend for themselves once hatched, few survive. The long-term close relationship that mammals, and even more so humans, have with their children is what has made us so successful.

Often, mammals, to raise their young, become involved in complex family and group dynamics. Wolves, for example, form packs in which often only the alpha individuals are allowed to procreate, but all members of the pack contribute to raising the offspring of the alpha couple. They are rewarded with the security and greater chance of survival that the pack offers. Claiming and defending a territory with one's group or family, is directed by this mammalian chakra. As humans, our territory may not just involve physical space, but also includes professional, emotional and intellectual territory. For this to work out, mammals and by extension, primates and humans, may organize themselves in hierarchical pyramids topped by a leader, whether this is in the political, business, military or sporting arena. Following a leader, called "being a team player" in corporate talk, is a capacity conferred by this sacral chakra. Being the leader is conferred by the next higher chakra, the navel chakra. These two chakras are closely interlinked, as we will soon explore.

The sacral chakra led to the formation of the limbic brain, i.e. the mammalian brain, which made us social animals. Having a limbic brain gave us the ability to enjoy each other's company (reptiles don't hang out with each other), and to enjoy touch. Humans typically recharge by being in the presence of family and friends. This function is enabled by the mammalian brain, which defines our sense of self by who we are, in relation to others and the collective. For example, I may feel good about myself if I consider myself a loving husband, a supportive father, and a breadwinner for my family. This belief in myself may incur dents, if my family communicates that they consider otherwise. This is because as a mammal and primate, my sense of self does not solely arise out of myself, but of my environment and the community around me, too.

One of the most powerful functions of the sacral chakra, and by extension the limbic brain, is that it allows us to manufacture a collective sense of self by recycling collective emotions. The evolutionary purpose of this is to weld individuals together as a pack, pod, pride or group, and to succeed as a collective. The mechanism by which this is achieved consists of obtaining a common sense of self. For example, I may define myself as a fan of a particular music outfit, and may derive a collective sense of self by going to concerts of that band, and then continue doing so by listening to their albums with friends. Another typical example would be that my sense of self is enhanced by considering myself part of the smart crowd because I use a particular brand of computer or handheld device, or barrack for a particular sports club.

More private examples would simply involve us getting together with our friends. When friends get together, they often do so with initially very different emotional charges. One person may arrive looking worried, stooped over, grey in their face, nervously looking around and gesturing agitatedly. Upon observing their interactions with their chosen group of friends, we may notice that postures, facial expressions, breath rhythm, tone of voice, etc., change until they reflect that particular group's average. The mechanism at play is that the group picks up the emotional state of the newcomer, or person in need. By duplicating her emotional state (through imitating its parameters) and then feeding it back to the newcomer, the group shows concern, acceptance, compassion, love and ultimately, that the newly arrived individual is part of the group. The emotional state of the newcomer is recycled through the collective, and with that, the newcomer experiences they have been seen, accepted, supported and loved. The next step then is that the accepted newcomer now adopts the common collective emotion of the group. The group has achieved this by recycling and equalizing their emotional charges. Once individuals depart from the group, to go about their own activities, they feel they are a valued part of a collective. The mechanism by which this is achieved, importantly is not human language, such as verbal solutions offered to problems. The mechanism consists solely of non-verbal communication, which is facilitated by our mammalian brain. The sacral chakra and the mammalian brain enable us to cycle and create collective emotions.

On the positive side, this forms a strong bond between groups of mammals or humans. We cannot live without this interaction, and it is an important part of our mental health. On the downside, the group to which we belong can censor, manipulate, or enforce behaviour by refusing to recycle emotions with us. We all are familiar with the phenomenon of rejection. We experience rejection, when those that we are emotionally close to, refuse to duplicate our emotional state, i.e. refuse to pick up non-verbal cues from us and feed them back to us. Through this method, any group of mammals, primates, or humans controls the behaviour of its individuals. To some extent, this is necessary for the group to function, but it is this very same mechanism, the refusal of acceptance and resulting rejection, that is used among humans to manipulate.

Acceptance and rejection today are playing themselves out on social media, rather than in direct interaction. Social media is so successful as a business model because it addresses the sacral chakra, and with it the limbic brain to a much greater extent than the neocortex, which performs rational processing.

CHAPTER 2.

There are now reports of people becoming so obsessed with the reaction they get to their posts and photos on social media, that their psychotherapists have to ask them to delete their social media accounts for mental health reasons. Some people take this step themselves to prevent further damage to their lives and minds. Especially teenagers are at risk. In this context, it is interesting to note that the brains of teenagers are wired so they obtain a dopamine hit, when obtaining the approval of their peers. That's one reason why teenagers desperately try to be seen as cool by their peers but may disregard to a great extent what their parents have to say.

The key word for the sacral chakra is connection, and in particular, emotional connection. A disfunction or blockage of this chakra leads to emotional disconnection, such as the disability to look someone in the face, understand their emotions and respond appropriately. We may then feel socially inept and awkward, and incapable of sustaining rewarding relationships. In this scenario, we will find it difficult to read, interpret and respond to other people's non-verbal communication, such as pitch of voice, posture, facial expression, etc. Some people have this pathology from childhood, but a mild version of it can be brought on through habits and occupation. For example, obsessive study, particularly of very abstract scientific subjects can bring about that life energy (*prana*) is wired from the sacral chakra to the throat chakra (the fifth chakra). The same can happen in a person extremely devoted to artistical pursuits, or to spiritual practice and mystical experiences. In these cases, the throat chakra (and in case of the mystic, often the sixth or even seventh chakra) will take up more life force from the sacral chakra. We may get less proficient in social interaction, and less comfortable in large crowds, or in front of the camera. The other side of that coin is that a person who is very outgoing, extravert, and a crowd-pleaser, may not be able to wire enough life force (*prana*) into the throat chakra. Because that *prana* is already taken up by extraversion and social intercourse, they may find it difficult to become outstanding at science, art, or mysticism. There is a natural trade-off here, as these three disciplines demand a certain introversion, i.e. to be comfortable to spend long hours in one's laboratory, library or studio with little social interaction.

When you look into the history of mysticism, you will find that most mystics, including Moses, Jesus, Muhammad, and Buddha, spent lots of time in seclusion, often in the desert or mountains, to purposely distribute life force away from the sacral chakra to the higher chakras. A way to integrate this trade-off into a modern life, may be to follow a certain rhythm with times of introversion followed by periods of social integration. In my own life, I feel that after intense teaching tours, I need time in seclusion in nature to recharge. Again after a few weeks in nature, there is an automatic urge to go back out to share. This reflects a rhythmic life force (*prana*) distribution between the sacral chakra on the one hand, and the throat- and third-eye chakras on the other.

There is actually a rhythm in the body that does connect the sacral and the third-eye chakra, and that is the rhythm of the cerebrospinal fluid (CSF). The sacrum, if floating properly in the sacroiliac joints, performs a bowing or nodding movement, called nutation, and the reversion of this movement is called counternutation. These subtle movements turn the sacrum into a pump of cerebrospinal fluid (CSF). CSF not only massages the brain, makes it pulsate and supplies it with nutrients, it also connects the sacral chakra directly with the third-eye chakra, in a CSF-filled cavity in the brain, the third ventricle. In this way, CSF and the sacrum are directly related to the phenomenon of Kundalini, the *pranic* force that resides in the two lower chakras and powers spiritual evolution.

The name sacral chakra comes from the sacrum, the sacred bone, a name formed in ancient Greece. The ancient Greeks considered the sacrum as the seat of the soul. We may assume that the Greeks understood the fact that the movement of the sacrum is linked to what in India called is Kundalini (another term for *prana*/life force, used when ascending). With the base chakra, also the sacral chakra is a seat of Kundalini energy, which needs to be conducted upwards to experience spiritual breakthrough experiences. The sacral chakra is named after the sacrum because the sacrum actually houses the chakra. If you look at the sacrum from the side, you will notice it curves, a curve that forms at its front a convex hollowing. In this hollowing, the *brahmaguha*, cave of Brahman, the sacral chakra is located.

There are two more reasons this chakra and bone may be called sacred, and they both are related to procreation and sexual intercourse. According to the Vedas, when we enter life, we incur a karmic debt to our ancestors for their service to deliver us a body. The most straightforward way to discharge this karmic debt is to pass on the torch of life and have children. Having children is really about learning selfless service. Our parents served us selflessly and we pass on this service to our children. This means that child-rearing actually has a profound spiritual dimension. In this complex, modern world, we must also consider that the single-most carbon-intense decision we make in our whole life is to bring more people onto Earth. We can ensure the continuation of the biosphere only if we simultaneously address the twin problem of overconsumption and overpopulation. The increased space a growing humanity demands, we are taking away from other species, which are plunged into extinction. I am not suggesting here that procreation in our times is inappropriate. And no person should deem themselves in a position to make rules on who is and who is not entitled to procreate. However, we cannot attempt to relate to pressing issues from positions established when 0.1% of today's human population roamed the Earth. I am attempting to create a nuanced representation of this complex issue, so individuals have as much information available as needed to make a high-quality decision.

The other function making the sacral chakra sacred is sexuality. The late psychologist Wilhelm Reich said that sexuality is not a function of procreation, how it is generally seen, but that procreation is a function of sexuality. At first this seems to be a baffling statement, but we need to remember that sexuality is unnecessary for procreation. Enough species have found methods less time- and energy-intense. However, according to the ancient *Brhad Aranyaka Upanishad* (IV.5–6), a husband-wife relationship acts as a device 'to recognize the Brahman, the Divine, in one's partner'. This is the secret of so-called sacred sex. It is not a method involving fancy positions or changing partners, but a discipline employing sex combined with awareness in a comitted relationship to increase the loving bond between two partners, until both can see the Divine within each other.

That is why in yoga there is such emphasis placed on the term *brahmacharya*. The term is etymologically not linked to sex, but means seeing the consciousness, the divine self, everywhere. It came to mean "having sexual intercourse only with one's lawful partner" (*Vasishta Samhita* I.44) because the close emotional and loving bond required for sacred sex is impossible in a promiscuous setting. I am not saying that from a position of theorizing. In my late teens, I was a member of the Rajneeshie movement, where free love was the norm. While such a setting may be "fun", which is the prerogative of youth, it is not conducive to recognizing the Divine in one's partner. This is an advanced spiritual discipline, and requires commitment and a level of intimacy and trust, that cannot be created when espousing multiple partners.

To understand that on a deeper level, we have to look at one of the Sanskrit terms for sexual intercourse, *karma mudra*. *Karma mudra* means seal of karma, and this name is used because sexual intercourse seals a karmic bond, let's call it a karma-collective between the two partners. On a *pranic* level, this can actually be "seen" because the subtle bodies of both partners are connecting with silver strings or bonds, which in common parlance are called heart strings. Many of us are familiar with the fact that a traumatic relationship break-up can feel as if something within us is actually breaking or tearing apart. This feels so because it actually does! This breaking and tearing of heart strings can easily take a year or longer, and I have seen cases of people, both male and female, who never recovered from this process but were caught in a downward spiral that ultimately destroyed them.

Back to the karma aspect of it. While I am responsible *towards* others (for example, to act truthfully), once I have had sexual intercourse with somebody I am now karmically responsible *for* them, whether I like it or not. Have you ever noticed that once you had intercourse with somebody, that they may act as if you are resonsible for them? Well, that's because they do have a point! Our modern, capitalist society may try to turn sexual

49

intercourse into a casual affair of consumption as much as it wants. However, the point remains you can have casual social intercourse with somebody, but not casual sexual intercourse, because during that time the subtle bodies merge. There are always karmic repercussions to this process, whether we are aware or ignorant thereof. If you make somebody open up to you and then dump them like a hot potato and cause them to suffer, it's your karma to have caused this suffering. In yoga, we call sexual intercourse by the name *karma mudra*.

Again there is a relating terminology in Hebrew and the Torah (the Old Testament). If you read the English version of the Bible, you will repeatedly find sentences such as "and Abraham recognized his wife", or "and Jacob knew his wife", with oddly, after this process of recognition or knowledge, the wife being pregnant. The reason for this is that in Hebrew the terms "to recognize, to know" on the one hand and "to have intercourse with" on the other are the same (la daat). Similarly to the Sanskrit language, Hebrew still confers today the information that intercourse is a sacred activity not merely relegate to conceiving progeny, but to recognizing the divine essence in one's partner. I don't want to lecture anybody here from a moral high horse. I was no saint in my youth, I came to pay the price, and a lot of my yogic efforts had to be devoted to repair the karmic damages caused. Then I was sorry and I wished somebody had properly explained the subject to me beforehand.

I need to discuss one more contemptuous topic in this context and that is the Bonobos. The Bonobos are the fourth species of large apes, a group which also includes Chimpanzees, Orang-Utan and Gorillas. Bonobos are smaller than Chimps and they are separated from them through the massively wide Kongo river in central Africa. Bonobos are vegetarians and they have a very different social structure from Chimps. Similar to humans, chimps are dominated by aggressive alpha males. There is a lot of fighting among them and access to females is reserved to the biggest and most powerful males, who are controling such access through their aggression.

The Bonobos are different. If one is depressed, other members of the pack will go over to that individual and have sex with them until they feel better. Bonobos don't seem to combine sex and hierarchy, which chimps and most other mammals do. Homosexuality and sex between family members is common among them, too (Disclaimer: This is a value-free primatological observation. I am not equating homosexuality to incest). Bonobos are a fascinating subject for anthropologists, and we may wonder, what would have happened had humans chosen the Bonobo model of sexuality, rather than the chimpanzee model.

This was not a straight forward choice. There were human cultures and tribes who practised Bonobo-like virtues. The reason our society today is largely following the chimp model, is because tribes, kingdoms, and cultures, in which sexuality was subject to power and suppression, cultivated more aggression. This aggresion translated into the fact that around the globe, and throughout history, so-called orgiastic cultures were defeated on the battlefield by cultures in which sex was a commodity to organize and control society. The Bonobos themselves only survived because they are separated from chimpanzee populations by the vast Kongo river, which the chimps cannot cross. Had they been able to do so, they would have wiped out the less aggressive Bonobos long ago.

To my knowledge, the late psychologist Dr. Wilhelm Reich did not know about the Bonobos, but their behaviour would have supported one of his main hypotheses, which was that fascism (including the Nazis and the Third Reich) was created through the suppression of sexuality in the petit-bourgeois family (the lower middle class). It is a class that does not own production facilities but has benefited enough from capitalism to stand above the industrial worker class. It was the class in which fascism most rapidly took hold and Reich traced the aggression, with which fascism spread in this class, to sexual suppression. Reich does have a point, and why his hypothesis does not explain fascism entirely, the typical hippie chants such as "make love not war", reflect a growing understanding that a healthy sexuality affects societal mental health.

I will now defuse the opposite argument: imitating Bonobo sexuality would solve many of our societal woes, such as war, aggression, and abuse. This argument fails to consider that while we have indeed inherited mammalian brain circuitry, we have gone far beyond mammals in our evolution. To my knowledge, the most recent large-scale experiment to expose humans to a somewhat Bonobo-like sexuality, was the Rajneesh movement, led by the already mentioned Osho aka Bhagwan Shree Rajneesh. One of the key features of the movement was the belief that as soon as one felt any form of sexual attraction to somebody, one should yield to the impulse and consummate the attraction. This philosophy did not lead to any long-term, societal improvements, and the main reason for that is that for humans, sex is mainly a mental rather than a physical process. To express the same fact in slightly colourful words, in humans, the main sexual organ is not between their legs, but between their ears. While the body will get enough of sex pretty quickly, the mind becomes hungrier the more you feed it. The Bonobo system did not work when transferred on humans with their complex, large brains and in many Rajneeshie-individuals simply led to sex addiction. Many members of the cult spent a great deal of time processing emotional, ego-based, and hierarchal outcomes of their sexual behaviour, which took cerebral bandwidth away from other creative avenues. The same conundrum was recently eloquently expressed in an article written by a young lady who confesses to her mum she is polyamorous. The mother's response, "Darling, sit down. You must be really tired. I'll make you a cup of tea".

This brings us to the next point covering the sacral chakra, that a blockage of this chakra could cause either an impediment of one's sexual function or its exaggeration, and therefore the inability to evolve beyond it. With Rajneesh culture, the founder of the sect had promised that the practice of free love would enable the members to quickly evolve beyond the sacral chakra and their sexual identity. The opposite took place. It led to excessively identifying with one's sexual function and to being stuck at this chakra, rather than going beyond. There was lots of talk of going beyond, but talk is one thing, actions are another.

The sacral chakra can therefore be under- but also over-stimulated. Its over-stimulation may cause frequent, explicit, sexual expression in one's language, but also in overuse of sexuality to define one's identity. An under-stimulation or blockage is present, if we cannot own our sexuality and cannot express ourselves sexually. This also relates to not being able to own, acknowledge and express our emotions when necessary.

The sacral chakra is also the seat of basic emotions, which we share with all mammals. I'm using the term basic emotions here because I do not consider divine love as a basic emotion. It is not actually an emotion. It is a quality of the self, the *atman*, the consciousness, and thus it is activated within the heart chakra. The love that the heart chakra enables us to feel, is a love that is unconditional. That means it is not limited to our spouse, children, parents, friends, members of our tribe or clan, but it is triggered merely from realizing that the entity across from us is a sentient, feeling being. If it is truly love triggered by the heart chakra, this love also does not rely on an empathetic or reciprocal response.

The sacral chakra confers an empathetic response, and it enables us to place ourselves in somebody else's shoes. This means we feel and understand their situation from their frame of reference, rather than ours. This can take place primarily, either on the level of emotions, mentally, or somatically, but all three levels are always present because body, emotions (which in yoga is the pranic level) and the mind, are always linked and never separate. The empathetic response is triggered by our ability to duplicate somebody else's physical, emotional and mental state. If I allow that to happen, I will feel their pain, confusion, sorrow, etc., the way they feel it. This then leads to empathy, that is, their suffering to some extent becomes mine, too.

This decides whether I allow myself to duplicate somebody else's state a socio-political dimension. For example, an important part of preparing a population for war, is to dehumanize the opponent, to denounce their humanity. Once this has taken place an army now can effectively kill "enemies" because they have become subhuman in our eyes. Erich Maria Remarque's book *All Quiet on the Western Front* contains shocking reports of WW1 trench warfare, including a scene where the main character kills an enemy soldier in close bayonet combat. He then witnessing the foes slow and agonizing death from close quarters. While initially, he hopes that the other is mortally wounded, as the enemy soldiers' condition rapidly deteriorates, the main character quickly develops concern, compassion, guilt and shame, at having killed another human. Once the other is dead, he searches his corpse and finds his ID, details, photos of his wife and a letter and realizes that the other was, like him, a human individual, veiled behind the dehumanizing, hideous propaganda of the war machine. The soldier eventually asks the dead enemy for forgiveness.

This fascinating passage demonstrates that the main characters' ability to empathize is initially switched off. This is caused by the shutting down of the sacral chakra due to the fear associated with warfare. During warfare, empathy must be intercepted so that only the base chakra, which powers the reptilian brain circuitry, is activated. We can then, at least in the short-term, act more or less like killing machines although in the long-term PTSD often catches up with us. This shutting down of the sacral chakra in most of us works only temporarily. That's why even during times of war our humanity may break through. Remarque's lead character resolves to deliver the ID of the enemy soldier he killed after the war to his wife. This humane gesture is intercepted by the fact that he himself is killed in action on a day, on which, according to headquarter briefings, *all is quiet on the Western Front.*

Another fascinating function of the sacral chakra is that it enables us to duplicate the emotional state of mammals, such as our pets. Recent research has revealed that if dog owners look into the eyes of their dogs, oxytocin (the cuddle hormone) levels in the blood of both dog and owner will rise. This was known to take place among human lovers, or mother-child couples, but was never actually measured to take place inter-species.

Although we humans have influenced the evolutionary development of wolves into dogs, via the sacral chakra, this influence has also gone the other way. Wolves communicate with each other mainly through gaze, and particularly through the direction in which they are looking. For this purpose, wolves have white sclera (the white in the eye), so each member of the pack can see from a distance at whom the leader is looking. Primates, from which humans developed, do not use this way of communicating, and because of that their sclera are black. You cannot see from afar which way they are looking. Humans are the only primates who, like wolves, have white sclera. It is thought that we developed this mutation because we co-evolved with wolves, that is the wolves caused this evolution in us, so we could better communicate with our canines. This shows the power of the sacral chakra and its associated mammalian brain circuitry.

The element related to the sacral chakra is water, which will play an important role when we get to the stimulant for this chakra. Element water is also related to the yantra of the crescent moon, which this chakra bears, and is connected to its empathetic and emotional nature. Water can adapt to any form and mould to any space, and in this way can be called empathetic. To duplicate somebody else's emotional state can be likened to embodying a liquid nature and filling their persona from the inside. That's how we can feel to "be in their shoes". Notice also that if you sleep close to large bodies of water, your dreams become more emotional and heavier. The emotional tides of our bodily fluids and hormones are in a similar way influenced by the moon, as the tides. I enjoy looking from mountaintops on bodies of water, but if I sleep right next to the ocean or a large lake, my dreams will be heavy as if I get sucked down into the collective subconscious. Similarly, the emotions of friends, family members and large populations around us will influence our emotions, too. When traveling around the world and coming back to particular cities, we may notice that many cities have a particular "feel" to themselves, that cannot be explained just through their history, ethnicity and culture. Metropolises such as New York, Tokyo or Mexico City, through their magnitude, take on an ocean-like character and one can "feel" the city simply by again being immersed into the collective emotion of their inhabitants, even without leaving one's hotel room.

Many yogic texts include sentences like, "It is always through bad company that novices lose all their yogic merit". The sacral chakra opens us to the collective emotion of those around us, and that can draw us into a downward spiral. That is why many yoga texts suggest choosing our company wisely. The Yoga Sutra (II.40) also speaks of the phenomenon of spiritual-emotional contamination. Contamination occurs if we carry with us subconscious, negative emotions. Because each subconscious imprint asks for its own repetition, we are drawn into the company of those who carry similar subconscious, negative emotions like us. In this way, we encounter the same hurts, rejections and disappointments over and over again, until we have released the program within us that caused them in the first place, i.e. the associated primary hurt. The Yoga Sutra suggests intercepting this mechanism of contamination by not engaging in any toxic emotions and thoughts. This stance in yoga is called mental and emotional hygiene.

The sacral chakra, different to the base chakra, is very complex and demands a large part of our brain's bandwidth, typically to decipher facial expressions and other forms of non-verbal communication. If this bandwidth is diverted towards, for example, mathematics or a similar abstract skill, a person can become proficient in it but may display a reduced capacity for basic human connection and warmth. In some mystics the opening of higher chakras can lead to life force shifting away from the sacral chakra, which may cause a certain level of social ineptitude, much like autistic behaviour. But continued social engagement can prevent or at least reduce any excellence in higher pursuits. Mystics often prevent this by seeking solitude. In modern society this conflict between deep introspection to bring about peak experiences and the ability to go out, communicate and share, has shifted to the electronic sphere. Continued, obsessive engagement with social media platforms can not only prevent spiritual and intellectual development, but also take on pathological forms so the person in question feels they cannot stay off social media, lest they should lose contact with the world. Meanwhile true engagement with "live" humans has been lost. Notice also, that excessive interaction with data feeds and social media can impinge on your intellectual development. This is because constant incoming messages, emails, posts and tweets constantly ask us to engage, but distract us from truly immersing ourselves deeply into the study of complex subjects. Our attention is kept at the surface and is used all day long to micromanage what, arguably, could be called trivia. While it is important to engage and interact with those around us, for the spiritual practitioner, a wise compromise must be struck.

The sense associated with the sacral chakra is taste. Notice that taste can only be conferred in a watery medium. If your tongue is completely dry, you will not taste much. Due to its association with water and emotions, taste is the sense with the strongest influence on our emotions. Against this backdrop we can understand modern society's preoccupation with food, taste, cooking, restaurants, recipes, etc. Due to taste's and food's propensity to change our mood, seeking comfort in food or drink is widespread. If we harbor deep-seated dissatisfaction issues, continued comforting through food and drink can easily lead to overeating, obesity and diabetes.

Both the base chakra and the sacral chakra (and also the next, the navel chakra) represent our evolutionary past. We would never exclusively meditate on these chakras (unless a serious pathology is present). Also the use of any stimulants or drugs related to these chakras (heroin, morphine, alcohol, cocaine, crack, crystal meth, coffee), are more likely to present spiritual obstacles, rather than not. Sometimes (alcohol, coffee) the detrimental effect on our spirituality can be kept in check by making consumption irregular and by keeping dosage low. In these cases, though, these substances keep Kundalini down, or at least form an obstacle for its raising. The opposite problem is presented by drugs and stimulants that can aid in raising Kundalini (such as psychedelics, hallucinogens, entheogens, etc.), which we will cover later. Often the uncontrolled and uncontrollable raising of the divine creative force can then lead to chemically induced psychosis, multi-personality disorder, paranoia or megalomania. This will be covered as we work our way up, chakra by chakra.

In yoga, we initially do not meditate on individual chakras, but work on the unimpeded flow of prana between the chakras up and down the central energy channel. Problems arise mainly from being stuck at a particular chakra. For example, the inability to go beyond the sacral chakra could lead to us defining ourselves excessively through our sexual roles. The widespread telling of penile jokes among males can indicate the inability to define ourselves outside of our sexual role, and hence the inability to go beyond the sacral chakra. The other end of the problem is the inability to own this chakra, which could cause an unfulfilling sexuality, infertility and inability to have any close rewarding relationships that require empathy, compassion and duplicating somebody else's emotional state.

The Briggs-Meyers test used in the corporate world, does assess whether an applicant's sacral chakra is functioning, although the assessors would likely be unaware of this. The Briggs-Meyers test, based on Jungian psychology, does for example, test whether we are sorting by *self*, or sorting by *other*. Sorting by other essentially means to which degree our sense of self is influenced by the feedback we get from those around us, a function determined by the sacral chakra. If we are strongly influenced by the sacral chakra, our sense of self is majorly affected by the feedback we obtain from those around us. If they approve of, or even communicate love, our behaviour is positively enforced. If instead they do censor us, we will likely change our behaviour to get good feedback, which will lead to our brain rewarding us with a dopamine hit. In corporate parlance, this would define us as a team player. A corporation understandably wants you to be pliable and responsive to the feedback of your team members and especially superiors.

If your sense of self responds little to feedback from the outside but is rather created by who you think you are, then you are said to sort by *self* rather than by *other*. On a chakric level, this is caused by a rather weak sacral chakra, which itself can be caused by different scenarios. Scenario number one would be if your sacral chakra is blocked and mainly your survival chakra is active. This is the previously discussed case of the psychopath who cannot feel guilt, shame or empathy. In this scenario, if others say you are bad or encourage you to change your behaviour, your inactive sacral chakra would make these suggestions pearl off you like water off a duck's back.

The second scenario would be somebody who has a healthy sacral chakra, but they have a very strong sense of purpose, which is coming from one of the chakras higher up and overrides the sacral chakra. This would be the case of a mystic whose sense of self and purpose is created by some form of vision or mission. They can then absorb strong censorship, not only from the community around them but also from those in power, and still pursue their mission, without becoming uncompassionate and non-empathetic. Typical examples would be Jesus Christ, Krishna, Martin Luther King or Mahatma Gandhi.

A worrisome scenario, which combines aspects of both, the psychopath and the mystic, is the case of the cult leader. Novices to the spiritual path sometimes naively assume that everybody with some form of higher insight automatically is a good person and can be trusted. This is not the case. A cult leader is only a psychopath in a mystic's disguise. They have activated higher brain circuitry but use their insights to impress their followers to get power over them. Their pathological state derives from the fact that their heart chakra is closed, which can easily occur if psychedelics are taken before the heart chakra is opened. This is less likely if one continues to work on one's spiritual evolution and opens the higher chakras in sequence with spiritual practices such as yoga.

The two lower chakras (base- and sacral chakra) are *tamasic*. *Tamas* can be translated as mass particle, which means the two chakras are under the influence of inertia. Gravitation and downward-pull, here, are strong. Nauli (churning of the abdominal muscles) is a technique that helps to overcome inertia, mass, and *tamas* at the sacral chakra, and lift the Kundalini higher from here. The further we get away from the area of these lower chakras, the easier it is to overcome this inertia. This is similar to a rocket ship leaving the gravitational field of the Earth. The further we get away from the Earth, the less impetus we need to maintain our speed. Any stimulant or narcotic we take related to the two lower chakras, will add to the existing gravitational pull that drags us back into our evolutionary past.

THE SACRAL CHAKRA DRUG: ALCOHOL

The sacral chakra is associated with the element water. The sacrum plays an important role in the body as a pump for cerebrospinal fluid, the liquid that engulfs, nourishes and massages the brain and spinal cord. Interestingly, the stimulant associated with this water chakra is the only liquid stimulant, alcohol. Alcohol will stimulate libido in small doses, but larger doses bring out its adverse effects as a neurotoxin. The libido-enhancing effect of small doses of alcohol is because it enables one to "own" one's limbic brain, which, among other functions, enables courtship and relating, but also to simply connect to others emotionally. If we cannot "own" our sacral chakra and limbic brain function, we may feel socially isolated. Because alcohol stimulates the sacral chakra, we then may reach to the bottle to overcome social or sexual isolation.

A key word for the sacral chakra is connection. If we feel disconnected with those around us, or feel too inhibited to connect, then alcohol is often used to overcome the feeling of inhibition and social awkwardness. Alcohol is also an anaesthetic. It's used to anaesthetize physical and emotional pain. As already discussed, emotions and emotional pain are related to the water element. Emotional pain can cause us to cry, again showing the connection between emotion and liquidity, and crying can be very healing. Particularly males who are taught to suppress tears, may instead reach to alcohol, which like tears, is a liquid.

In our spiritual evolution, our sense of self expands. First, it involves only our body (reptilian/base-chakra stage), then our family and clan (mammalian/sacral-chakra stage), and eventually our tribe/nation, or various ideological/religious groups (primate/navel-chakra stage) that we adhere to. Our sense of self can then continue to grow to involve the whole of humanity (humanoid/heart-chakra stage), all life, the whole biosphere and planet (animistic/throat-chakra stage), the cosmic intelligence that expresses itself as the whole of creation (bhakti, third-eye-chakra stage), and even to cosmic consciousness (jnana/crown-chakra stage). This evolution and expansion of sense of self is not always smooth sailing. At some point, we need to connect with and feel the collective pain of all beings ever felt, an event described in the *Bhagavata Purana* as "he is a yogi who feels the pain of all beings". St. John of the Cross described this level as "the dark night of the soul". The German language contains a beautiful term describing these sentiments, *Weltschmerz*, the pain of being. Being is essentially painful. Not all the time, but there will always be moments, whatever our state of evolution is, when it hurts to be alive. In moments like this confusion can take over, and we may wish to never have started spiritual evolution. Alcohol then offers itself as a straightforward solution because it readily contracts our sense of self back to where we were, to the sacral and mammalian chakra from where the world looks simple again, if only for a short time.

Alcohol consumption is surprisingly common even among mystics. Although I never had a sustained habit of alcohol consumption, I used it a few times to "ground" myself. During the late seventies and early eighties, quite frequently, I took large quantities of LSD and other psychedelics. I did so usually by myself, alone and in the forest. I enjoyed the beautiful nature around me and spent my time meditating and reflecting on the big questions of life. While I was quite happy alone in the forest, I noticed upon returning and mingling with people that psychedelics, at least sustained use of high doses, make you socially inept. This is due to their drawing life force (*prana*) away from the lower chakras and towards the higher. Most forms of spiritual practice share this tendency with psychedelics to power mystical experiences. Psychedelics have this effect in a more concentrated form (there are dangers to that, too, and they are covered in great detail in the respective chapters). After I had taken too many psychedelics too often, that I became socially isolated. I discovered then, that I could rectify this problem through occasional alcohol consumption. Alcohol made me outgoing, friendly, downright silly and a socialite. All a far cry from the brooding mystic, who spent his time in the forest by himself and didn't talk to people. I want to clarify that I am here describing a pattern I had during my late teens, which I do not recommend today. We would be justified in saying I was combating one pathology with another. I am telling this, not to suggest alcohol as a therapy countering societal isolation caused by psychedelics, but to describe why alcohol is attractive to many including mystics.

Because alcohol activates our mammalian, emotional brain circuitry (at least in low doses) it makes us open to tune into strangers we would otherwise have no interest in (whether that is a good thing is debatable, but understandably for many it makes parties bearable). Alcohol also makes us social, outgoing and both emphatic and empathetic, that is we are congruent in our communication, but also can tune into others (again on low doses only). Alcohol triggers the sacral chakra, which is so crucial for forming human bonds and non-verbal communication. You can speak the most eloquent words, but if your posture, breath rhythm, pitch and facial expression do not meet the communication code of your audience, nobody will understand what you say, nor will they care.

The reasons against taking alcohol are pretty much the same as for it. It stimulates the 2nd chakra. The yogic goal is to be able to consciously place life force (*prana*) into the chakra pertaining to the task at hand. The yogi aspires to do this through mental concentration and spiritual practice alone, and not by relying on the crutch of a chemical or plant agent. The problem with using a stimulant to activate the chakra necessary for a particular function, is that during the active time of that stimulant it will be difficult to activate a different chakra, should the need arise. People who consume alcohol often may act in a grossly inappropriate way if the situation suddenly changes. If a particular chakra/evolutionary brain circuit is activated consciously through mental concentration, then in a split second, you can change to another one, if a changing situation requires this. If the 2nd chakra is chemically activated, the ability to change the circuit may only arise once your hangover has eased off. That's how people wake up in a police lock-up, instead of in their own bed.

If you have to use alcohol to activate your mammalian brain circuitry, then you are the slave of this chakra and not its master. This is true for all other chakras and their associated drugs as well. It is this point that ultimately got me to quit all drugs whatsoever. The activation of chakras with chemical and plant stimulants ultimately is not feasible, nor sustainable. If we would stick to this avenue, it would force us to carry an apothecary around with us, containing stimulants for each chakra. I actually had a friend 40 years ago who did that. His nickname was "chemical". Even then, if our present situation changes (it constantly does), and a different chakra would be required, we would still have to wait until the stimulant for the previous chakra has worn off, which may with some substances, take a long time. Mastery of life is really the ability to play the chakras up and down like a xylophone. It is something that cannot be reliably done using substances.

If you let go for a moment of any memory you have grown up in a society where alcohol was legal and part of daily life, then you have to admit that the only objective reason for it to be legal is that it is less concentrated than some other drugs. Many more people are dying from alcohol-related deaths than any other drug (besides tobacco, which doesn't appear mind-altering to me). Perhaps it was tried to make it illegal during the prohibition in the United States and it didn't work. That argument is a cop-out. Neither does marihuana prohibition work, and for that fact, even opiate prohibition. The main effects of prohibition are that it makes the drug lords wealthy, it reduces the quality of drugs available, and it pushes people into the penal system, who are actually requiring support with mental health issues rather than penalization. I'm not dead set on legalizing all drugs, but I can't quite see the point to make them all illegal, and yet keep tobacco and alcohol legal.

CHAPTER 2.

The only other argument I can see that works in alcohols favour regarding legality, is that it makes the electorate more emotional. Being more susceptible to emotional arguments, the electorate then often throw reason away. In the two decades I live in Australia I have witnessed a particular party winning the federal elections repeatedly, on a xenophobic platform. As far as I can see, Australia has quite a few urgent problems that would need to be addressed. No other country in the world is hit every day by so much sunshine, yet the electric grid is run by ancient coal-fired power stations. This leads to regular power outages (as the outdated power generators fail) and poisons the atmosphere with CO^2, mercury and other toxins. The ones profiting are the coal barons. The entire manufacturing sector has been sacrificed for the mining industry, which doesn't actually supply a lot of jobs. Australia has the largest per capita greenhouse emissions, and regarding its indigenous population, it has one of world's poorest human rights records. However, inevitably when election time comes around, this party almost every single time convinces the electorate that the one burning issue Australia has is to keep refugees (the boat people) off the coast. The ruling party does so by portraying 'them' (the refugees) as being different to 'us', that 'they' threaten our national identity and that 'they' cannot be integrated into our society. Alcohol, by activating our mammalian brain, fires up the emotional-territorial brain circuitry of our ancestry. With increasing alcohol consumption it becomes easy to differentiate "they" from "us" although at close inspection we are all similar. This so-called "othering" is an important feature of the sacral chakra, as it defines us as part of a group or clan.

Compared to most other drugs, alcohol is a mild stimulant, that is you have to take rather large quantities to have a strong effect. It shares this classification with coffee and marijuana. If alcohol is consumed in moderate doses and irregularly, it has comparatively little impact on spiritual development.

Chapter 3.
THE NAVEL CHAKRA AND COCAINE

THE NAVEL CHAKRA

The navel chakra represents an important step in our natural and spiritual evolution. It is a complex chakra with many important aspects that need to be discussed. The Sanskrit term for this chakra, *Manipura*, means city of jewels, with its nature said to be blazing due to its associated element fire (*agni*). It is in the spinal cord on the height of the navel as the name suggests. The expression of this chakra is fundamentally different from the two previous ones, which were both inert (*tamasic*) in nature. The Manipura is frantic (*rajasic*), and since we have come under its sway, there has been a frantic striving for change, development and progress, often merely for itself and little apparent benefit.

Related to the element of this chakra, fire, is the visual sense. This chakra is the subtle blueprint for primate brain circuitry, i.e. the monkey brain. Developing most parts of the neocortex (the third tier of our brain) is the evolutionary outcome of the collective activation of this chakra. The neocortex enabled us to enlarge our sense of self from mammalian packs, pods or prides to complex tribes, kingdoms and modern states, for all its worth.

I name chakras by their location (such as navel chakra) rather than their function, which is often too complex to be described in a single term. In the present case, however, the term power chakra, describes this chakra reasonably well. The term power chakra comes from there being two storehouses of life force in the body, the solar storehouse, associated with the navel chakra and the lunar storehouse, associated with the third-eye chakra, described later. At the outset, we need to understand that the storehouse is not the same as the chakra, but it is related to it because it is adjacent to it. A chakra represents evolutionary brain circuitry, whereas a storehouse is more aptly described as a *pranic* battery. The solar battery adjacent to the navel chakra powers the following functions:

- Left analytical brain hemisphere
- Right solar nostril
- Fundamentalist mind
- Sympathetic nervous system
- Extraversion
- Efferent (outgoing) nerve currents
- Motor-neurons
- Catabolism (breaking down tissue)

This chakra is more male in nature than the previous one. Notice that most primate societies and many human ones, are male dominated. Under the sway of the navel chakra our society also became more science-oriented and empirical. To be outgoing rather than introverted is esteemed in our culture. Modern life is becoming more and more stressful due to the overload of the sympathetic nervous system (which activates fight-and-flight, whereas rest-and-relaxation are receding into the background). Because our efferent (outgoing) nerve currents are overloaded, we suffer from sleep depletion. It is expected of us to have a strong physical presence, and people who don't, are rarely elected as leaders, even if they are ethically and intellectually highly developed. Our entire culture is highly catabolic (breaking down tissue, and by extension, any structure). Through our unsustainable activities our culture is breaking down the entire biosphere, with many species of plants and animals being made extinct daily. Rather than being caused by fate or being predetermined, the imbalanced state of modern humanity came about through the cultural choices we have made over the recent millennia, influenced by this chakra. Individuals can contribute by returning themselves to a state of balance through pranayama. I have described the method in great detail in *Pranayama The Breath of Yoga*.

The term *Manipura*, by which this chakra is also known, gave rise to several important English words. One of them is *manipulate*. Those under the sway of this chakra are preoccupied with abandoning the many truths to the benefit of a single truth (this being the definition of fundamentalism, in its many guises). There is a tendency to expressing oneself (extraversion) to the detriment of listening and feeling others (an introverted tendency). If allowed a sole reign, this chakra gives us a tendency to override conflicting opinions and push ahead with our own agenda. Because of its focus on the left brain-hemisphere this chakra gives us the linguistic ability to talk others out of their rightly held positions, and to convince ourselves that our opinion is the only correct one, even if it is ludicrous.

The Sanskrit *mani* = jewel is the etymological source of the English *money*, and the name of the *Manipura* chakra became *money pool*. We are now in late-stage capitalism where giant money pools, hedge funds, have become more powerful than many national governments on Earth. Trade agreements are being negotiated where multinational corporations can sue democratically elected governments for compensation, if these governments dare to pass legislation that prevents corporations from exploiting their natural resources, and impinging on the profits of these corporations. Our modern world is ruled by money pools, and populations and nature are becoming more and more obsolete in the attempt of these money pools to turn all of nature and all relationships between living entities into money and profit. In this context, it may help to remind ourselves of the prophecy of the Cree, "When you have cut down the last tree, poisoned the last river, shot the last buffalo and caught the last fish, you white people will finally realize that you can't eat money."

This historical drama that plays itself out, is not simply caused by the navel chakra, but by our obsession with it, our reluctance and failure to evolve beyond it, ultimately by our lack of spiritual evolution. Please remember this paragraph when we discuss the drug of this chakra, cocaine. The excesses described here regarding this chakra, are to a good extent enabled by people addicted to cocaine and power. Some people are so good at it they do not even require cocaine.

The element of the Navel Chakra is *agni*, fire. Again, it is easy to see the relation between the Sanskrit and English to looking at the related *ignite* and *ignition*. The term *agni* refers to pure fire in its elemental form but in the body in its impeded form, it is called metabolic fire (*pitta*). *Pitta* can be re-converted into elemental fire, fire of intelligence (*agni*). Many yogic practices such as Nauli, Kapalabhati, external breath retention (kumbhakas), and Kundalini-raising meditations do this. The human has an inbuilt desire to understand the cosmos. For this to happen, metabolic fire (*pitta*) has to be converted into the fire of intelligence. Fire of intelligence here does not mean a high IQ or high score in trivial pursuit. It means to understand the cosmos and to place oneself into the service of life in its totality, by acting life-affirmatively. If this does not happen, then intelligence is often placed into the service of darkness. The monsters of history (such as Hitler and Stalin) were often seemingly intelligent people, but they used their intelligence to serve wrong ideas.

The keywords and key functions of the navel chakra are acquisition, accumulation and assimilation. On a biological level, via the metabolic fire this applies to food. If *pitta*, the metabolic fire in this chakra, is impeded, one can develop a voracious appetite and gain weight. On a deeper level, though, we as a society created hierarchies sorted by acquisition, accumulation and assimilation of wealth and power. We may use the function of this chakra also for accumulation of sexual exploits, or numbers of likes or friends on social media, or whatever else can be acquired on an economic, societal or political level. Important again to understand is that we did not have to develop into that direction. There was a potential for that, and through our choices as individuals and as a society and civilization, we gradually over millennia developed into this direction, which we now consider as normal. It is not normal! It is only that we cannot see the forest for the trees. We all need to work together and develop visions how we can organize our societies along other lines, rather than just accumulation of wealth and status. This is a toxic program that leads to converting our environment and communities into money, and if adhered to for much longer, will lead to our collective undoing.

There are also positive sides to this chakra. It assimilates and stores life force (*prana*), thus promoting health. In breath retention (*kumbhaka*) life force can be extracted from the retained air, and stored in the solar battery, associated with the navel chakra. Also closely related to this is area is the metabolic fire that assembles the body from the building blocks derived from food. The navel chakra is also the seat of medical knowledge. This is confirmed by Patanjali, one of the founders of Ayurveda, the Vedic science of medicine, when he says that he derived his medical knowledge by meditating on this chakra (Yoga Sutra III.29).

The navel chakra develops economic, business and entrepreneurial skills. The more open the navel chakra, the more one can stand one's ground in modern capitalist society. A person with an underdeveloped navel chakra may have great business ideas, but whenever they apply them, they go broke. Another less ingenious person, equipped however with a fully activated navel chakra, may come along and turn the same business idea, "borrowed" from a failed visionary, into a monetary success. I have given approaches to activating the navel chakra in my books *Pranayama The Breath of Yoga* and *Yoga Mediation: Through Mantra, Chakras and Kundalini to Spiritual Freedom*. However, it is questionable whether our already commerce-obsessed society needs more activated navel chakras or rather awakening of the subsequent, higher chakras. But having this chakra defunct can be crippling to one's life, as all of one's material aspirations may come to naught. As the humanistic psychologist Abraham Maslow has pointed out, it is difficult to follow through with your higher aspirations if the basic needs are not covered.

The navel chakra is also responsible for developing leadership abilities. Leadership in human society is determined predominantly through non-verbal communication, similar to that used by our primate ancestors when choosing their leaders. This shows again the link between this present chakra and the primate brain. If you are baffled by so-called enlightened societies regularly electing buffoonish right-wing populists over intellectuals with a brainy program, then look no further. The monkey-brain often feels safer to follow the person who conveys through their body language they are convicted in being the right person to lead you, and that they have all the right answers. It is probably futile to point out that to the degree the intelligence of a person matures, to that degree their conviction in being just the right person to lead you and having all the right answers, will decrease. To the degree to which our intelligence matures through spiritual evolution, we will eventually come to admit with Socrates, that the only thing we know for certain is that we know nothing. We will also ask ourselves how we actually developed the belief to know something with great fervour? The more we learn, the more we realize how much we don't know, the more do we question what we believe to know. That is why great intellects rarely make great leaders. However, much of these considerations are beyond the scope of this chakra, which simply expresses the urge to lead and dominate, no matter what.

In this context, it helps to quote Donald Rumsfeld, secretary of defence during the George W. Bush administration. Rumsfeld was interviewed by a journalist about the data and evidence supporting the case for the US invasion of Iraq. Rumsfeld's response was there were two types of people. Those who simply go and make history (and obviously can't be bothered about asking themselves too many questions) and then there are the others who write about the first group. Rumsfeld's obvious point was that he counted himself as belonging to the first group and the journalist to the second. As such, he couldn't be bothered explaining his motivation to a mere mortal belonging into the second group. This, more than anything, explains the drama of the navel chakra and the fact that we are so obsessed with it. It is because we are obsessed with power.

In this book I am focusing on the spiritual outcomes of drug use and I'm only skimming the subject of neurology, which may, however, interest some. Dr Gabor Maté sums up neurological research regarding addiction to drugs like heroin and cocaine in his *In the Realm of Hungry Ghosts*. To look into latest research regarding neurology and psychedelics (i.e. LSD, psilocybin, etc.), then Michael Pollan's *How to Change Your Mind* might be of interest. For a general understanding of the matter you can't go past Robert M Sapolsky's *Behave: The Biology of Humans at Our Best and Worst*. Sapolsky is an eminent professor of neurology and as an empirical materialist his and my beliefs overlap little. But I admire anybody who devotes that much work and dedication to a subject to create such expertise. In *Behave,* he quotes the report of a primatologist who observes the fight of two alpha-male chimpanzees. Eventually, one of them beats up the other. The loser runs off and wants to cool his temper somehow. He encounters a female and, after serious resistance from her side, he rapes her, at considerable pain to her because she is outside of estrus.

This somewhat sobering example clearly proves the long-held claim that rape is not a function of sexuality, but of domination. The losing alpha male needed to go off and dominate somebody else to pass on his emotional charge. Had he encountered a weaker male, he would have beaten him up, but since he encountered a female, the avenue by which domination was pursued, was through rape. This is a common mechanism, by which the power chakra will use the sacral chakra to exert itself. This needs to be considered when looking at cases of rape, or sexual abuse, in humans. Too often, women are still seen as at fault and are criticized for provoking a male. But to force a woman into sexual activity is not primarily a sexual act, it is about subduing her. It is about power.

The archetype of womanhood in our society used to be the female who is open-hearted, receptive and kind, but she is then paired up with a male, who is brooding, short-fused, and can't verbally express himself. In spiritual terms the female has an open heart chakra, and but is disconnected from her power chakra. The male on the other side, can neither express himself emotionally, nor can he show his affection, but has all the power on his side. This is also reflected in males' using to be the sole breadwinners in families, and until recently also had all family property and assets in their names. The female here can exert power only through her male, and the male can feel his ability to love only through his female. These standard role models, while looking attractive to some, in reality present us with two incomplete, psychologically crippled human beings, who have to metaphorically lean against each other, to stay upright.

One cannot be an integrated human without an active navel/power chakra. To serve society in any complex task, it is essential to activate this chakra, without which no leadership is possible. If the navel chakra is closed and higher chakras are open, you may become a seer, but you cannot assert yourself in society, you will be trodden upon. An inactive navel chakra is often associated with a victim mentality. Somebody with an active navel chakra can be powerful, yet still compassionate, which is the case when the heart chakra is also active. Note, that it is said about Jesus, "and they were surprised about his words because he spoke like one of power and not one of the scribes" (Mark 1:22).

The term *scribe* here is significant. What is meant is that scholars who excessively stick their noses into books may have overdeveloped intellects, but this often draws life force (*prana*) away from the navel chakra. In this scenario, you may pronounce something that is accurate, but your words do not convey power. You will then be ignored. Spiritual practitioners should understand this. If you have learned and understood much, accept responsibility and offer leadership. However, you cannot do so if your power chakra is inactive. All your efforts will go to waste because without an active power chakra you cannot make a valid contribution to the life of others.

For the individual, it is essential to place life force (*prana*) into the navel chakra, when addressing a congregation or audience, when wanting to convince someone, when making business decisions, during board meetings of a corporation, when engaged in the legal profession, when performing surgery and other medical services, when leading a military unit, during food intake and digestion, during political negotiations and any commercial dealings, and during many scientific activities such as study. The ability to place *prana* into the navel chakra as such will not determine whether these abilities are used in an ethical way. This needs to be considered separately.

The differentiation between history and pre-history is usually determined through the availability of written sources from a particular period. Since it is the navel chakra that enables us to create abstract writing, we can argue that the collective activation of this chakra started history. The navel chakra gave us the possibility to increase our sense of self to include tribes and nations, rather than just bands, families, packs, pods and prides. However, so far, human history is little more than one of warring tribes and nations. Until recently (early 20th century) we gave little importance to human rights and dignity. It is only recently that we concern ourselves with such things as "international morality" in the sense as it was used by the Ethiopian emperor Haile Selassie in his 1963 speech to the United Nations General Assembly, when he so eloquently said,

"that until the philosophy which holds one race superior and another inferior is finally and permanently discredited and abandoned; that until there are no longer first-class and second-class citizens of any nation; that until the colour of a man's skin is of no more significance than the colour of his eyes; that until the basic human rights are equally guaranteed to all without regard to race; that until that day, the dream of lasting peace and world citizenship and the rule of international morality will remain but a fleeting illusion, to be pursued but never attained."

We are now finally concerning ourselves with ethics governing the relation between nations and ethnic groups, rather than just "the winner takes it all", as it was still en vogue during early 20th-century colonialism. This is a welcome portent, showing that as a species we are again increasing our sense of self by collectively embracing the heart chakra. At the level of the heart chakra our sense of self here will increase to take in the whole of humanity. The navel chakra itself can give us little in terms of ethical considerations for the whole of humanity. The navel chakra is forever stuck in "greed is good" and "survival of the fittest". This worked just fine when we were technologically undeveloped. However, our technological prowess, which has not yet paired with similar prowess in ethical and spiritual development, has now become a threat to our survival. Science enthusiasts naively believe that technology will fix all our problems. Nothing is further from the truth. The vast majority of our problems are caused by technology, not abetted by it. Our problems can be fixed when our spiritual evolution finally catches up and overtake our technological development and only then. Our spiritual evolution since several millennia is stuck in reverse. This is due to the influence of the sky-religions (opposed to Earth-based spirituality), who propose that spirit is opposed to matter, and that the spiritual goal is somewhere else, not here and now. According to the sky-religions the goal is in heaven, nirvana or emptiness and often embodied through the projection of a giant, bearded, irate, white male into the sky. Science and technology can solve problems only in the hands of those who can use them, rather than are used by them. Humanity has no idea how to deal with the threat of AI (artificial intelligence), or genetically modified humans or cloned humans. AI is a cat we are letting out of the bag just because we are not in control of our collective actions. We are acting as if AI, cloning and genetic modification will take place because we, who have invented them, can't stop them. Here science is using us rather than us using science. In that regard, we are acting like a person high on drugs.

The sense associated with the navel chakra is the visual sense, which is again related to this chakra's element, fire. Seeing relies on light for images to be conveyed via the retina to the brain. Any form of light, whether emitted by the sun, reflected by the moon or created through artificial lighting, is only a form of controlled fire. Analytical intelligence is also a function of this chakra; hence its importance for scientific thinking. The power of intelligence is a form of fire, i.e. a higher form of metabolic fire. As the sun sheds light on Earth, so does the fire of intelligence shed light on things of which we were hitherto ignorant. We need to be very cautious though as in the last few centuries, our intellect rushed ahead of our spiritual and moral development, or it might be clearer to say we ignored our spiritual development to the advantage of mere scientific progress. Technological development spurred by scientific intelligence now threatens to unleash a fire consuming most of our biosphere and making us extinct. That one of the greatest threats now comes in global heating and the age of fire (climate scientists are proposing the advent of an age of fire marked by frequent, all-consuming mega bush- and forest-fires), is because we continue to emphasize this fire chakra, without mellowing and cooling it enough with the love and wisdom of the higher chakras.

Connected to the fire-nature of this chakra is also the fact that it is frantic *(rajasic)*. Move from the bucolic bliss of a landscape largely untouched by human hands to any modern metropolis and you immediately notice the frenzy *(rajas)* of modern humankind. What is it exactly that we are trying to achieve with all this senseless scampering around? The only things we collectively seem to achieve is creating trillions of tons of waste, poisoning the oceans and atmosphere, and making more and more species of plants and animals extinct. But this we notice only when zooming out and taking in the big picture, a function, which this chakra does not possess. Nor do any of the stimulants that foster this chakra's brain circuitry encourage us to do. What this chakra allows for, is competitiveness with the people around us, and ambition to outdo them. This is caused by the frenzy *(rajas)* of this chakra, which creates an enormous amount of movement with no constructive direction.

Like the sacral chakra, so also the navel chakra uses the limbic system to communicate with others by using non-verbal communication such as gesture and facial expression. But in contrast to the sacral chakra, the navel chakra does not do so to feel secure and appreciated by forming bonds, but it hijacks the limbic brain to lead others. Its evolutionary purpose is to do so to the advantage of the whole group. A group of primates or humans will always choose somebody with an active navel/power chakra. However, the possession of an active navel chakra does not necessarily guarantee this chosen leaders' beliefs are useful for the group. It just means that leading will come naturally to them. If we can understand the navel chakra, we can activate it in large groups of capable individuals, who can then make a more informed decision as to who has the right program and not just the charisma. A leader should also have activated the higher chakras, so they are compassionate, all-inclusive and visionary and not just pander to a section of the electorate.

The blockage of the navel chakra is brought into effect by the Vishnu *granthi*, with *granthi* meaning knot or blockage. The term knot indicates that the life force (*prana*) cannot flow into or beyond this chakra. The name Vishnu blockage (*granthi*) is awkward, with Vishnu being one of the three main Hindu deities. It makes one automatically conjure up the image of an anthropomorphic god who haphazardly blocks somebody's *pranic* channels (*nadis*) and lets somebody else's flow. This is not the case. The blockage is so named because Vishnu in Hindu mythology is the maintainer of society. The navel- and heart chakras are the chakras that deal with society, determining how individuals interact with the larger society around them. The blockage (*granthi*) is then that knot that blocks the flow of

Vishnu's realm, the maintenance of society. In modern parlance, this blockage stops you from becoming a fully integrated human, asserting yourself from a position of power (navel chakra) if necessary, and coming from a position of unconditional love (heart chakra) if feasible. I clarify this distinction here because the view that unconditional love carries you through all possible scenarios, may be an entertaining hippie- and fairy dream, but any comprehensive study of human history will reveal many a situation in which acting from the navel/power chakra is more appropriate to benefit society.

The Vishnu *granthi* can block the navel chakra in two ways. First, it can prevent life force (*prana*) from entering the chakra at hand, so the evolutionary brain circuitry associated with this chakra is not available to you. This is the typical scenario of a powerless person, who may get victimized and cannot take the mantle of the leader, even if necessary. I am not indicating that victimization is the fault of the victim. It always takes two to tango. A perpetrator will scan for a suitable victim, but the karmic responsibility is still with the perpetrator and the civil code of law must protect any victims.

The other way Vishnu blockage (*granthi*) blocks this chakra, is that it prevents one to go beyond it, in this case, to activate the heart chakra. And this is the present dilemma of our human society. Although increasing attempts are being made, our society still creates hierarchies according to wealth, power and status. Access to healthcare, education, legal services and influence on lawmakers (lobbyism), are similarly determined by the fatness of your wallet and asset portfolio. In many Anglo-Saxon societies, the social net is rolled back. Many services that during the 70s and 80s were still in public hands and supplied for free to all (or at a reasonable cost), have been privatized and are scarcely affordable by the many. At the time of writing this, during the first 12 months of the COVID pandemic, the world's 10 wealthiest individuals have increased their net worth by a staggering 450 billion dollars, whereas a billion people have sunk back into destitution and poverty.

To understand that collectively humanity is blocked by Vishnu *granthi*, look no further than at the fact that every year more wealth and power is controlled in the hands of fewer and fewer, obscenely wealthy individuals. The dream that equality, freedom and liveable conditions for all will be achieved soon and that everybody can have a fair go (that's Australian lingo for the belief you always will be rewarded if you work hard enough) is just that, a pipe dream, that is moving further away by the day, a move fuelled by hardcore-capitalist, neoconservative ideologies. Failure to go beyond this chakra leads to defining oneself through one's wealth and looking for profit and material advantage in all situations.

It is easy to criticize capitalism but harder to come up with an alternative. Let's look at communism. In his *Communist Manifesto*, Karl Marx proposed three historical phases, which eventually would merge into communist society. The first phase, slaveholder society, can clearly be identified with the reptilian base chakra. His second phase, medieval feudal society, with its emphasis on binding families and clans to small territory and their often tyrannical leaders, closely tracks the sacral chakra. During the third historical phase, industrialism, its leading class, the bourgeoisie, developed production facilities. From a yogic perspective, Marx's bourgeoisie is the class that fully opens the navel chakra and develops its potential. It is interesting to note the importance Marx places on developing modern industrial and entrepreneurial capacities. He has precisely analyzed the development of human society, which equates with yoga's view of the first three chakras. But where to turn to from here? If humanity remains stuck at the level of the navel chakra, the industrial production facilities created under its thrall, will, through unbridled greed, destroy this biosphere (and us with it) by exhausting its resources and poisoning it. It is, therefore, even from the viewpoint of survival, a must that our spiritual evolution progresses to the next chakra, the heart chakra. As a professed atheist, Marx was silent on any such possibility.

Marx defined communism as the dictatorship of the working class (proletariat), whereas we could define capitalism as the dictatorship of the production-facility owners (bourgeoisie). In capitalism, we can usually see opposition to the ruling formation. At the time of writing this, a simplified view of US democracy sees it to be mainly a shifting conflict between Wall Street (backing the Democrat party) and the military-industrial complex (backing the Republican party), which are two rivalling factions within the bourgeoisie. This assessment may sound sobering, but on the bright side, it means there is at least some form of opposition. In a country run by the central committee of the Communist Party, we will see no opposition besides clashing personalities of officials, of which the one with the stronger navel chakra will assert himself, with little differences in program between the contenders. That's even more sobering.

Before turning to the group of drugs activating the navel chakra, there are yogic methods to achieve both the activation of the chakra, should it be underdeveloped, and the so-called piercing of the Vishnu blockage (*granthi*), should evolution beyond the chakra be impeded. However, these methods involve daily practice, so often it's just more convenient to take a drug and instantly be under the sway of the power chakra and its frequently questionable pursuits. Yogic ways of activating the navel chakra and reducing the activity of Vishnu blockage (*granthi*) on this level, include Nauli (churning of the abdominal muscles), external breath retention (kumbhaka after exhaling), Uddiyana Bandha (a muscular lock of the lower abdomen), *Bahya* (external) Uddiyana (the sucking up of the abdominal contents into the thoracic cavity, Nadi Shodhana pranayama (alternate nostril breathing), and particularly Surya Bhedana pranayama (a breathing technique during which all inhalations are taken through the right nostril and exhales are performed through the left), which are described in *Pranayama: The Breath of Yoga*. Another important technique is to meditate on this chakra exclusively while striking RAM into it (these set of techniques being described in my text *Yoga Meditation: Through Mantra, Chakras and Kundalini to Spiritual Freedom*). As with all previous chakras, after activating it, the most important step is to go beyond it and on to the next one.

THE NAVEL CHAKRA DRUG: COCAINE

With everything just described in the section on the navel chakra, no wonder drugs activating this chakra would be some of the most frequently consumed in our society. Simply get a hit and have instant power, but at a cost. Drugs in this category are cocaine, crack-cocaine, powder- and crystal meth (ice), amphetamine (speed), and the ubiquitous coffee. Coffee is much milder than the others but drink a triple-macchiato on an empty stomach and you are close to a speed-hit.

The quintessential drug in this category is cocaine. While under the influence of cocaine, even people who are generally meek and non-assertive can have the feeling they are in charge of a situation and in control of their lives. Cocaine also increases one's linguistic skills to where people who previously have difficulties expressing themselves, can suddenly become apt manipulators. It is commonly used by salespeople, by people working in the legal profession, and by high-powered businesspeople. When I was a student, I worked as a chauffeur for a high-end limousine service. My boss charged $1000 a day for my services, including the Mercedes 600, which assured that we would get as clients the wealthiest and most powerful people coming to town. Cocaine usage amongst our clientele was so widespread that a significant part of my job was devoted to vacuuming spilled coke from seats and the floor of the car at the end of my shift. This went so far that to reduce the mess, I asked my boss to insert retractable mirrors with engraved grooves into the armrests of the rear seats, which unfortunately he refused to do. I thought that was a real shame as it could have improved our service, as everybody anyway knew that we were the "powder-express".

Listening to the conversations between my clients, en route to driving them to their hostile take-overs or board meeting presentations, while snorting their rocks, was one of the most educational periods of my life. Typical conversation openers after the first toke were usually along the line of "Okay, how are we going to screw these guys this time? How are we going to make them bend over, let their pants down and …?" I don't want to give too many more of these colourful examples, but I recognized the language clearly when I saw *The Wolf of Wall Street*. Language under the influence of cocaine consists of a mixture of manipulation, adversarialism, puerile penile phantasies, and hunger for power and wealth, usually combined with pleasure in using coercion, deceit, trickery and cunning, to gain advantages over another. And usually, this game is played in the spirit of an athletic pursuit, meaning the more ruthless and successful somebody is at the game, the better they feel about themselves and the more they would boast about it to other passengers in the car.

A common feature in all these conversations was the complete lack of well-wishing and compassion for any others. Cocaine is so powerful that even in a person with a certain ability to access the heart chakra, it will generally impinge on accessing any of that chakras brain circuitry. In the extreme (which is usually the fact when activated via cocaine) the navel/power chakra will see other people merely as an asset or resource to be exploited. This was never clearer to be seen, when my clients, after a day of hard work on coke, asked me to get them a "piece of meat", with the term meat reserved not for a steak but for a human in the sex trade.

The beautiful part of the world where I live (Australia, northern-NSW) boasts one of the last vestiges of the hippie movement. The local constabulary is engaged in a serious war of attrition against the local hippies with mobile drug testing. Drivers are constantly pulled over and tested whether any illicit substances can be found in their saliva. If you have smoked pot in the last 14 days, you'll lose your license and get a criminal record, but until recently they didn't even test for cocaine. And that is because cocaine is what the big end of town is on, and they don't want to lose their license. It was only after a huge outcry from the population, that cocaine-testing was officially included in the regimen, but people in >$100,000 cars are rarely pulled over, so it remains mainly a gesture.

History's most insidious and famous cocaine-user must have been Josef Goebbels PhD, Hitler's propaganda minister.

CHAPTER 3.

To experience all of cocaine's scary power without having to ingest any, then listen to Goebbels *Erklärung des Totalen Krieges* (declaration of total war)-speech at the *Sportspalast* in 1943. That the war for Germany at that point was lost, was obvious but to the most convicted Nazis. Even just to read Goebbels speech reveals mastery of rhetoric and demagogy, but the soundtrack lifts it to a completely different level. As with all his speeches, Goebbels was high on coke to his eyeballs and he masterfully whipped the 100,000-attending crowd into an unsurpassed frenzy. After having had already endured 5 years of war, with retreat and defeat ensuing on all fronts and the German cities suffering bombing day and night, by the end of the speech, the rambunctious audience was screeching for a totality of war the world had never seen before to be unleashed. It was to come, and it cost Germany alone 12 million dead and its cities to suffer destruction of up to 90% of its buildings. Hail Coke!

The Führer himself was no minnow either. Throughout the war, his physician Dr Morrel kept him high as a kite on a cocktail of morphine, cocaine and methamphetamine (ice). Ice is another drug stimulating this chakra and it is the secret behind Hitler's blitzkriegs (lightning warfare). In the olden days, during war, fighting only took place in daytime. Besides a few guard posts, everybody went to bed, and battle resumed next morning after breakfast. Hitler understood that the secret to success in war was to avoid long, drawn-out campaigns, but instead to keep pushing non-stop against enemy lines until they collapsed. No army in a sober state of mind can do that. In the run-up of WW2 Germany established huge methamphetamine production facilities and the soldiers were kept on these drugs until battles were decided. The method only failed during the war against the Soviet Union, which was so vast that the Russian armies could afford to withdraw until the Germans had run out of thrust (and methamphetamine). You can read more on this subject in Norman Ohler's *Blitzed: Drugs in Nazi Germany*.

Another well-known but less infamous cocaine addict was Sigmund Freud. While being a genius, Freud's psychology excessively focusses on the pathology of the human psyche. One can only wonder what he could have done without cocaine and whether his work and teaching would not have developed more into the direction of humanistic psychology and developing human potential akin to Jung and Maslow. With cocaine being the most expensive drug on the market, we need to ask ourselves why many people sacrifice their otherwise successful lives to support a habit that can cost in extreme cases north of $1000 per day. A person aching to achieve a position of power over others, is doing so because they are trying to overcome a place of hurt and humiliation they have experienced early in their life. This could, for example, be an emotionally abusive relationship with a primary carer, or long-term sexual abuse they could not escape from, both being situations where any form of control was taken away from them. Such individuals are often processing healing from their own trauma by putting themselves into a position of power, so they can control everybody they come in contact with. This works all fine in one's daytime business, but come the night, and with it, the dawning of unfulfilled desires, those in power often need to return to the situation that caused the original trauma but this time with reversed roles, as explained in the next paragraph. Thus they can achieve a moment of relief. This then explains the correlation between power and cocaine. Power is sought to alleviate a trauma caused by a feeling of powerlessness during one's infancy. This feeling of powerlessness is momentarily halted by consumption of cocaine. The same drug also helps us to attain power in the world, in our pursuit of activating the power chakra.

Parallel research covering a different scenario shows that perpetrators of sexual abuse are often those who themselves have been abused in their childhood. They are compensating for a situation in which they were traumatized and powerless by passing on the trauma to somebody else, within the framework of a situation in which they are totally in control. That's why the abused is often a child or a person under their control, such as a student, follower or employee. How does this relate to cocaine? There must be a hurt, a pathology of the power chakra, for a person to become seriously interested in cocaine. Cocaine will give relief from pain caused by disempowerment. During our childhood many of us were humiliated in situations outside of our control. If that was done by a parent, they may have meant well, may have wished to toughen us up, and make us capable of competing and surviving in a cruel world, but this may have left such a deep trauma and feeling of being powerless in the child, that now as a grown-up she is hankering for a constant feeling of being in charge and control.

This tallies with the personal experience I had with cocaine, which is also corroborated by many tales I heard from other people. I got sucked into it because I had friends who used it, and as a teenager, out of fear of being rejected, I tried it out a few times. And then nothing happened, I felt nothing. Or almost nothing, never anything stronger than a triple macchiato could give you, too, at a much lower price. I found cocaine utterly boring, and it did nothing for me. I simply stopped using it out of boredom. I never had a craving for it at any point in my life, not before, during or after taking it. I'm not saying this to point out my inherent greatness but right the opposite. I was inoculated against cocaine addiction through the absence of adverse childhood experiences, for which if anybody is to be acknowledged, then not me but my parents.

When I'm saying that cocaine couldn't get to me because I did not carry the trauma that made me vulnerable to it, I am also not disseminating this from a moral high horse. But what I'm saying is that we should not look down on people destroying their lives through addiction because it is not through their choices they brought on this situation, but their environment and upbringing made them vulnerable. Addicts don't deserve our condemnation and judgment but our compassion and support. Dr Gabor Maté, in his *In The Realm of Hungry Ghosts – Close Encounters with Addiction*, explains that it is not the drug itself that is addictive but that the drug fills an already existing void. Maté repeatedly calls it a "spiritual void" and points out that with a gambling addict, we would not claim that a deck of cards itself has addictive qualities. Yet when we look at substances, we ascribe to them addictive powers. However, we are vulnerable to addiction because we are spiritually empty and our society does this to us. This void, says Mate', has been created by trauma and he shows how the likelihood of addiction statistically rises with the number of adverse childhood experiences (ACEs) you had in your life. ACEs are, for example, cases of sexual, physical or emotional abuse, witnessing one parent beating the other, witnessing addiction of a parent, etc. In these experiences, the child is powerless and a navel/power chakra lesion occurs, which makes us later vulnerable to cocaine and similar drugs. In a typical example, Maté quotes an addict who remembers as a child trying to sleep on the floor while attempting to block out the sounds stemming from the interaction between his sex worker-mother and a procession of customers.

Understanding that an addict is not a person performing wrong choices or an inherently weak or morally inferior person is important. A cocaine addict is a person trying to come to terms with a deep, emotional hurt and trauma. The well-quoted trope of self-medication also holds regarding cocaine, and it is something difficult to understand for those not holding such hurt and damage. Like many other addictions, so also cocaine use is often handed down in family lineages, which is due to parents often passing on their own traumas to their children. When looking at the biographies of addicts, whose life has been destroyed by drugs, it is easy to judge their parents. But their parents often received their trauma from their own parents and so on. Nowhere clearer is this visible than in First Nations communities. Drug addiction was literally unknown to them until their cultures were destroyed by white colonialists. And it is wrong to say that drugs were not available to them because they were, and typically they were used only rarely and then for ceremonial and initiatory purposes, but never recreationally. The problem of recreational drug use and passing on of intergenerational trauma amongst indigenous people, is caused by colonialists trampling their previously well-functioning cultures under their boots.

A quick word on other navel-chakra drugs like speed, crack and crystal meth. Speed is a general term for amphetamines, which are similar to cocaine but often not as psychoactive. Crack-cocaine and crystal meth (ice) are considered even more powerful but weren't en vogue when I was young, so my understanding of them is a., theoretical, and b., based on observation of their users. Crack and ice seem to have a faster deleterious effect on the life of their users, but their basic pathological mechanism is still the same as for cocaine, that is, adverse childhood experiences and vulnerability due to childhood trauma.

What seems to become trickier as we work our way up the speed/cocaine/crack/crystal meth ladder is spiritual rehabilitation. All addiction and the tendency to get infatuated with drugs in this category is ultimately caused by spiritual disconnect (such as through the destruction of one's family or culture), but it also becomes harder to rehabilitate, the deeper we slide into addiction. Although I never become addicted to cocaine, I noticed that its use conferred a contracted sense of self, i.e. my meditation became dry and less rewarding. The ultimate reward of meditation is ego-transcendence, which is only another way of saying an expanded sense of self. The great humanistic psychologist Abraham Maslow towards the end of his life included ego transcendence into his hierarchy of human needs. He stated that humans first need to cover their basic needs such as food, shelter, etc., but as soon as that is done, they will strive for self-actualization, they need to express the purpose of their existence through what they do, for example, their profession. Maslow found that people who succeed with that too, eventually yearn for ego-transcendence (on a sidenote, Maslow is pretty close here to the four Vedic human objectives (*purusharthas*), which are wealth (*artha*), sexual satisfaction (*kama*), right action (*dharma*), and spiritual liberation (*moksha*)). Ego is only a piece of software that limits your identity, i.e. who you believe you are, your sense of self, to the highest level at which you can operate. For somebody whose highest level is the navel chakra, this means the apex of their sense of self is reached in their ability to lead, coerce, manipulate and dominate others.

I'm not saying that everybody who is a leader is a dominator and manipulator. But for us to go beyond the urge to manipulate and dominate, the navel chakra must act in service of a mission it receives through one of the higher chakras. This was for example, the case in leaders such as Christ, Gandhi, M.L. King or Nelson Mandela. They had received a vision of their lives higher purpose, and their navel chakra acted in service to this vision.

The problem with cocaine and the other drugs in this category is that they activate our navel chakra, but only for it to be used for its own sake. While routing great amounts of life force (*prana*) into this chakra, these drugs prevent us from going beyond it. They make us stuck at the navel chakra (this is a theme that repeats itself, to some extent, for pretty much every drug). For a person with an extreme spiritual urge, it may still be possible to conduct *prana* further up, but if using navel-chakra drugs we are always fighting an uphill battle regarding spirituality. *Prana*, when directed by cocaine, gets stuck at the navel chakra and it requires extreme resolve to conduct it any higher against the force of the cocaine. Due to our current evolutionary stage and limitation, it is difficult to conduct life force (*prana*) any higher at the best of times, but cocaine and the related drugs make it so much harder. This category of drugs should be avoided by spiritual practitioners.

On the bright side, when you leave the drugs of the cocaine-category behind, their effect will linger on for some time, making your meditation dry, but this eventually will pass. The evolutionary blueprint sees for us to open the navel chakra during puberty, but then during adolescence to realize that true meaning in life comes from serving others, from contributing to their growth and blossoming. When we do not mature to this point, the world looks like a dangerous, heartless place full of reptile-like beings that need to be controlled, lest they should attack us. Cocaine and similar drugs give us the illusion we are in control and in charge in a heartless world. When replacing these drugs slowly with spiritual practice and true human connection, we need to be compassionate and patient with ourselves. This does not happen in a short time.

The most widely used drug in this category is coffee. Coffee is much milder than the other drugs, but that does not mean it's harmless. I will argue here that if you do drink strong coffee, the coffee created with a barista-type espresso machine, try to not make it a daily habit. If you have to use it on workdays, then try to stay off it on weekends. If you have to use it daily, try to use less coffee powder. If you use double-shots, try to go down to single-shots, etc. And the reason for that is that although coffee is milder, spiritually speaking, it still has a similar effect to cocaine. We could liken it somewhat to homeopathic cocaine.

There is a widespread belief you do get more done on coffee. However, studies have shown that people on coffee actually spend a lot of time going back and correcting mistakes, which they made when performing tasks on coffee-induced haste. The advantage that coffee seems to confer, is then eliminated. This is beautifully expressed in the popular coffeeshop-sign, "Coffee: Do more stupid things faster with more energy". This sentence sums up not only the drama of coffee but also of our entire coffee-fuelled culture. Our modern capitalist, consumer culture likes to do things fast and with lots of energy. Unfortunately, we never stopped long enough to sit down and really contemplate whether it was such a great idea to clear-fell the ancients forests, which were the lungs of the biosphere, to make thousands of species of plants and animals extinct, to deplete the oceans of fish and instead fill them with plastic, to shoot down the massive herds of bison, and deplete the skies of billions of passenger pigeon and hundreds of millions of Eskimo curlews, to take nutrients out of the soil and instead hammer it with pesticides and chemical fertilizers until it is salinized and then washed away, to poison the atmosphere until the pole-caps melt and the oceans rise, and finally to poison our psyches until the question is not anymore, whether we do have mental disorders but the question becomes, "how many and which ones?"

These things are connected, and they are caused by us not being gentle, not stopping long enough to contemplate whether something really is a good idea, not listening to the suffering all around us, of other people, of the animals and the earth. And coffee, while it may not have caused these problems, is part of the Great Acceleration To Nowhere, which in reality drives us into a cul-de-sac of evolutionary stagnation. Uh well, at least we are going full pelt at it! And that's the problem. Because we are going so fast, we don't have time to sit back and notice we are going in the wrong direction. We need to slow down, relax, find new meaning in our relationship with each other and with the non-human life all around us.

Have you noticed that you have much more energy when you drink a strong coffee? Where do you think that energy is coming from? Energy is mobilized *prana*. Coffee helps you to mobilize *prana* that was stored in your body waiting to be expended on a rainy day, when you need it, particularly in old age. Coffee simply helps you to deplete your *pranic* storehouse deeper than you can do without coffee. You are still using the same battery; you are just discharging it faster.

If you find you don't have the energy to fulfil a particular task, it's more holistic to lie down and have a nap, or go for a walk in a forest, or go to the beach to watch a sunrise or sunset. These activities are re-charging. But our fast-paced, off-kilter, de-natured, unbalanced society and economy, forces us to do tasks now. But if we constantly force ourselves to do them, although we don't have the energy, we are ultimately working ourselves towards burn-out. And if we can override that, then towards an early death. To constantly deep discharge our *pranic* battery depletes our vitality, and ultimately makes us age faster, both as individuals, but also as a culture and civilization. This is true on a mild level about coffee, on a stronger level about speed, cocaine, crack and crystal meth. While their intensity is different, their tendency is the same, and that is to deplete your *pranic* storehouse and make you go faster, ultimately to nowhere.

Chapter 4.
THE HEART CHAKRA AND ...ECSTASY?

THE HEART CHAKRA

There are seven main chakras. Some yoga schools break some of the chakras down into several sub-chakras, but the seven chakras are sufficient to explain evolution, history and all transformational states. Of these seven main chakras, the heart chakra is the axis, the centre piece. It provides the axis around which the three basic chakras, which contain our evolutionary past, and the three higher chakras, which contain our evolutionary future, revolve. Besides the heart chakra geometrically being the central chakra, the reason yoga considers it the most important one, is that the heart chakra is suitable as a base from which to venture into most situations and mental states. This means it is functionally central, too. The three higher chakras, to be discussed in great detail later, will give us spiritual insights and revelation of three levels. However, once we have received these initiations and revelations, we need to return to the heart because it is from here, we can meet others and communicate with them. For that purpose, the higher chakras are unsuitable. And the heart chakra forms a good point of departure from which to venture into the lower chakras, if needed.

But why do we have to leave the heart chakra at all? Can't we just approach all problems and situations from here? Survival, procreation, taking care of one's children and spouse, and assertion or assimilation, cannot succeed when coming from the heart chakra. For example, from the vantage point of the heart, all people you meet are equally worthy of love. The heart chakra does not realize that you have a unique karmic relationship with your children and your spouse. For this, the sacral chakra is required. Similarly, when Jesus drove out the moneychangers and vendors from the temple of David, he did not do so from the heart. The heart chakra would hold the position that everybody should be able to act according to their own needs and desires. It is the power chakra, employed by Jesus that realizes that sometimes there are greater things at stake than the individual's right for free self-expression. In this case this was the need for cleansing of the Temple of David from inappropriate commerce, an act of re-consecration.

The heart chakra is the next major step on humanity's journey of spiritual evolution. If we liken the navel chakra to our primate brain, then the heart chakra is our humanoid brain, the brain that directs and determines what it is to be truly humane. Whereas the more basic emotions are linked to the sacral chakra, the heart chakra contains the more complex sentiments that drive much of human society, for example, our need to be acknowledged and respected by others, love, shame, guilt, honour, righteousness, chivalry, nobility, etc. It is the activation of this chakra that made leaders like Gandhi, M.L King and Nelson Mandela who they were. Also, Jesus Christ and Krishna were masters of the heart, but as we will see later, both had an uncanny ability to play the scale of the chakras up and down, much like a xylophone. That's why both were so baffling and unpredictable to their audiences, and it is this capacity, the ability to evenly access all chakras when required, that is the goal of the true yogi.

What the element air is for the macrocosm, that is the heart chakra for the microcosm, the human being. The element air manifests itself in the microcosm as the heart chakra. Both air and the heart chakra are related to the sense of touch. The movement and temperature of air are felt by the skin, the tactile organ. Similarly, sentiments of the heart are often expressed through touch. Note that hugging involves embracing the heart area of another person. If we see another person in great pain, we embrace them to bring the magnetic fields of our hearts together. This is often more powerful than to speak many elaborate words.

Our society is dominated by the navel chakra and often we act as if that's all that matters. For example, we go to work mainly to earn a living. However, while being at work, we are not just a robot going through the motions in a perfectly programmed way. We are interacting with our work colleagues and qualities such as respect, acceptance, rejection, avoidance of shame and guilt become driving motives. For many people, to work in a particular workplace does not just mean to perform a certain function, but honourable (rather than self-demeaning) communication and interaction with others at the same workplace takes on great significance. If the management of a particular workplace does not ensure a dignified and supportive environment, we may leave our job and apply somewhere else, although the first workplace gave us a decent income. This is because the heart chakra represents the evolutionary stage of the fully integrated human being. At this point, we are not just concerned about making enough money, but how we do that becomes paramount. We are asking questions about ethics and whether the activities of the entity for which we are working, is reconcilable with our values.

The function of the navel chakra is assimilative/accumulative, but here at the heart chakra, it becomes relative, the focus now becomes how we are relating to other human beings. What makes us truly humane is our ability to relate to others from the heart, rather than in a mechanistic, calculating fashion. For a teacher, it is very important to relate to students in a heartfelt fashion. Particularly for spiritual teachers, it is very important that they come down from the lofty heights of the still higher chakras, and centre themselves in the heart. A teacher very adept in doing so was Jesus Christ. By washing the feet of his disciples, Jesus showed us that the teacher cannot tower above the student, but the teacher must demonstrate that he recognizes the Divine in the student. This cannot be a mere verbal statement but must be demonstrated in action.

According to the Upanishads, the atman, the self, is in the heart. That's why with the opening of the heart chakra, we will recognize that the Divine embodies Itself in the same way in others, as it does in us, too. That means the same divine self, which is in us, is also in the person across from us. On a deeper level, we realize that we do share the same self, the same consciousness. So says Krishna in the Bhagavad Gita, "I am the self in the heart of all beings." In the Bible, we find Jesus saying, "he who has seen the son, has seen the Father". When Jesus uses the term "son" or "son of God", he does not refer to himself, but to the divine self in all beings, whereas the term Father implies the cosmic self. True seeing of the "son" the divine self in the body, leads to seeing the Father, the cosmic self.

At the level of the navel chakra, we cannot see the divine self in another. We see them as a resource to be exploited, an entity competing with us, unless we cunningly manipulate them. Once we see, with the opening of the heart chakra, the divine self in others, we cannot anymore do evil unto them. Because they share the same self with us, any pain and suffering incurred to them, also incurs to us. That's why we see saints and mystics acting "selflessly". Selflessly is not really the right term here. We use that term only because we identify "self" with the pathologically contracted self of the lower chakras. At the level of the base chakra, our sense of self is limited to our body. At the level of the sacral chakra, our sense of self expands to include our family and territory. At the level of the navel chakra, our sense of self grows to include our professional association, nation, religion, etc. But still we believe in the concept of "other", we believe that we cannot love another, who is not included in our sense of self, because they do not share our religion, culture, nationality, etc. It is only at the level of the heart chakra, that we recognize the Divine as the core of our self. However, this is only just the beginning, and the following step is even more important. It is the realization that the same self is contained in others, too, the cognizance we all share a common self, the Divine. At this point then, our sense of self increases to take in the whole of humanity. Then the injunction, "do unto others as you would have done unto yourself" does take on a new import because there are no more human others.

Note, how much conflict in our society exists because of "othering", the definition of a group or category we identify as us, and a different one we call others. It is thus, that whites can enslave blacks, that Christians and Muslims, men and women, believers and infidels, conservatives and progressives, capitalists and communists, have's and have not's, can fight each other down the aisles of history. Once the other is included in your sense of self, any basis for strife and conflict has fallen away.

Due to this expanded sense of self, the heart chakra promotes compassion. On the level of the navel chakra, becoming wealthy or powerful, or possessing excellent skills, are the highest goals we would strive for. Once the heart chakra is activated, however, we learn that the greatest gift in life is to make a positive contribution to the life of others. And it is not because others then believe us to be great, but because we realize that true happiness and freedom do not arise from receiving but from giving "selflessly". It is this that makes us truly human and humane, the ability to give without expecting reciprocity. It is the urge to give, to simply contribute to the flowering, blossoming, unfoldment and evolution of another human. Unlike the sacral chakra, which reflects neediness, and the navel chakra, which wants to receive and take, the heart chakra is giving. To open the heart chakra, means to allow a greater force of infinite potential to express itself through us for the good of all. There cannot be a greater feeling of happiness and freedom for the individual than to become a conduit for that force. The ability to selflessly give to others liberates us from our past. To serve others then becomes our own liberation from our robotically conditioned past.

It is easy when reading these lofty passages to become dejected upon noticing how far we as a civilization and species still have to go to become a truly humane or "enlightened" society. But there are also green shoots everywhere. As I am writing this in my own home country, Australia, rages a discussion around Australia Day, Australia's national holiday, the day all Australians celebrate their national identity. Controversially, this is the date on which the first fleet of colonialists landed in Australia (26th January), and which heralded the beginning of mass slaughter and cultural genocide for Aborigines. Our indigenous people refer to this day therefore as invasion day, or survival day, and for them, understandably, it is a day of mourning and not celebration. Every year a greater number of white people come out in support of the Australian indigenous people in rejecting this date as incapable of being celebrated by all Australians. Truly, the 26th of January can never be an all-Australia day, but only a white-Australia day. This acknowledgement and change in sentiment are taking place because white people are including people of colour in their sense of self, they are identifying with them rather than seeing them as *other*. A similar change is taking place in the United States with the Black Life Matters movement and globally with the MeToo movement. For millennia men simply looked the other way when other men treated women as their property. This took place because according to the logic of the sacral chakra, any woman other than a man's mother, wife and daughters, was excluded from that man's sense of self. Today, men worldwide are slowly waking up to, what Buddha called for, in a bygone age. And that is that men should look at all women with the same respect as if they were their mothers.

A similar progress brought about by a gradual collective activation of the heart chakra, is taking place in the judiciary. Although a fully opened navel chakra is essential for a judge, the evolution of our judiciary has gone far beyond this point. Whereas Hamurabi's law could be reduced to the simple tenet "an eye for an eye, a tooth for a tooth", today a judge, even in a murder case, has to consider whether a murder was executed cold-bloodedly or with internal turmoil and whether the perpetrator appears to regret the action, and even the degree to which any remorse shown is authentic. Because of its complexity, any such judgement could never be handed down by a machine such as a computer: it needs a human with at least some intuitive access to functions of the heart chakra. Today we are looking more and more at how far a perpetrator themselves was victimized by the circumstances in their own life. A sentence today is also less aimed at mere punishment but as an attempt at reintegration, a "corrective service". While at this point this may be touted by legal systems as mere theory, a beginning has been made and a slow progress towards this theory is being implemented.

While great spiritual leaders of the past activated their heart chakras and gave us a vision of true humanity, most of our current political leaders are still evolving to that point. If you look at the human as a promise, a bridge that spans the chasm from the animal towards the Divine, then the heart chakra is the exact midway. Here the human looks at its most precarious, most vulnerable and most precious. For if we look at those teachers of the heart, many were slain through our own hands. At the point human life becomes most humane tit looks to us so utopian that we are inclined to destroy it. And why would we do that? Because the mere presence of these teachers is a painful reminder to all of us this is where we are heading. A painful reminder to the rest of us how far behind we are with our "survival of the fittest" and "each to themselves and the last eats the devil". So painful that it is easier for us to eliminate and kill these advanced souls rather than keep the provocation alive in our middle. But those teachers have shown that it is exactly into this direction that the evolution of humanity points. Whereas the base chakra sees others as competitors or threats, the sacral chakra as guarantors of security, and the navel chakra as possible add-ons to one's followers, the heart chakra relates to others from the position of wanting to give unconditional love.

Open the heart chakra after the navel chakra has been activated but before animating the still higher chakras. If one opens the heart chakra without activating the navel chakra beforehand, one is likely to be taken advantage of. This is the scenario of the healer who takes on the disorders of their patients, or the lover who becomes victimized and taken advantage of. But if the higher chakras are opened without the heart chakra being activated beforehand, one is likely to become something akin to a cult leader. For if you understand sacred law (throat chakra) and obtain divine knowledge (third-eye chakra) and combine this with entrepreneurial skills (navel chakra), but without the joy of giving, serving, forgiveness and compassion (heart chakra), the result may be a self-serving cult leader, where followers count only in relation to their ability to fatten their wallet, or increase his sphere of influence. No spiritual teaching, and indeed teacher, are worthy without the ability to selflessly serve the student.

An opening of the higher chakras with both the heart chakra and the navel chakra blocked may lead to schizophrenia or a multi-personality disorder. If your higher chakras open (for example, through psychedelic agents), a sudden enormous influx of data not directly pertaining to your personal life, can overwhelm you, and if the middle chakras (navel and heart) are not fully active this data and information cannot be meaningfully integrated into your worldview. This condition will be discussed in more detail when dealing with psychedelic drugs (LSD, psilocybin, DMT, mescalin, etc.) in chapters 5 and 6 of this book.

The higher chakras can also be opened too fast by extreme forms of spiritual practice, such as in the case of the Indian civil servant Gopi Krishna, the author of the 1970 book *Kundalini, Evolutionary Energy in Man*. But this did not happen spontaneously in an instant. For 17 years, Gopi Krishna concentrated daily for 1 to 2 hours on the crown chakra while sitting in the lotus posture (Padmasana). Such an extreme form of practice can bring about these effects. Before engaging in extreme practices aimed at opening the higher chakras, for mental sanity, we need to first complete the groundwork. This means that the chakras need to always be targeted from the bottom up. This is also exactly how the natural evolution of life works. When we were reptiles, the next evolutionary step was not the neocortex and primate brain, but we first needed to develop the mammalian, limbic brain. In spiritual evolution, we need to first take the next appropriate step and not jump three steps ahead and leave out a few.

Let me explain why: The opening of the third-eye chakra can lead to visions of an infinite number of beings being exhaled (coming into existence) by the Brahman (the infinite consciousness or deep reality) and a similar number of beings again inhaled (being reabsorbed) by the same Brahman. When the heart chakra is open, there is an incredible freedom in that vision, as you can see that the state of the eternal self (the heart or *atman*) of all these beings does not change in that process. You can also see we all share the same *atman*, which means that in the birth of one, we are all born and in the death of one, we all die. With an open heart- and third-eye chakra you can also see that the pure consciousness within every individual (*atman*) is the very cosmic consciousness (Brahman) that does all the giving birth and annihilating. The bodies die, yet the self is immortal. This is the meaning of St. Paul's cryptic words, "In

CHAPTER 4.

Adam we all die yet in Christ we all are reborn". Adam, the first human, is here taken as a metaphor for the body, and Christ is the self-realized consciousness within us.

This is all nice and easy with both chakras activated, but with the heart chakra closed, the same third-eye chakra induced visions (of which psychedelics are a stimulant of) can turn into a spirit-crushing and soul-maiming machinery of destruction. So, the question is not how on Earth can we get such a vision and divine revelation as fast as possible. The question is how we can appropriately prepare ourselves because this type of vision will eventually come on your spiritual journey, if you want it or not, and when it comes, you had better be prepared, or else there is no chance of integration.

These visions are powered by the higher chakras, and we need to prepare ourselves by opening and activating the medial/intermediary chakras, the navel- and the heart chakra. The two lowest chakras are tamasic or mass-like in nature. They constitute the animalistic impetus of our evolutionary past. The navel and the heart chakra are rajasic in nature, representing the frenzy of human society and its unease of ever being content with where we are right now. The higher chakras (throat and third-eye) are sattvic in nature, they show us sacred law and order of the cosmos, and the intelligence that crystallizes itself as everything. We can neither understand nor integrate this if the heart chakra is closed. The inactive heart chakra has given rise to the myth of the Kundalini accident, where people report mysterious body sensations coming from nowhere. These so-called Kundalini accidents are caused either by psychedelic drugs (and can take place with a long time delay, as the unravelling may go on in the subconscious) or by intense spiritual practices (*sadhanas*) that are done aggressively without understanding of their impact. Today, these practices are all advertised on the internet with no understanding of their impact. Before we engage in them, the heart chakra and before it, the navel chakra, have to be unblocked.

The blockage of the heart chakra is again the working of the Vishnu *granthi*, the blockage of the force that maintains human society. If the Vishnu blockage (*granthi*) is powerful, it may block the navel and heart chakras simultaneously. If so, no higher spiritual exercises (such as meditation on awareness or the higher chakras) should be practised: these middle chakras need to be opened first. If through an accident the higher chakras open, while Vishnu *granthi* blocks the two middle chakras, schizophrenia is likely. Schizophrenia means that people cognise such powerful knowledge they cannot integrate it into their lives. When the navel- and heart chakras have been opened, most things that life throws at us can be handled. Especially the heart chakra fosters submission to a higher intelligence and power.

The exact method of unblocking the heart chakra is beyond the scope of this book and I have described it in previous textbooks. I will nevertheless quickly sketch the development. Firstly, one should prepare oneself with as much *asana* (posture) practice as feasible. I have practiced postures for 40 years with varying intensity, but there was a decade where I practiced *asana* for over 3 hours daily, partially to undo the damage done to my astral body through drugs. I have described this process in great detail in my first two books. I realize that the Ashtanga vinyasa method is not suitable to all and other gentler approaches may be more applicable for some. In my case, the high-powered approach was exactly what I needed to mitigate the hardwearing effect of my prior life.

The next step then is to synchronize the lunar and solar energy channels, the holistic/integrative brain hemisphere on one hand, and analytical brain hemisphere on the other. This is achieved through a pranayama technique called Nadi Shuddhi, which has several pre-stages and must include mantra and visualization. The next step then includes internal and external breath retentions with simultaneous application of all three bandhas (internal locks) called Mahabandha. This complex process is also known as Stage 1 *granthi*-breaker. Only when Stage 1 *granthi*-breaker has succeeded, do we go on to the next step, which is Stage 2 *granthi*-breaker, also known as Bhastrika. If you are not properly prepared for Bhastrika, you can have a similar disorienting effect as when taking a hallucinogen. Some teachers advise going straight to Bhastrika and there are some crazy versions of it on the internet. No surprise then that people blow fuses and have Kundalini-accidents. The process briefly listed so far is described in great detail in my textbook *Pranayama The Breath of Yoga*.

A few more words on Bhastrika: inhaling and expanding the ribcage increases the space we allocate to ourselves. The ability to do so is directly linked to self-worth and self-love. A collapsed and rigid ribcage is often linked to armouring and protecting the heart but also to denying ourselves the additional territory that a full inhalation would allocate to us. Bhastrika is a dynamic breathing technique that includes thoracic bellowing – quickly inflating and deflating the thorax. This is the prime method of breaking through the energy blockages, particularly the Vishnu *granthi*, which blocks the heart chakra. Bhastrika is the most powerful breathing technique in existence and can be practised only when other more basic forms of *pranayama* are mastered, reflecting the need to open the lower three chakras first.

Once you are established here, you practise conducting life force (*prana*) through the chakras, a method I have described in my text *Yoga Meditation: Through Mantra, Chakras and Kundalini to Spiritual Freedom*. The ability to consciously place *prana* into the heart chakra is a great asset for an individual. It helps us to stay centred in the heart and connected to the greater good during trials and tribulations. It also helps us share merit we gain when riding a wave of success and are on top of the world. Placing *prana* into the heart chakra is also important during conflict resolution. It helps us to understand that the needs of the individual in front of us are very similar to our own or those of the group we belong to.

The heart chakra can also be opened by meditating directly on its location combined with visualizing it and by using the *mantra* YAM, the syllable of air. However, this is not a method suitable for beginners. Firstly it is only suitable if the chakras beneath the heart, especially the navel chakra have already been activated. Secondly, meditation on a single chakra does not help with conducting *prana* in and out of a chakra. A typical example of a situation in which this would be needed would be if you are sitting in a park watching over your children playing when suddenly your children are threatened by danger. The right thing to do here is to drop your *prana* down into the sacral chakra (the one that allows you to mobilize massive amounts of energy in defence of your progeny) and to protect your children. If in such a situation, you would meditate exclusively on the heart chakra, this would do nothing for your ability to protect your children.

Among the *asanas*, back-bending assists in opening the heart chakra, but postures are only ancillary in this process. The relief that one feels upon getting the brick-load of age-old conserved emotions off one's chest through back-bending differs from opening the heart chakra. Opening the heart chakra means to love others without needing anything in return. The process of resolution (*sankalpa*) that I described in my text *How To Find Your Life's Divine Purpose* is also paramount for this chakra.

The dichotomy between the navel- and the heart chakra represent our present situation, with the navel chakra responsible for complex human social structures that rely heavily on organizing a society by competing for scarce resources, and by rewarding individuals by allocating them pleasure units (wages) or demerit (fines) if their actions do not align with the societal majority. Still somewhat in the future beckons the heart chakra with its message of love, reconciliation and healing the wounds of the past, which obsession with the lower chakras has surely brought about in us. Both of these chakras are frantic (*rajasic*). *Rajas* (frantic activity) provides energy, and we need the energy surge of these two chakras to move human society forward across the bridge that spans the chasm between the animal and the Divine within us. To make our path across this chasm, the inertia of the past has to be left behind and great energies have to be mobilized. This also expresses itself as the many stresses and tensions that modern society exposes itself to.

We now come to the mystical qualities of heart chakra. The Sanskrit name of this chakra, *anahata*, means 'unstruck'. The reason for this is that the *mantra* OM is heard in this chakra. It is the primordial sound, the sound that brought forth the vibratory pattern that today we call the Big Bang, the birth of our universe. Note that the primordial sound OM itself came forth from a form of void, the unified field. Usually, a sound is produced by two objects striking against each other. There was nothing to strike against when OM was projected forth; hence it is called unstruck.

The reason OM is heard in the heart chakra is explained in the *Chandogya Upanishad* (VIII.1): 'Within the human heart there is a triangular shrine and within that shrine a small flame the size of a thumb. And within the flame miraculously is this entire vast universe with all its worlds, oceans, rivers and mountains.' The small flame is the pure consciousness, the self. Within that self the sound OM occurs and within that sound is the whole of the universe.

In the *Maitri Upanishad* (VI.35), we encounter more mystical knowledge about the heart. 'As a fire dies down once we stop providing fuel, so when the fuel of the senses is withheld, the mind is reabsorbed into the heart.' That is a baffling sentence, but it reflects the realization that the mind is projected forth from the heart and not the head. That's why we use the adage, "follow your heart," because the mind needs to be in service of the heart. With the opening of the heart chakra, the mind will become the servant of the heart. Then humanity can take the place it is destined to be, that is, the guardian of the garden of life, the biosphere, rather than what it currently is, its pillager, ransacker and looter.

The *Upanishad* explains in the above quote that, if external stimuli are withheld, the mind will be reabsorbed into the heart. In ancient society, the heart was the natural resting place of the mind when the mind does not need to work. Notice how different this idea is from that of modern society. Firstly, we bury ourselves under a constant input of sensory stimulus so the mind can never come to rest in the heart. This situation has become exacerbated through the prevalence of hand-held devices, who through their constant audible alerts inform you that your reply to some irrelavent post of some digital passer-by is required. Secondly, when no sensory/external stimulus is available our now hyperactive mind, instead of being reabsorbed into the heart, complains about boredom and out come the drugs, the sex, the television, the computer game, the real estate portfolio, the academic degree, the business empire or whatever else we can come up with to keep it frantic. This means that in our culture, the mind never gets to rest in the heart, at the bossom of the Divine (the *atman*). For this reason self-love, self-acceptance and self-esteem are an anathema to our culture.

You will find that members of most ancient cultures when asked where they reside within their body will not, like modern westerners, point to their forehead but to their heart. Patanjali, the author of the *Yoga Sutra*, says (III.34) 'Knowledge of the mind is produced by meditating on the heart chakra.' This takes on a much larger significance when we understand that yoga itself is the science of the mind (and not that of the body, which is Ayurveda). Patanjali is the founding father of the science of mind, of yoga. In this stanza, he tells us he gained this knowledge by meditating on the heart chakra.

The heart chakra itself can be pure (we even use the expression *being of pure heart*) or it can be defiled by lower sentiments, such as greed, avarice, infatuation, ambition and competitiveness. The heart is cleansed by abstaining from harbouring toxic thoughts and emotions, such as revenge, desire, ambition, greed, aversion, hatred, infatuation, jealousy. Modern society espouses the belief we are slavishly subjected to these lower emotions and thoughts, and these emotions are somehow natural. We ourselves manufacture these emotions, and we spend a lot of energy and time doing so. It is only due to our being not producing them consciously that we are completely unaware of the process. We are, however, producing them subconsciously by constantly repeating and reinforcing subconscious imprints (*samskaras*) and conditioning (*vasana*). To keep the heart pure, it needs to be daily cleansed through the process I have outlined in *How To Find Your Life's Divine Purpose*.

Ambition tells us to want more and more – and it always pushes happiness into the future until another goal is accomplished. However, this future never comes. A heart poisoned by ambition will never be happy; it will only ever produce more goals and ambitions, and even at death, there will be a longing for a distant future when all ambitions may finally be fulfilled. Contentment means realizing that the heart, the pure consciousness, is forever complete, and no ambition, no goal, no becoming, can make it complete. Contentment leads us into the triumphant here and now of pure consciousness, the *atman*.

There are four levels of divine realization and with the activation of the heart chakra, we experience the first, to see the Divine, the *atman*, in others. This means to see there is one common self we share with all humans. For completeness, I will mention the next three levels, which will be discussed in greater detail while covering the upcoming chakras. At the throat chakra level, our sense of self expands so we now recognize the entire material cosmos and all life forms as the crystallized body of the Divine. With the opening of the third-eye chakra, God-realization expands to include the cosmic intelligence that crystallizes as the cosmos and all life. God-realization peaks at the crown chakra, at which we know infinite consciousness as deep reality and the unified field, out of which everything emanates and to which everything returns.

CHAPTER 4.

The heart chakra confers a lasting experience of the essential goodness in every being, and it constitutes an essential step in human evolution. It enables us to switch from mere justice, settling scores and getting even, to compassion and forgiveness. People sometimes think they place themselves in a disadvantageous situation if they forgive, as if holding on to one's grudge and vitriol against somebody was an asset. A person very dear to me once told me they would take their hatred against their own father into their grave. They had been treated cruelly by their father and thought that if they forgave him, they would let him off the hook. But when this person died, their hatred, which they had intended to be directed against their father, turned against themselves and their death became very unpleasant.

We let not others, but ourselves off the hook when we forgive. By holding on to grudges and negativity, we punish ourselves and hold ourselves in the past. Through forgiveness, we heal ourselves and become able to move forward. Realisations, such as these herald the dawn of the heart chakra. When moving forward to the heart chakra, we become able to give up conflict with ourselves, and it is this conflict with ourselves that expresses itself in crime, warfare, hatred, competition and so on. If we truly embrace the heart and forgive ourselves for our own shortcomings and failure, we can stop fighting against their manifestation in others. When Jesus said (John 13.35), 'People will recognize you for being my disciples if you have love for one another', he talked about a new, future humanity that was directed by the heart chakra.

There is another issue relating to the heart chakra we need to inquire into before we return to the subject of drugs. And that is our continued reliance on leaders and especially on spiritual leaders. We are witnessing a transition towards the era of the heart chakra. This change is necessary; otherwise, our planet Gaia will pull the curtain on humanity. This transition towards the heart chakra is not something that leaders can do for us; leaders themselves are still part of the old paradigm. A leader asserts themselves via their navel chakra over others, who is primarily operating on the level of the sacral chakra.

During the era of the heart chakra, the Divine will be expressed less by strong leaders who deliver one truth in a linear, top-down fashion. It will be expressed through what happens between us, how we interact with each other, how we treat each other, what and how we communicate. The Divine revelation during the heart chakra phase will come as interrelatedness, humanity will change to operating like a decentralized brain in which all neurons are wired to each other rather than in a vertical fashion, and that's why the old linear guru-paradigm can no longer serve. In the old paradigm, a guru is somebody who is trying to convey the evolved messages of the four higher chakras through the vehicle of the third, the navel- and power chakra. That cannot work. The vehicle, the teacher, herself must be transformed by the message and can therefore not remain a leader anymore who is towering over their followers.

The new guru is not a person, but it is what emerges as we teach each other, as we take the next step of human evolution together, as we experience an awakening of the heart chakra. Newly emerging Christian theology calls this "the second coming of Christ as the whole of humanity receiving the Sonship collectively." Also, here we find the concept of the Divine expressing itself through the entirety of humanity. Interestingly, this was already announced when Jesus said, "And have I not said ye all are gods. Ye all are children of the most high" (Psalm 82:6). In Buddhism, too, this same thread was continued when Thich Nhat Hanh said that the Maitreya Buddha (the coming Buddha) would not be a single person but the emerging consciousness of the *sangha* (community of practitioners) as a whole.

The outgoing sacral- and navel-chakra paradigm still forms our ideas about the guru and spiritual teacher. Many of us remain dominated by the mammalian chakra and limbic brain psychology; that is, we are looking for a leader who will safely guide us, like sheep to a fattening meadow. Those who have activated the navel chakra are desperately looking for just such a flock of sheep to lead. To paraphrase the great Abraham Maslow, we might say, "For a leader to be ultimately at peace with themselves, they have to lead." Along this line of enquiry, I have to say that much of the years I spent following gurus was ultimately about the drama of the leader, the guru, and not about the life of the followers. Although so much seemed to happen in our lives back then, we followers were really only pawns on the boards on which the gurus acted out their own drama, their own needs. One such need was to be seen and loved by a large number of people, similar to a rockstar or celebrity actor. If you have that need, you will develop any sort of charisma to obtain it. But charisma is still just a reflection of sacral- and navel-chakra dynamics. Although in our case, the vehicle of a spiritual teaching is used, the structure of a sacral- and navel-chakra relationship does not differ from that of a commander to their private, a boss to their employee, or a warlord to their mercenary—it is one-dimensional, top-down and linear. This must change now.

As we are reeling from the abyss of ecocide, to which the belief in and exertion of authority has driven us, the heart chakra teaches us to relate from an entirely new paradigm. The

Divine at this level wants to express Herself as interrelatedness, inter-being, compassion, forgiveness, love, and gratitude. Part of that is realizing that the structure, not just the content, of human relationships must change, must grow. Activation of the heart chakra means realizing that together, we receive the Divine as a collective. Nobody is an exclusive incarnation or avatar of the Divine. We all need each other to take this next step together. The Divine is now expressing itself collectively through all beings, from the greatest genius down to the most insignificant amoeba. There is no single person who can express this; the nature of the game has changed.

Life and modern society have become too complex for a single person to have all of the answers, or for humanity to be divided into a two-caste system of "enlightened ones" and "unenlightened ones." So what can we do to receive the Divine? Listen to it, feel it, and become it. Try to see the Divine in the eyes of every person you meet. See their struggle to embody the Divine. Maybe they can only see it in themselves and not in others and therefore are trying to revive the old paradigm game of "I'm the guru."

When the heart chakra collectively activates, there will still be spiritual teachers, but the focus will be on how much their conduct reflects their teaching. How do we interact with each other? How do I convey my experience through my actions? More important than the fact that I have recognized the Divine within me is whether I can now see the Divine in the person across from me. Most important is how I treat this person. Only through my conduct with them can I convey what I see within them. In the outgoing navel-chakra model, the guru produced our evolution. In the incoming heart-chakra paradigm, we collectively evolve spiritually, as one humanity. In the old system, I would ask myself, "How can 'I' attract the grace of the Divine? How can 'I' spiritually awaken? How can I enter nirvana? How can I attain Jnana?"

The heart chakra has us rephrase these questions: "How can we foster the emergence of the Divine through our collective? How can we co-create our evolution? How can awakening manifest through us?" The shift is away from the individual. What liberates us is not personal attainment but service. However much I have personally attained is still relative, if the person next to me is stuck in the mire. We either evolve together, or not at all. I cannot isolate myself against the pain and anguish in the world; I can only numb myself (such as through drugs or so-called success). When I experience yogic super-conscious states, I realize at some point that my being does not end at the surface of my skin but transcends all boundaries. At some point, literally all pain experienced by any being in the past, present, and future (and all glory, too) becomes mine. Would I enjoy my own shabby, small-scale enlightenment when others are depressed and suffering? That would suggest this so-called enlightenment isn't worth much. Future spiritual evolution is no longer relegated to individual attainment. Through our interrelations and our expressions of gratitude, through forgiveness, love, and compassion towards each other, the Divine will emerge collectively as *us*.

The Divine is embodied in all beings, particularly humans, but only if we can consciously feel it and be it. Collectively we are now becoming the guru. And now it is time for us to grow up and share this responsibility. We must withdraw our projections from all forms of authority and reclaim our own power. Let's create an equal humanity in which we are united as free, and unconditioned individuals under one super-intelligence, the

Divine. In collectively realizing the Divine in these manifold forms, we may co-create our destiny. We are invited to stop being part of the problem and start being part of the solution.

IS ECSTASY THE HEART CHAKRA DRUG?

Firstly, ecstasy or MDMA (Methylenedioxymethamphetamine) is an amphetamine and should be in the navel chakra group. However, the case is not so clear. Ecstasy is one of those drugs that cannot be clearly allocated to a single chakra. So, let's look closely.

During the 1970s, ecstasy was a popular drug in psychotherapy and particularly in couples counselling. The substance has been shown to increase empathy for and closeness with others. It also increases self-confidence. Similarly, it helps people who are too bottled up to access and own their emotions. It reduces inhibitions. All these effects made it very popular for members of the Rajneesh-movement (a popular cult I was a member of), too. It was only made illegal as a Schedule 1 drug (severest category) in 1985 and against the resistance of many psychologists and psychiatrists. It took until 2017, that is 32 years, for that stance to soften after evidence was recognized that MDMA supports treatment for post-traumatic stress disorder (PTSD), and it is now used, for example, in Israel to treat war veterans.

Let's look at some of the negative effects: Because ecstasy today is often used on raves and in nightclubs, it can lead to dehydration and demineralization, which occurs when people drink too much water and dilute the electrolytes in their bloodstream. A significant danger also comes from the fact that when buying ecstasy on the black market, you may end up with something different than intended, and often with something much more toxic. Black market pills of ecstasy often contain only around 40% MDMA and the rest may be bath salts, or worse. The coroner of the Australian state of Victoria recently urgently recommended introducing drug testing at music festivals, after it was revealed that five young men died after taking what they believed was MDMA. It turned out the pills did not contain MDMA but a dangerous combination of two new psychoactive substances.

When I was a member of the Rajneesh-cult, the myth was circulated that ecstasy was absolutely pure, non-toxic and within an hour, it would break down to nothing in the body. That's a fairy-tale. MDMA emits your dopamine and serotonin (pleasure hormones) stores in one huge hit. That's why you can get very euphoric and hedonic (open to pleasure) but may feel depressed and depleted afterwards. If you watch people on ecstasy while you are sober, it's peculiar to see what little things can give them pleasure and joy but see them the next day and serious impulses that would usually elicit a positive response are now met with bland gazes. Because ecstasy exhausts our pleasure hormone storehouses, we are now much harder to please. Most people who come off an ecstasy habit, feel depressed for some time. Another effect of serotonin is that it helps you sleep well. With serotonin depletion through regular use, sleep deprivation often results.

Let's have a look at the toxicity: with the around two dozen times I took ecstasy, I am still classified as a moderate user. But I was surprised by its toxicity and the time needed to repair my body through yoga. I practiced yoga through the entire time of my ecstasy use and somehow, with all the Rajneeshie-talk around me, I brainwashed myself into believing it was safe. It wasn't. From my subjective experience, ecstasy was harder on my body than any other drug I took. I did lose a lot of life force (*prana*), it depleted and weakened my navel chakra and my energy channels (*nadis*). It took extensive high-intensity yoga to fix the acute and chronic damage caused by this drug.

Would I still consider it worth taking against PTSD? Yes, in PTSD therapy, you may take it one to three times and in a setting in which you work intensely on your issues. That's a completely different situation than mere recreational use. We will encounter this problem again when talking about the hallucinogens. Users are quick to point out that certain drugs have shown to be beneficial in a therapeutic setting. That's a far cry from a habitual, recreational self-medication, in which a lot of time is wasted in simple hedonistic settings such as raves.

My description of self-sustained damage incurred by ecstasy is anecdotal and, for others, hard to verify. I can, however, see it in my yoga students, too, if they suffer from a similar post-ecstasy condition as I did. But let's look at hard science. Ecstasy has been shown to damage the axon terminals of serotonin receptors and they repair only very slowly (as I discovered in my practice). It also negatively affects both the white and grey matter in your brain. It reduces neuroplasticity in white matter and density in grey matter. Furthermore, it reduces the total volume of your grey matter, and it can even reduce in size your orbitofrontal cortex. That's the part of your brain behind your eyebrows that has the final word in decision-making. All data from other brain parts are wired to this one for final cognitive processing. This is one of the most recent parts of our human brain to develop and if you look, for example, at the Indian epic *Mahabharata*, its main character, Yudhishthira, is a walking orbitofrontal cortex. He's constantly busy collecting massive amounts of data to spend a long time considering the right decisions to make. You don't want that part of your brain to decrease in size! If we should take any drugs at all, it should be ones that increase the size of the orbitofrontal cortex (I haven't found any yet).

In line with my personal reports above, ecstasy, if taken regularly, may also cause damage to your serotonin transporters, meaning for being more upbeat for a short time now, you pay by being more downbeat for longer in the future. Your attention span may also reduce, with your memory and your visual processing. This depends on how much you use. One of the worst effects is the link with depression following ecstasy use, but an increase of anxiety is also clearly linked. Generally, science says that some of those negative effects are reversible when you stop using. You can reverse it through a long life of yoga, at least so I think, but I wonder whether it wouldn't be better to start your yoga without having to first reverse negative side effects incurred through drug use? I've always wondered that during the last 40 years of my life, and I can never answer that question.

With all of that covered, I'd like to revisit my own experiences with ecstasy in a therapeutic setting. During the early 1980s, I spent a big part of my income on Rajneeshie therapy-groups, some of which employed ecstasy. While I did learn a lot, some of what was touted as great insights did not stack up in hindsight. One of the purported advantages of ecstasy is that it increases empathy for and closeness with others. This could be of great advantage in couples-therapy, but if you come in a group therapy with the general public, you may not want to get close with everybody. In Rajneeshie-therapy, which today is widely emulated in general New-Age culture, we were told there is no reason we should not get close to everybody and not doing so was dubbed "withholding". Today, there is a reason we don't click with some people and that is because we don't harmonize with them. If you need to take a drug to biochemically override this impulse, it's probably not worth it. The most destructive and damaging relationships I ever entered in my life, I entered on the back of an ecstasy-session. While the accepted effect of ecstasy is that it increases closeness and connection, my experience is that it biochemically simulates these, where they actually aren't.

Ecstasy is also said to increase your emotionality. That can be a good thing up to some point. If somebody bottles up their emotions and cannot feel nor express themselves, they can become shut-off and others may find it hard to relate to them. But I found that ecstasy simply makes you more emotional for no good reason and purpose. Intense emotions are like a rush, a sensation, and people with borderline personality disorder appear to get addicted to the intensity of their own emotions. You get used to them and ask for more. In the end, you don't feel alive if you don't feel them. You become addicted. The trope of the drama queen is that of a person who conjures up intense emotions because otherwise, they feel they are not truly alive. Here emotions are a form of stimulus like any other.

Note also that emotions are always related to something that has occurred in the past. For example, experiences I had in my childhood with my mother have traumatized me in a particular way. My wife now could react so it subconsciously reminds me of the way I appeared to be treated by my mother, and this may trigger reexperiencing the anguish bottled up during a whole lifetime. That's an emotion, and if it led to an outburst, my poor wife wouldn't know what hit her. I would now project the remote past experienced with my mother onto the present moment and my wife would have no way to understand how the present situation could have triggered such an exaggerated emotion. Important here to understand that just because an intense emotion is expressed, it does not need to reflect any form of authenticity but can easily be a robotic projection of the past onto the present.

A common place sold in therapy groups was that the feeling and expressing of intense emotions would liberate us from the past. But did that really change who we were in a positive way? I don't think so. The expressing and the changing are two separate things. You can feel and express something and not change, and that's what usually happened in those group therapy sessions back in the 1980s. You can feel something, become aware of an underlying programming, and then change it. In my experience, the expressing of an emotion of itself doesn't seem directly linked to the changing of a behavioural pattern and program. This is so because the expressing of emotions related to a past hurt often return us back into their grip instead of liberating us.

Another widely accepted effect of ecstasy is that it decreases your inhibitions. Again I would argue that not all inhibitions are useless. Some are there for a reason. You may not act out in a certain way because people will judge you. On ecstasy, you can learn to override that and act out nevertheless. That may be good sometimes but in others, it just makes you a fool.

Summary: Ecstasy is not a heart chakra drug, although it can reveal certain aspects of it. True ecstasy consists of opening the heart chakra and experiencing the revelation of the Divine seen in the heart of all beings. This leads to the recognition we all share the same *atman*. When assessing whether somebody has opened their heart chakra or not, don't listen to what they say about their experiences, but see how they treat others. See whether their treatment of others reflects the claim they can see God in everybody. The key is not what we believe to have seen or experienced, but to what extent the vehicle has been transformed by what it has seen. Our actions matter more than our words.

Besides its possible therapeutic effect, ecstasy is a physically hardwearing drug, and that is especially true for the *pranic/astral* body. Ecstasy should therefore be limited to professional therapeutic situations in cases such as PTSD.

Of all chakras, the one that has no direct stimulant to activate it, is the heart chakra. I think there is some deep significance to this. Of the seven chakras, six have a clear stimulant or group of stimulants that target the respective chakra, but one chakra, the central and axial chakra, which holds the key to successful application of all, has not. The mystery of the heart chakra is that once opened, you realize that the greatest joy to being alive is not to receive, to get, to take, but it is to give, to serve others, to contribute to their life and awakening, to be grateful, to forgive and to love. That is where freedom lies. And with that key, the other chakras can be unlocked.

Chapter 5.
THE THROAT CHAKRA AND THE PLANT HALLUCINOGENS

THE THROAT CHAKRA

With the opening of the heart chakra for the first time, our sense of self expands so much that it engulfs the whole of humanity. During the previous age of the navel chakra, we developed tribalism, nationalism, patriotism, and conflicts between the many dimensions of "us" versus "other", whether this is male and female, intergenerational conflicts, black and white, have's and have not's, etc. With the collective opening of the heart chakra for the first time, the entirety of humanity is included in our sense of self. The collective opening of the heart chakra will lead us to a humanity living life guided by love. Some may say this is a dream, but it is not. It is rather an absolute necessity. As a species, we cannot survive if we do not take this step. Otherwise, in our navel chakra obsession, we will simply eat up this planet, Mother Gaia, the guarantor of our survival.

So, if the whole of humanity with the activation of the heart chakra is already included in our sense of self, where else is there to go? Where is the next frontier? The throat chakra will take us even further beyond the heart chakra. Many will say this is impossible, as we are still so far away from collectively opening the heart chakra. It must be understood, however, this confusion, this inability to look forward, has taken place every single time we have switched from one chakra to the next. A chakra is truly understood only once it opens. A reptile cannot understand the complex emotions and considerations of a mammal, just as a base chakra person looks at a sacral chakra person as an alien. The same happens at every single step of chakra evolution.

With the opening of the throat chakra, our sense of self will expand to take in all life forms of the planet. Notice that even as we are becoming one humanity, to what extent, geological formations, plants and animals are still excluded from our sense of self. During the 2019 Australian bushfires, I was dismayed to see the extensive coverage that the unfortunate death of 28 humans garnered, whereas losing billions of animals and trillions of trees were barely mentioned. Don't get me wrong. I'm not saying that the death of 28 people is to be taken lightly. What I am saying is there is a complete disconnect from the value and importance of non-human life.

There are two ways we need to understand the value of non-human life, intellectually and spiritually. Let's look at the intellectual side first. Human life on this planet is not created, supported and ensured by humanity but by non-human life, the entire biomass of the biosphere, including animals, plants and microbes. You can observe that at play everywhere in nature. For example, the physical parameters here on Earth allow for life to exist. But most are not produced by the bare rock of planet Earth. Instead, they have been created and are maintained by the biosphere. For life to continue to exist on this planet, we are relying on a process called homeostasis of the bio parameters. Homeostasis means that the bio parameters, such as temperature, chemical make-up of the atmosphere, salinity, PH, and temperature of the oceans, precipitation, seasons, soil consistency, etc., oscillate and fluctuate only within a very narrow bandwidth.

That the bio parameters stay within that band, is not due to the geological formation of the planet but due to the sum total of Earth's organisms, its biomass. So is the atmosphere on Earth created predominantly by plants and animals. In the beginning, there were plants only. They created so much oxygen that the air became oxygen-hyper-enriched. A single lightning strike set the whole world alight. After that, animals came about. Animals take up the oxygen, turn it into carbon dioxide and feed it back into the system. Then plants metabolize the CO^2 and turn it back into oxygen. Note that for plants, oxygen is a useless by-product, and so is CO^2 for animals. But together, they metabolize each other's metabolic wastes and use them as food to thrive. This means that plants and animals are interdependent. So are we dependent on all other organisms.

This principle occurs everywhere on Earth. Let's look at ocean salinity. Ocean salinity has been more or less constant, operating within a very narrow band for 2 billion years. When ocean levels drop or when giant continental salt deposits crack open through tectonic movements and get washed into the oceans, salinity will rise. All oceangoing organisms will sense that and as directed by a common intelligence, they will filter out salt via their kidneys and deposit it in their bones. As they die, their bones sink towards the bottom of the ocean and get sequestrated away through sediment. This process goes on until salinity is returned to the average level. When Earth heats up and ice shields melt, water levels rise and salinity in the oceans decreases. Maritime organisms will then exude salt into the oceans until salt levels are back to normal. This way, maritime organisms have maintained ocean salinity as if directed by one common intelligence. And not only "as if" but they are directed by such an intelligence. The biosphere and the cosmos themselves are intelligent. We could compare both to a supercomputer but only in as far as raw intelligence is concerned. Because the biosphere and the cosmos are sentient, whereas the supercomputer is not.

With the opening of the throat chakra, for the first time, humanity viscerally understands that the entirety of life on Earth nurtures and supports us. Have a look now at how this plays itself out as biodiversity. If the sum total of all organisms will excrete a by-product that is toxic to all existing organisms, a new organism will appear that can metabolise it. The new life form will then return the metabolized substance into the biosphere in a form that can be consumed by the already existing organisms. As time goes on, more organisms get introduced, and the biosphere becomes more and more complex, i.e., biodiversity increases. The more biodiversity, the more different organisms there are, the more stable the joint superorganism will be, the more it can weather crises. Hence, as humans, we should not think that we don't need the delta smelt or the monarch butterfly (two of the many endangered species that human activity has pushed to the brink of extinction) just because we can't put a monetary value on them. Their purpose is in supporting an extremely complex superorganism, Gaia, which supports us, with the complexity of the superorganism being completely beyond Homo Sapiens capacity of understanding. We should not consider ourselves entitled to make decisions about which species is allowed continued existence and which ones are in the way and should die out.

CHAPTER 5.

Next, let's consider methane. One of the greatest concerns climate scientists have, is that the rising temperatures on Earth will lead to a release of giant amounts of methane, which is often more toxic than carbon-dioxide. Methane is locked into the frozen tundra, but recently these areas have begun thawing and methane is released into the atmosphere in constantly increasing amounts. This process is well out of humanity's hand, and no present technology can harvest and sequestrating away such enormous quantities of methane. The only question is: will methane-consuming microbes multiply fast enough to metabolize the methane and return it into the biosphere in harmless compounds? Theoretically, this is possible, but it is made less likely through our war on microbes. Microbes are our friends; they are on the same team. We need to support them. Without microbes, we are toast.

To take this subject further, consider that the more specialized an organism is, the narrower a band of homeostasis it requires. The more specialized an organism is, the more sensitive it is to fluctuations exceeding that band. The most specialized organisms on Earth are we, humans. Hence, it is in our interest to support the homeostasis guaranteed by the current biodiversity, as we need it more than any other organism on Earth.

There are organisms such as archaea (a basic single-cell lifeform) that can live millions of years without oxygen, deep down in the Earth under massive tectonic pressure, in extreme heat and under extreme toxicity. For example, in the Mariana trench (the world's deepest oceanic trench between Japan in the north and Papua New Guinea in the south), are located undersea volcanoes that exude toxic, sulphuric burps. On the spouts of these volcanoes, archaea have been found flourishing not only in the presence of this toxic cocktail but also under

CHAKRAS, DRUGS AND EVOLUTION

atmospheric pressure 1000 times higher than what we are used to, with 11km of water weighing down on them. Imagine how a human would fare under those circumstances?

Archaea have also been found when drilling through the sediment under Lake Titicaca in the Andes, the world's highest navigable lake. The lake is at an altitude of 3500-metres above sea level, and it is 280 metres deep. The sediment deep under the lake has not been in contact with oxygen in hundreds of millions of years. It also is exposed to one of the highest tectonic pressures on Earth (which is still raising the Andes skywards). In this sediment, archaea have been found, happily flourishing. They are being squeezed, but they are good sports and don't mind a bit of foul play. Again, imagine humans under these sorts of circumstances. What I want to show here is that we are an incredibly fragile species, yet for the last 400 years, we have been throwing our weight around on this planet as if we are the crown of creation, which we so obviously aren't. There are much, much tougher guys on this planet, and most are microbes.

We are supported by all the other organisms on Earth. We are standing on their shoulders, but we are not returning the favours. We are making 100 species of plants and animals extinct every day. One hundred species less every day who were working on keeping the biosphere safe and stable so complex organisms like us can thrive. The indigenous people, who looked at themselves as the guardians and keepers of the garden, were on the right track. But we modern people always seem to know better because we supposedly manufacture progress. At least that's what we are duping ourselves into.

The opening of the throat chakra gave us indigenous religion, that is animism and shamanism. Animism means to realize that everything, the entirety of creation is only crystallized spirit. To use a more poetic wording, the entirety of creation, including all matter and beings, is the crystallized body of God, of the Divine. The sky-religions (term used collectively for all non-indigenous religions, juxtaposed to earth-based spirituality) developed a rather strange concept of the Divine as something far away in heaven, Nirvana or emptiness/nothingness, and this bodily existence and matter are an obstacle or an illusion (maya). This is a huge misunderstanding, as all matter and bodies are only crystallized divinity. To see matter as crystallized spirit is exactly the understanding that indigenous people and especially shamans have. A shaman is a spiritual warrior or practitioner that actively works on bringing a biotope, a particular area of the biosphere, back into balance. Biotopes are in a state of dynamic balance where distributions of lifeforms are constantly changing. A shaman is a human who perceives this consciously and supports nature's tendency to seek balance.

An essential part of that is to accept plants, animals and microbes as spirit-guides. This is something hard to understand for modern, agricultural-industrial people, but we should look at the effect we had on the planet and biosphere during the last 8000 or more years (accelerated during the last 400 years, and again accelerated since the 1960s and 90s) and the devastation we have wreaked. This should teach us that with our limited, modern worldview, we are missing out on a lot of information. The opening of the throat chakra will enable us to experience the spiritual wisdom of animals, plants and microbes, and to co-exist and co-create with them as a unity.

But the shaman goes even further. If you look at our bodies, they are made up to a large extent of minerals (element earth) and fluids (element water). Related to those two elements, there are two more forces. One is the force that moves things around (element air), and the force that consumes food and turns it into energy or thought/intelligence (element fire). Indigenous people always understood these forces within us and communicated with them and worshipped them outside of us as rock spirit, water spirit, wind spirit and fire spirit. For a shaman, this is not an abstract process, but it is a practical thing and expresses itself in the worship and respect for natural phenomena and geological formations. For example, in all ancient cultures' mountains, rivers, oceans, large forests, etc., themselves were sacred. Not that the gods lived in or on them (this idea came later) but that the geological and natural formations themselves were sacred.

This is a view we need to urgently come back to. If you look at the Bible, you will find the myth of the Garden of Eden, where we lived naked in harmony within the garden, and off it. This describes the historical period when all of humanity was indigenous. The expulsion from the garden describes only our own, self-created exile from nature, and the subsequent destruction we have wreaked upon it. Have a look, for example, at the fact that we give the status of a legal person to corporations who often do nothing but loot and pillage nature and human communities, and convert relationships, communities and nature into money. On the other side, we think that mountains, oceans and forests are insentient. They are not. They are alive intelligent beings and must have our love and protection, much more so than corporations, to whom we currently extend legal protection and recognition.

The throat chakra enables the individual and society to live in harmony with divine law, as the whole cosmos is only a crystallization of divine law. This chakra gives us knowledge of the sacred laws according to which creation unfolds. Upon evolving to this chakra we realize there is a clear master plan according to which everything is happening. One sees that the world and the human are not the senseless accident, as some modern scientists would have it. At the level of this chakra, the meaning and purpose of everything is understood. Questions such as 'Why is God doing this to me?', end here, as we realize that cosmic intelligence is enacting itself simultaneously through everything rather than "is doing things to us".

The Sanskrit term for the throat chakra, *Vishuddha,* means 'of greatest purity'. This is the first chakra where one gets a view entirely impersonal, rather than egoic. Even the heart chakra still thinks in terms of 'How do *I* relate to other beings' ... 'How can *I* serve others'. At the level of throat chakra, there is no more I. There is only pure vision of the cosmos as crystallized divine law. In practical terms, this means that the throat chakra is the first purely *sattvic* chakra. This means that here there is none of the torpidity (*tamas*) of our lower urges and chakras (base and sacral), nor is there the mental frenzy (*rajas*) of achievement of the medial chakras (navel and heart).

The most workable translation for the term *sattva* is intelligence-particle. All matter and all phenomena, according to yogic philosophy, contain three elementary particles with are mass (*tamas*), energy (*rajas*) and intelligence (*sattva*). While atoms contain mass and energy, they also contain intelligence that informs them how they should configure at the subatomic, atomic and molecular level to form more and more complex structures that eventually lead to superstructures such as galaxies, black holes, or human brains that can understand and research galaxies and black holes. This chakra enables us to decode this information and understand our role in the cosmos. In this, it is the informer not only of the shaman but also of the scientist and artist. In all these disciplines, we are going beyond ego. It is not important which individual is disseminating these systems of knowledge, but important is that the individual becomes an empty conduit, so pure knowledge can flow through.

This chakra is the microcosmic representation of the element space or ether. Space is not an element in the way air, fire, water and earth are elements: it is more subtle. But without it none of the other four elements could display themselves, which is why it is more fundamental than the others. The sense associated with the throat chakra is sound (*shabda*), but *shabda* means much more than what we understand by the term sound. This includes that it needs air or a similar medium in which to travel. *Shabda*, however, is the sum total of all vibratory patterns, including the vibratory speed of quasars, black holes, supernovas, galaxies, elementary particles, molecules, quarks and photons. These patterns have one thing in common: they need space to arise, but they go far beyond air.

The entire universe, in fact, all universes, consists of multiple layers of vibratory patterns, which make energy crystallize into matter. The original vibratory pattern that gave birth to all others was and is OM. OM arose out of that infinite intelligence that is OMnipotent, OMnipresent and OMniscient. That infinite intelligence is the intelligence of the Divine, of God, and its infinite potential and divine will to make the world reality. In Sanskrit, the state out of which OM arises is called *Shabda* Brahman. *Shabda* Brahman, which in physics we call the unified field, is the potential but yet unmanifest ability of the Divine to manifest itself as an infinite multitude of crystallizing vibratory patterns, which at any moment are giving birth, sustaining and annihilating an infinite number of universes. Since the *Shabda*

Brahman is pure consciousness and infinite potential and creativity, it cannot say no to anything that possibly could be. Everything that can be, will be!

The whole world – from the original projection forth of the sacred sound OM down to the smallest, most unassuming insect or mineral – is a manifestation of divine law. The whole world manifests itself according to law. There are physical laws, laws of harmony in music, civil laws that regulate society, linguistic laws that enable us to understand others, laws of architecture that, if abided by make buildings stay upright, laws of aerodynamics that, if understood and applied, make aeroplanes stay in the air, etc.

Those who have activated the throat chakra, relate to others by experiencing, understanding and passing on divine law. The evolution of human society was and is usually powered by those few individuals who have opened or had spontaneous access to the throat chakra, for whatever reason. We call them geniuses, but often we do not understand them, and they may not understand themselves either, as we can see in tragic cases like Mozart or Van Gogh. The function of the throat chakra is to make us see and understand divine law. While the yogi aims at systematically and methodically growing in him/herself the ability to perceive and understand divine laws, it is the great visionaries with intuitive access to this chakra who have advanced our society. Newton, for example, could see the laws of classical physics in a way that others before him had not. Mozart had the same ability in relation to laws of harmony, whereas Shakespeare understood those of language. Albert Einstein had the uncanny ability to cognise divine law related to relativity. Those visionaries did not invent the laws, but they could see already existing divine law manifested through divine will.

This ability is related to an opening of the throat chakra. It is extremely powerful and should be tampered with only once all the chakras below it, are activated. If the throat chakra opens spontaneously through previously accumulated merit, the opening, as in Mozart's case, may be beneficial to the whole of humanity, though the benefit may not extend to the individual in question. Mozart died young and in an unfortunate situation, like many other geniuses before and after him. Another great example falling into this category was Vincent van Gogh who could make us see things like nobody before him. Unfortunately for van Gogh, this made his life very painful as his navel and heart chakras were inhibited.

You may ask how come people like Mozart, Einstein or van Gogh downloaded information enabled through this chakra even if we never saw them performing spiritual practice? Remember the Yoga Sutra stanza in the preface of this book? The Yoga Sutra in stanza IV.1 says that chakra activation can be brought on through birth, drugs, mantras, austerity and concentration practice. Chakra activation through birth means that in previous births, we have performed actions that have caused the chakra activation in this life. But because we cannot remember what we have done or even that we have done it, the activation comes suddenly over us and usually as a force of nature, which means we cannot switch it on or off as required, nor can we understand and integrate it. For example, a yogi who brought on activation of the throat chakra through conscious practice in this lifetime would not choose to activate it while driving a car or heavy machinery, as the deep insights of the chakra may interfere with the current activity of operating machinery. The activation of a chakra brought about by past life activity, however, can completely disorganize one's life, for example, if chakras beneath the one in question are still closed. This was the case in Mozart and van Gogh, who were geniuses but were beset by suffering and ultimately created their own undoing.

Traditional spiritual practices such as yoga provide us with the opportunity to open the chakras step by step. Once the heart chakra is opened, we can provide great service to all who come in contact with us, but it is the opening of the throat chakra that allows us to provide help for generations far into the future. Both chakras rely on the integrating power of the navel chakra, if this process is to remain a positive and useful experience for each individual. Spiritual practice (*sadhana*) has incredible power. For its effects to be harvested properly, techniques have to be practised in harmony with the capabilities of the individual. When discussing the opening of the throat chakra through plant hallucinogens, we will learn how our life can be turned upside down if chakras are not activated in order. This is akin to taking future steps while presently needed, supporting steps have not yet been taken. Here, we cannot integrate what we experience, similar to the roof of a house cannot stand if no supporting walls have been constructed beforehand.

If the throat chakra is fully open, the result will be the cognizing of what the *Upanishads* call deep or sacred knowledge (*vijnana*) and what Patanjali calls in Yoga Sutra I.48 sacred order (*rta*). In most of the sky religions (the Abrahamic religions, Buddhism, Hinduism, Jainism, Sikhism, etc.), however, mystics often leave out the throat chakra and go straight from the heart chakra to the third-eye- or crown chakra. If the throat chakra is left out, this can lead to the erroneous perception that the world is an illusion. The world is not an illusion; it is real. It is the most sacred, precious gift of the Divine to all beings. It must be appreciated in all its beauty. The lack of focus on the throat chakra led also to our metaphorical expulsion from the Garden of Eden, our disconnect from indigenous Earth-based spirituality, the desecrating and destruction of nature and, for example, the ownership and domination of women through men.

Another important aspect of this chakra is that it connects you with the spirit(s) of a particular location. Notice, for example, that the sky religions all are entirely transportable. Their goal is sky-based, either heaven, Nirvana, Shangri-La, emptiness/nothingness, etc., and these goals are not location-sensitive. Their approach is the same from all places. The throat chakra, and the indigenous Earth-based spirituality informed by it, give you experiences that are location-sensitive. Amongst indigenous people, it is common that if you travel to a particular location, you approach the local people for an "introduction to country". They are the people that know the spiritual forces of a particular desert, mountain range, river or ocean. They have maintained them, made offerings to them, and performed ceremonies for them often for thousands, and with the Australian Aborigines, for tens of thousands of years. With an active throat chakra, asking local indigenous people to intervene on one's behalf with the local spirit(s) makes a lot of sense. But for a person with this chakra dormant, this may sound like complete mumbo-jumbo. Tragically, in most modern white people, the throat chakra is dormant. That is why during colonialism, we could not see value in traditional Earth-based spirituality, and subjected indigenous people to, at least, cultural genocide, if not often actual genocide. And this is not relegated to the past but it is still going on as we speak.

CHAPTER 5.

On an interesting side note, the word spirit exists in many languages only in the plural, for example, Japanese *kami* and Hebrew *Elohim*. Directly translated into English, these terms mean God, but in their local languages, they exist only in plural. This means that ancient stratas of these languages date to times when their speakers were indigenous and animistic. Particularly the Japanese state religion Shinto is a fascinating mix of sky-religion and animistic stratas. For example, the sacred Mount Fuji has a spiritual power that cannot be transported but can be worshipped only in this location. A similar function has the Besakih Mother Temple on the slopes of the holy Mount Agung for Bali, the Sierra Nevada de Santa Marta for Columbia, the Pahá Sápa (Black Hills) for the Lakota Native Americans and Uluru (formerly Ayers Rock) for the Australian Aborigines. These geological formations form the spiritual heart of these cultures and anybody activating the throat chakra can clearly perceive this mountain as spiritual forces conveying the highest teachings, whereas a person without these abilities may look at them as mere large piles of rock.

While the navel chakra's function is assimilative, and the heart chakra's is relative, the throat chakra's is legislative: it opens us to divine law. If, however, your throat chakra is open and some of the lower chakras closed, you may become a visionary who dies ignored and misunderstood, only to have your work discovered and celebrated years after your death, as happened to J.S. Bach, van Gogh and many others. Or you may go mad in pursuit of your genius and have others reap the benefit, as happened in Nicola Tesla's case. If your heart chakra is open too, you are likely to be in harmony with the community around you and get its support. If the navel chakra is open as well, you can change the world and manage your contribution during your lifetime. This is a very auspicious constellation.

An important way how modern humanity conceives divine law is science because all scientific laws are only divine laws. There is an apparent conflict between both is in no small part because our theology, our ability to describe the Divine, has not kept up with the progress of science and this is due to our losing any appreciation for mysticism. To create more up-to-date approaches to theology, we need modern mystics who have at least a basic education in the major sciences and to attain authentic mystical and divine revelations. Otherwise, a theology is just mockery.

Like art and shamanism, so also science depends on an at least partial activation of the throat chakra. The problem is that with our self-engineered expulsion from the Garden of Eden, a metaphor for placing ourselves above nature rather than in its service, our religions became a barely concealed tool to manipulate and control people (and nature, too). Notice also, that although there is this supposed conflict between religion and science, both actually agree that matter is dumb, dead, spiritless and meaningless, and therefore can be exploited and manipulated to our heart's content. Notice again, that for the first 300 years of Western scientific development, all the founders of Science were very religious people. Men like Rene Descartes and Isaac Newton simply followed the biblical injunction to "make the earth thy dominion". The term dominion comes from the Latin dominus and means Lord/master, but it is actually the name of the roman slaveholder caste. Now it becomes clearer why humanity could disregard the spiritual value and beauty of nature, wilderness, rivers, mountains, forests and oceans. Our religions firstly devalued the divinity of these entities.

CHAPTER 5.

Only then, with science, did we coerce, manipulate and destroy them, so that now in the 21st millennia, we are looking into the yawning abyss of environmental holocaust, ecocide and our own extinction.

But ironically, the supposed conflict between religion and science is still narrated to keep the population from seeing that together they performed a concerted attack on nature and Earth-based spirituality, with the objective to declare indigenous people inferior so colonialists could take their lands away and industrialists then exploit them (with indigenous populations today often employed as cheap labour and in the sex trade, while sprouting we are lifting them out of "poverty"). Rene Descartes, for example, traced the beginning of his scientific career to an experience he had as a young man. An angel reportedly appeared to him and said, "Control of nature is obtained by number and measure". Descartes then went on to lay a big part of the foundations of today's mathematics, geometry and physics. Our obsession and preoccupation with measuring and controlling, unfortunately, is caused by a religious and supposedly divinely communicated misunderstanding that sees us as separate from nature rather than an integral part of it. The results of this view now are becoming apparent. Centuries after Descartes, this belief of separateness has led us to where we are destroying nature at an ever-accelerating pace and are sawing off the very branch on which we are sitting.

The compound of religion and Science have provided us with an evolutionary cul-de-sac that leads nowhere. To understand that, we need to differentiate here between the scientific method (science) and the philosophy of Western Science, which is materialistic reductionism and objectivism, but more on that later. By realizing the divinity of the material cosmos, we come to understand that humans were meant to be guardians of this garden of Eden and not its looters, ransackers, pillagers and plunderers. But unfortunately, that is what we have predominantly done throughout the last 10,000 years. There is, however, a human culture that has existed for over 100,000 years that managed to live in harmony with nature, and that is the indigenous culture. When analysing indigenous spirituality, we understand that indigenous people have always looked at the whole of the world and nature, including all life as divine. It is possible then, after all!

Another example showing that religion has created Science, is Occam's razor. Occam's razor is one of the most important principles of science today. It states that if various explanations of a phenomenon are available, and one is simpler or requires fewer components, then the simpler one should be preferred (one shouldn't construct unnecessary complex models to explain something). So, who exactly was Occam, the founder of this principle? Occam was a 14th-century Benedictine monk. Until rather recently, most scientists came either out of the spiritual profession or had a spiritual worldview. Today, Science and religion seem to have gone separate ways, and it is exactly this illogical split of spirit and matter, or more precisely, the idea that matter is not spiritual, that has brought us to the abyss of ecocide, environmental holocaust, and our possible extinction. All our destructive actions are informed by this erroneous and illusory split. We cannot escape catastrophe unless this split is healed.

This split is not only metaphorically treated in the Bible as the expulsion from the Garden of Eden, but also in the *Puranas* (a class of Indian sacred scriptures) as the Four-*Yuga*-Model, according to which we now live in the *Kali Yuga*, the age of darkness. Both of these models, the Biblical and the *Puranic*, describe how we lost our Earth-based, indigenous spirituality and replaced it with sky-based religion, in which a remote Divine is placed either in heaven or even further away into nirvana and nothingness. But the Divine is here! Every square inch of this Earth is a sacred site and Gaia a living super-intelligence. The philosophy of Science, with its separation of nature and its materialistic reductionism (which like religion is monistic), is only the brainchild of religion. With the complete activation of the throat chakra, however, science can be placed into the service of Earth-based spirituality. At this point, Western Science itself a religion based on coercion, control and manipulation of nature and a tool of suppression of vast swaths of humanity by those in power (see AI, cloning, satellite surveillance, cyberwarfare, etc.) can ultimately be returned to serve nature, and not only in a speciesist service of humanity (serving only one species), but in service of all species, of life as a totality. Thus the collective activation of the throat chakra can bring about a fusion of divine science, divine art and divine engineering, as divine law. To understand why this urgently needed process is taking place so painstakingly slow, we need to understand Planck's principle. Max Planck, the father of quantum mechanics stated, "A new scientific truth does not triumph by convincing its opponents and making them see the light, but rather because its opponents eventually die, and a new generation grows up that is familiar with it. An important scientific innovation rarely makes its way by gradually winning over and converting its opponents: it rarely happens that Saul becomes Paul. What does happen is that its opponents gradually die out, and that the growing generation is familiarized with the ideas from the beginning: another instance of the fact that the future lies with the youth."

(Max Planck, *Scientific Autobiography*). This statement is often summarized in the phrase, "Science progresses one funeral at a time". It again highlights Science's similarities with religion. New data is often not sufficient to change a scientist's mind.

THE THROAT CHAKRA DRUGS: PLANT HALLUCINOGENS

In this section, I will describe the major, true activators of the throat chakra, the plant hallucinogens such as Ayahuasca, psilocybin, mescalin, San Pedro, Peyote, Magic Mushrooms, DMT, and Datura. Marijuana and Hashish form a special case as they share characteristics with this group but not others. They will be covered in an extra section adjunct to this one.

All drugs in the group of plant hallucinogens share that they contain psychoactive alkaloids. None are addictive and mostly, they require too much work to get addicted to. Many show no adverse physical health effects (some do, such as Datura), but they can have deleterious mental health effects, if previously existing conditions such as bipolar-, dissociative personality disorder or paranoid schizophrenia are present. Plant hallucinogens have shown encouraging effects in treating depression, drug addiction, repeating unexplainable headaches, and fear of death in terminally ill people.

The most common of these drugs are magic mushrooms, which contain psilocybin and psilocyn, which have also been synthetically produced. Peyote (Lophophora williamsii) and the San Pedro cactus contain, among other alkaloids, mescalin, which again is synthetically available. DMT (dimethyltryptamine) is another synthetically available psychoactive drug and it is one of the two active constituents in the ayahuasca brew used by Amazonian cultures. Datura (thornapple, jimsonweed, yerba di diablo) is another alkaloid-containing plant. All these are used by traditional shamanic cultures, predominantly in North-, Meso-, and South America but also elsewhere, and in the last half-century found induction into the worldwide canon of recreational drugs. There are many others of these plants, such as deadly nightshades, mandrakes, amanita muscaria, etc., which are used by shamans, but whose recreational use is less common. And there are other chemical stimulants, such as STP or 2CB, which also stimulate this chakra, but are not as commonly available.

All these drugs are precisely targeting and activating the throat chakra and are giving some facilities described in the section above. What they don't do is activate the navel and heart chakra, i.e. if somebody is deficient in these chakras and then consumes these hallucinogens, they may be met with temporary or longer-lasting psychosis. There is a great misunderstanding amongst modern recreational drug users that indigenous shamans use these drugs to find themselves or to sort out their own psychological problems. Shamans, before they take these plant agents, firstly undergo a long training in which they learn about themselves and sort out their own personality problems. When they finally do take entheogens, they do not take them as a psychological agent but for the purpose of healing, sorcery, magic, mysticism, research and cosmology. They take them to get abstract knowledge independent from their own psyche, or typically represents knowledge about somebody else's problems. A shaman is most often somebody who is the medicine person, ghost- or spirit-healer of a particular tribe. An afflicted person goes to the shaman and describes their problem, often a disease. The shaman will then enter an extensive trance, often absent the patient and will try to drive out or appease the spirit that has afflicted the patient. Importantly, a shaman does these things only once they have cleared their own psyche through forms of ritual and austerity. And in indigenous societies, shaman-apprentices are hand-picked, often during early childhood, for their propensity to enter mystical trances and communicate with the spirits.

Today many young westerners call themselves shamans, but in indigenous societies, nobody chooses or wants to be a shaman. To the contrary, they are often chosen against their will and need convincing. While today we may think the profession as being "sexy", the Maya shaman Martin Prechtel describes in his *Secrets of The Talking Jaguar* that a shaman is usually a lonely person. A lot of the diseases that shamans have to counteract are caused by sorcerers and so-called black magic. When counteracting this magic, the sorcerers that caused it will inevitably fall foul of the shaman and try to destroy him or her. Martin Prechtel says that all good shamans have ways of protecting themselves. Otherwise, they don't live long. If they do know how to protect themselves, the opposing sorcerers then attack the family of the shaman, and should that fail too, then the friends of the shaman. A good sorcerer, says Prechtel, has to constantly maintain what we could call an astral shield around their family, but for this very reason, nobody wants to be a shaman's friend. Because as a shaman's friend, you are the next in the line of fire of sorcerers taken on by the shaman.

The present author has taken most substances in this category and can attest to their capacities regarding this chakra, but several caveats have to be made. Their traditional usage differs greatly from modern recreational use. In traditional societies, these entheogens are taken in a sacred and ritualized context. The effect of these drugs is similar and that is because they are all activating the same chakra. However, their effect on individuals differs vastly. Mescalin has been popularized long ago by Aldous Huxley and he has given a good description in his classic *The Doors of Perception*. Two cacti that contain mescalin, the Peyote and San Pedro are used almost in the entire Americas. Their effect lasts about 10-12 hours, and the experience is more visual, auditory and synesthetic than the other alkaloids. In the 1970s the anthropologist Carlos Castaneda gave us useful descriptions of the work and life of a shaman. Castaneda's teacher Don Juan calls the spirit of the San Pedro cactus, "Mescalito". Peyote is recognised and used as a sacrament of the Native American Church. There is ongoing discussion amongst Native Americans about the feasibility of these substances. While some are enthusiastic, others, such as John Fire Lame Deer, a Lakota holy man and previous peyote user, eventually concluded that "every butcher boy can have visions with peyote" and a skilled person would stay away from it. Mircea Eliade, historian of religion, in his *Shamanism: Archaic Techniques of Ecstasy* states that drugs are a vulgar substitute for pure trances and that intoxicants are a recent innovation and points to a decadence in shamanic technique. According to Eliade, intoxication is used when shamans are no longer capable of attaining it otherwise. Some of that harsh assessment is actually true. The most archaic indigenous cultures, such as the Australian Aborigines, do not yet require drugs or plant agents to access mystical states. It is a natural part of their culture. Daniel Pinchbeck in his *Breaking Open the Head- A Psychedelic Journey into the Heart of Contemporary Shamanism*, describes the Huaorani, an Ecuadorian hunter-gatherer tribe who seem to be in a state of spiritual perfection, but are the only tribe in their region who do not use entheogens because they do not need them. It is a tendency we find all over the world, that the cultures that never espoused agriculture and little or no domestication of animals are still in a state where they do not yet need substances to achieve animistic trances.

Forty years ago I knew a young man, let's call him Joe. He bought a motorcycle and shipped it to Tierra del Fuego, to the southernmost tip of South America. From there, he rode all the way to Alaska. That's almost the distance from the South to the North Pole. He did that alone. We must assume that a person who performs such a feat is in a serious process of soul-searching. Joe was a sincere person really looking for something. When I met him again after his return, Joe told me he had attended a Navajo-led peyote ritual somewhere in New Mexico. The day after the ritual (peyote is active for some 10 hours), he had jumped on his motorcycle and pulled out on the highway. As he drove, he felt a spirit entity (his words) coming up behind him. He accelerated his 1000cc motorcycle to full speed to escape the entity, but to no avail. He felt the entity impacting on him from behind and lost consciousness. He regained consciousness beside the road after what he believed had been 2 days spent unconscious. In the two years following the event, his mental health deteriorated more and more, to the point of paranoid schizophrenia. Eventually, he took his own life. I researched the frequency of such occurrences related to peyote, mescalin, etc., and apparently, they are rare. Usually, they are thought to occur when previously existing mental health conditions, such as schizophrenia, are present. This was apparently the case with Joe. I knew Joe before the event. I wouldn't have picked that he had schizoid tendencies. This, then, is a tale of caution.

I will next report my experience with a drug that has an extremely high correlation with psychosis and death, Datura.

CHAPTER 5.

The vast majority of my substance use, and particularly that of psychedelics, took place between the ages of 16 and 19, and during those years, I spent a significant time on one hallucinogen or another. I did notice that among other users I knew, visits to the mental ward were quite frequent. But what was not down to previously existing conditions could often be allocated to unfortunate settings, that is, the circumstances under which hallucinogens were taken. For example, usage in nightclubs or during political rallies involving altercations with riot police and subsequent detention was not conducive to mental health, yet people still used psychedelics in these settings. Years later, I found out that psychotic episodes of psychedelic users in my social surrounds were often not due to LSD or magic mushrooms, but to a drug called Datura. Had I known, I may not have dared to touch this most potent of plant agents.

A long time after I encountered Datura, I would read in Carlos Castaneda's various books that you go to the *yerba di diablo* (Datura) only when she calls you. You go out in the desert on a full moon night to the spot where she waits for you. If you don't find the spot without using artificial light, then the search is over, and you wait for the next call. If you do find her in exactly the spot seen in the vision, you grab her lightly, and with a particular incantation, she needs to come out of the ground without resistance. You then prepare leaves, stem and seeds separately, using many ingredients and incantations. You also prepare yourself, and both together take around 8 months. There are only a few dates per year auspicious enough for you to take the *yerba*. If you miss the date for whatever reason, you have to wait for months. You can't ingest the *yerba* in a town but need to be in nature. There are many other rules which for brevity's sake I will not repeat here.

CHAKRAS, DRUGS AND EVOLUTION

I was ignorant to this and even had I known, I may have thought I needed none of that. I cut a handful of leaves off a plant and visited a friend. On the way, I passed by a bakery and grabbed a baguette. I arrived at my friend's place, chucked the leaves into a kettle, poured hot water over them and watched them brew, while I munched my baguette. In a sacred context, entheogens require extended fasting and especially the *yerba*, as I was about to find out, does not like baguettes. Datura really dries and parches your throat, so I ended up with the remains of the baguette sticking out of my throat for the next 10 hours. I was so paralysed I could not move.

While I was drinking my tea and eating the baguette, I was sitting at my friend's bar on a bar stool. Suddenly the effect of the yerba came on fully and it was too late to get off the stool. For what seemed to be aeons, the legs of the stool grew longer and longer and lifted me first out of his house, then towering above the city, and eventually above the continent, the planet and the solar system. I suffer from vertigo at the best of times, so sitting on a chair several lightyears tall was extremely uncomfortable for me. Eventually, my awareness homed in on the baguette still stuck in my throat due to its complete dryness. I looked past the baguette down into my throat (dissociating from my eyes) and noticed that my body was hollow and made from a clay-like substance. I then noticed that my body was also growing to humungous proportions. It was as if my awareness had contracted to this minute photon inside this sky-wide, hollow clay statue. As my body expanded with the five-lightyears tall chair, which had by now also changed its consistency to clay, I saw that all the clay was cracking up. My whole body collapsed into itself, and with the debris of the chair, fell into an endless, bottomless abyss. I remember feeling fear, but the fear was strangely remote, as if I were watching a character in a movie falling into an abyss. I thought, "Alright, that's it, I'm going mad now. I'm falling into some endless hell." I kept falling for what seemed to be an eternity. There was a clear feeling I could never, ever get back, that I had lost my mind. I'm sure things happened that night I can't even remember. I woke up many hours later, still sitting on that chair with the remains of that baguette still sticking out of my throat. I gradually climbed off the chair, poured water down my throat and eventually got the baguette out. I never took Datura, nor eaten a baguette, ever since. I also have a loathing for barstools to this day. To be honest, I have no idea how I ever got out of that state, certainly not due to any merit or skill on my behalf. When studying Castaneda's notes on Datura, I was taken by the emphasis that his teacher Don Juan places on finding out whether the *yerba* "liked" his apprentice, Castaneda, or not. After my experience with the yerba, in hindsight, I gathered that she did really like me. I would have hated to find out how she would have responded to my disrespectful approach, had she disliked me.

The problem with Datura is that its potency varies greatly, depending on the richness of the soil and other growth conditions to which the particular plant was exposed to. Another problem that should deter anybody remotely sane is that the lethal dose is only about double of the dose necessary to have psychoactive effects. You have very little leeway to get the dosage right. To see a representation of how the world looks on Datura, then go no further than the 15th-century Dutch painter Hieronymus Bosch's *The Garden of Earthly Delights*.

Let's look next at magic mushrooms and their active ingredient, psilocybin and psilocyn. The vast majority of my experiences with this category of substances took place with magic mushrooms. Compared to some of the other drugs, they are relatively easy to dose, a gram of dried magic mushrooms contains very similar amounts of active ingredients, wherever and in whatever circumstances harvested. Apparently, some skill is involved in differentiating psilocybin-containing mushrooms from other, more toxic variants, which can seriously impair your health. Again, I knew little of that and must have been just plain lucky. I took mushrooms about 80 times, usually in very high doses during the late 70s and early 80s. The late Terrence McKenna, who was back then the leading authority on plant hallucinogens, suggested we take heroic doses of 7 grams of dried mushrooms alone, on an empty stomach, in a dark room, with telephone unplugged and doorbell disabled. These recommendations are related to controlling the setting, that is, to let no unforeseen distractions disturb your experience. It is needless to say that the most unfortunate distraction to a mystical experience would be a previously existing mental health condition such as bipolar or schizoid tendency. These are collectively called the set, that is the sum total of mental expectations of the user towards the psychedelic experiences. These also include subconscious conditioning of which we are not aware of when beginning the experience.

In my case, I was lucky, and my psyche turned out to be incredibly robust whatever psychedelic shenanigans I subjected it to. Your expectations of a psychedelic experience play an immense role. But any subconscious fears that surface, have to be addressed. In my case, fuelled by early non-psychedelic mystical experiences, my rocksteady expectation was that all I could see of the world was only the surface, and beneath that surface there was a deeper, miraculous, beautifully mysterious and enchanting reality just waiting to show itself. It was this expectation, amplified by psychedelics, that was revealed repeatedly. What stops us in normal day-to-day consciousness from having mystical experiences is that our sense of self is limited to our body. We believe that the world around us is the other, the environment. We are duping ourselves into this belief with the ego, which is a brain software that limits our sense of self to the body. If the set (our psychological expectations) and the setting (the environment in which one takes a substance), are skilfully prepared to avoid any nonsense, then the drug may chemically dissolve the ego for a time.

If during the psychedelic experience we skilfully keep ourselves in what essentially is a state of meditation, we may have an oceanic experience, during which the ego completely dissolves, and the trees, the rocks, the forest, the mountains, everything that surrounds us, form with what we previously believed to be our body and mind, a new expanded sense of self. When I am using the term meditation here, I don't mean to control, reject or expel thoughts, but a form of surrender, in which whatever comes up from our subconscious is not held onto, but exhaled and let go of. The big difference to normal non-substance-induced meditation is that here you have the motor of the psychedelic chemically dissembling your ego. This means the only thing left to do is to surrender, surrender and surrender more.

Psychedelics are unpredictable and things can easily get out of control. That you never know what comes next was confirmed by Jerry Garcia, the leader of the Californian psychedelic band The Grateful Dead. Garcia was one of the most experienced psychedelic users, but he stated that you could never be certain what would happen on your next experience. If we can let go completely, trust we are held and nurtured, we can see the alpha and the omega and everything between, we can see the beginning, end and the middle of the world, we can experience cosmic consciousness. The reason this is the case, and this understanding also dawned on me while on psychedelics, is that the brain does not create reality. The brain is not a creator of thought in any way. The brain is actually a filter, a reduction valve. During day-to-day functioning, the brain will filter out 99% or more of all data available to you. It does this because none of those 99% are necessary and helpful for your survival. The brain makes sure that you get your education, get a job, pay your taxes, have a drink on the weekend, maybe go to the beach, find a mate, procreate, and pass on your genes.

To do this, the brain is incredibly active in screening out the vast majority of information that is unnecessary for you to survive. Psychedelics can be a chemical help to reduce the activity of the brain (and so are meditation, yoga and other methods), so your rigid perceptual biases are temporarily suspended and the whole of the cosmos suddenly floods in. An experience of oceanic ecstasy can then ensue. Things can just as easily go pear-shaped. To interrupt this process of having an oceanic experience, the subconscious may throw up any type of negative conditioning, holding on to our painful past. This is so because this new oceanic experience is totally outrageous and revolutionary to our narrow surface-self. Who the hell gave you the key to the pearly gates? How dare you? The solution to this dilemma between the conflict of a revelation on the one hand, and subconscious self-depreciation on the other, is to let go of everything and breathe out whatever it is that the surface-self and subconscious are throwing at us and to always surrender to what comes next.

CHAPTER 5.

It is an endless process of transformation taking place before our eyes and nothing in this psychedelic world is constant, there is only flux and change. As soon as we are trying to hold on to something, such as a thought, this holding-on will interrupt the revelatory impetus of the experience. To stay with the experience, we need to practice an endless succession of letting-go exercises. The keys in this process are firstly the breath, meaning to let go of everything that comes up with the exhalation. You literally breathe it out. Secondly, an attitude of the mind we could call disidentification, that is the refusal to identify with and attach to anything the mind thinks. These are basic, day-to-day meditation instructions, but during a megadose psychedelic experience, they not only become paramount but take on a surprising urgency.

We could use the riding-the-tiger metaphor to describe megadose psychedelic experiences. As long as we follow the above description, we stay on the tiger, and our sense of self could theoretically continue to expand until it includes most of the world. Once we identify with something, the tiger will throw us off and it could even turn around and bite or devour us. I mean with that expression that the identification with a particular sensation, formed in a split second, could turn into a negative self-enforcing loop, a negative, contracting psychedelic experience, among psychedelic users known as a horror trip. I've had plenty of those, too. Let me give you an example: Let's say we are undertaking a psychedelic journey with somebody who triggers negative emotions in us, who is sabotaging our self-worth, shames or gaslights us, attempts to manipulate or places a guilt trip on us. When having such interactions while on psychedelics, the subconscious may become triggered and throw up memories and imprints connected with similar episodes in the past. If we hold in our subconscious enough painful imprints of a similar nature, a strongly negative experience can ensue. As everything is totally amplified on hallucinogens, also this effect will be much amplified.

It is also not enough to say, I will simply avoid such people. The awareness that our interaction with another person is tainted by such elements, may only dawn during a psychedelic experience. It could also happen that the recognition we ourselves are doing this to another person dawns on us only during a psychedelic experience.

Probably the most important precondition for any psychedelic experience is that the setting is right. The term setting refers to the sum total of circumstances in which the experience is set. I learned that the location must be a place where I was safe and protected and sheltered from sudden adverse encounters. Back in the 70s, we youngsters would get together and explore hallucinogens together. That can be a really non-sensical idea. If one gets stuck on a negative experience, the person next to us is unlikely to be of much help if they also are under the influence, unless they are a really experienced and wise and preferably even saintly. They may be just as scared as us if they see us going through a fearful state. I learned that the most predictable way to experience psychedelics is to take them alone. However, that might not be the best approach for an inexperienced person. One needs to at least be familiar with pulling oneself out of negative psychological states, if needed. Using the services of a sitter or caretaker would be helpful only if they are experienced in counteracting negative states. There are now underground psychedelic guides who do that for a living. I do not envy them as they must be able to draw on extensive skills, what they are doing is nevertheless illegal and considering the risk, also probably poorly paid.

A psychedelic guide would need to have both psychological and shamanic skills. It is actually very difficult to combine both these skills. Psychology is an extremely analytical and left-brained subject. Studying such an academic subject actually draws you away from shamanic skills, which you may possess. Shamanism is more akin to witchcraft, magic and the work of a ghost- or spirit-healer. It's completely intuitive, artistic, non-empirical and right brained. It would be very difficult to learn both these skills and then nurture them both in the same brain. It would be a fantastic and worthy endeavour to do so, and provide a great service to humanity, but there is little societal support for it.

The reason a psychedelic guide must have psychological skills is that all major psychological issues of the client need to be dealt with before the psychedelic experience. The client would have to be screened for adverse conditions like bipolar disorder, psychosis and schizophrenia, and in these cases, they must be strongly deterred from using psychedelics. But even moderate conditions like self-loathing, lack of self-esteem, etc., which we all suffer from to some extent, would need to be addressed beforehand. Only with such preparation, can the client identify them during the experience and will then know how to handle them. Recreational users generally approach psychedelics expecting their psychological problems will be sorted out by having a powerful mystical experience. I strongly advise against this approach, as there is not enough emphasis on the prior learning of how to not get stuck on negative subconscious content.

The approach by which one works with a psychologist on a psychoanalytical level before taking a hallucinogen is called psycholytic therapy and the psychiatrist Stanislav Grof is a great exponent of this method. The approach by which psychedelics are simply taken to sort out one's psychological problems, on the contrary, is called psychedelic therapy and I am doubtful of its basic tenets. You have a deep transformational and mystical experience (i.e. a chakra 5, 6 or 7 activation), and this presumably will sort out your psychological, lower-chakra problems. The fallacy here is that psychedelics do not influence the lower chakras at all; they cannot solve problems present in those areas.

To understand this problem, simply look at the many reports of sexual abuse, rape, coercion, and manipulation in spiritual movements around the world. The teachers in these movements have usually, one thing in common, and that is that they have practised only methods that address the higher chakras (and have left out the heart chakra). If, for example, you provide somebody suffering from narcissistic personality disorder with a mystical experience (whether brought about through traditional techniques or psychedelics), this experience will not necessarily turn them into a nice person. I would love to confirm that mystical experiences solve all our problems, but it is not something that I have regularly witnessed. Far from that, a narcissist may actually weaponize their mystical experience by forming a cult to live out their narcissism via the adoration conferred by their followers. This is something I have witnessed repeatedly. Similarly, the case with somebody with psychopathic tendencies. A good example here would be Charles Manson, who used LSD to form a psychopathic cult. This will be covered in great detail in the section on the 6th chakra drug, LSD.

I do not contend that psychedelics can positively change your life. Michael Pollan describes one such example in his book,

CHAPTER 5.

How to Change Your Mind. During a psilocybin trial conducted by doctors and psychologists, a terminally ill cancer patient is given the hallucinogen to treat his extreme fear of death. He does experience some form of divine revelation, accesses deep love for himself and those around him, and says he will die the happiest person in the world. Wonderful! Right there and then the proof that psychedelics work. So, can we extrapolate this experience to the general audience? Not likely, because the terminal illness is actually part of the set (the sum total of the user's expectations and mindset), it's what supplied the framing of the psychedelic therapy session. The patient undertook this journey, looking for some deeper meaning to get over his crippling fear of death and that's exactly what he found. Already from the outset, there was a very strong incentive to bring about that very outcome. Notice also that an experience of pure consciousness (what the Yoga Sutra calls objectless samadhi) confers on you the experience you are eternal and infinite and therefore do not end with the death of the body. This experience teaches us how to die gracefully (called *moksha* in Sanskrit), but it does not teach us how to live rightly (called *dharma* in Sanskrit). Somebody may have a mystical experience that teaches them how to let go in death, but they may still not know how to deal with one's life. For this, a different type of experience is required, one that the Yoga Sutra calls objective samadhi and the Bhagavad Gita calls *svadharma* (your life's divine purpose).

An example to understand how expectation of one's impending death influences one's spiritual state, is the spiritual awakening of the Indian mystic Sri Aurobindo. Aurobindo, a freedom fighter battling the British Raj in India at the beginning of the 20th century, was on death row due to an act of terrorism. Upon request a yoga master visited him in jail and taught him a stock-standard, run-of-the-mill meditation technique. Aurobindo succeeded in only three days and became spiritually awakened, whereas his teacher, to his great chagrin, even after lifelong practice never did. The difference between both was that Aurobindo was on death row, and he needed the technique to work, whereas his teacher wasn't. Although we all in some way are on death row because we all know that our body has a use-by date, in reality, we dupe ourselves in subconsciously believing we are immortal. To some extent, this is understandable because it's always the others that seem to die and never us. True, until it isn't.

This principle led the late Armenian mystic Georg I. Gurdjieff to suggest that to increase our chances of spiritual awakening, we needed to have implanted an organ that reminds us at all times that we are mortal. During the mid-80s, when I had come off psychedelics, my friends and I jested that maybe this "organ" was the AIDS virus. My jesting ended when I did return a positive HIV-antibody test. With my pre-existing focus on mysticism, it was not rocket-science to predict what would happen next. I said good-bye to my girlfriend and friends and spent the remainder of my days meditating day-in, day-out at my favourite location beside a deep lake in the middle of the forest. I remember one particular night during the dark moon, when I swam at midnight out into the lake. I was gliding across the still surface of the lake with the starlight reflected in it. It felt like being suspended in liquid crystal in the middle of space with the stars all around me. There were no psychedelics needed here, my presumed impending death was enough to completely absorb me and to surrender to the experience. I was in this state of bliss for about six weeks. Because my health did not decline (back in the eighties, there was no treatment yet for AIDS, and cases usually rapidly declined), I had another test, this time using a different test method. My test came back negative and only then I discovered that the rate for false-positive tests was 10%. What I learned from that was that your life expectancy plays a huge role in your likelihood to experience deep meditation and mystical states. If you believe you have no future, nothing really stops you from diving right in. From that test result onwards, my meditation practice presented itself again as a more uphill task.

I mentioned earlier the first two phases of a skilful psychedelic experience. Phase one is preparation, which entails screening for serious adverse conditions, such as psychosis or, for example, heart disease. Another big part of this phase is analysing one's conditioning for negative imprints, such as self-loathing, bloated ego, megalomania, etc., and how to deal with them when journeying on psychedelics. Phase two is the actual psychedelic experience, including the right setting and instruction to let go of everything on the exhale, and surrender to and accept everything that comes up. Now comes phase 3, and during my 40 years of being off psychedelics, I came to understand that phase 3 is the most important phase. Without phase 3, the only thing we gain from a psychedelic journey is flowery yet empty tales, which are not backed up by personality changes. Phase 3 is integration.

We need to ask ourselves, "How will we integrate what we see?" The obvious answer is "through spiritual practice and discipline (*sadhana*)". Experiences will not integrate by themselves. Integration is not their responsibility, but ours. Which type of spiritual work one chooses is by and large a question of personal preference. My preference is classical eight-limbed yoga, but I have seen practitioners doing good work with Sufism, Cabbalism, Daoism, Shamanism and other methods. We need to simply decide which one works best and then sincerely commit to it. It is my belief, after a lifetime on the spiritual path, that even with psychedelic help, it is not actually the substances, but our spiritual practice and discipline afterwards, that produce the breakthroughs and integration.

I have already disclosed the fact that I took magic mushrooms 80 times (most of them megadoses) and in the next chapter, I will further describe that I took LSD around 150 times (again, most of them megadoses). I'm a slow learner, but at some point, even I asked myself why do I have to do this over and over again? Why can't I get the message? Why do I take psychedelics like going to the movies or having a meal and a few hours later, I'm hungry again? The answer was because I was incapable of integrating the experiences. The cabbalist and occultist Éliphas Lévi in *Transcendental Magic, its Doctrine and Ritual* stated that an intelligent person takes a drug only once. Then they've seen what there is to see, and what they cannot then see, they will not understand on later excursions either. The great Swiss chemist Albert Hoffman wrote in *LSD: My Problem Child*, that he could see a responsible usage of LSD (to be covered later) taking place four times in one's life, each time a culmination of one of life's major crises. Repeated use of psychedelics, then, is generally an admittance of failure to integrate one's past experiences.

The psychiatrist and medical doctor Rick Strassman, among other books, wrote *DMT The Spirit Molecule*. Strassman was the first after Timothy Leary to get FBI and FDA approval to legally experiment with LSD, DMT and psilocybin on life human specimens. Strassman took 20 years to get this approval. He then put around 140 individuals on the three aforementioned psychedelics. After that, he gave the license, which took him most of his adult life to procure, back because he was disappointed with the result. What he hoped for was that many, or at least some, of his research subjects would, after their psychedelic experiences, take up some form of traditional spiritual practice, but none did. It is exactly this point that is the crux of psychedelics. To integrate into your life what you saw, you need to perform traditional spiritual practices, but few people do so. The reason for that is that with psychedelics, we are obtaining the experience too easily in the first place. Indigenous shamans, yogis, Daoist, cabbalists, they are working for decades to bring them about these experiences. They have a lot of skin in the game. A psychedelic user may pay only $10-30. Is it surprising then that they don't value this experience enough to afterwards practice decades to integrate it?

I live close to a fascinating little town on the Australian east coast, called Mullumbimby. What Little Big Horn was to General Custer, that is Mullumbimby to the Australian hippies. It is their last stand. For an undercover-anthropologist, who wants to conduct the long-term effects of psychedelics on a large sample group of specimens, Mullumbimby is a paradise-found. Everybody here has taken them, often lots of them, and everybody talks about their mystical experiences. But few people seem to do something about it. The problem with experiences happening on psychedelics is that we often don't even understand their significance, nor can we clearly remember them. During his DMT studies, Dr Strassman gave his subjects two doses of DMT, one low dose, followed later by a strong dose. Strassman, who recorded what his subjects said and how they acted, was surprised that, when later questioned, many of his test candidates did not even remember what they experienced on the high doses. Strassman then understood that we simply will not remember, what we cannot come to terms with. What we cannot understand will simply get sequestrated away in our subconscious and is not consciously accessible.

I stopped using psychedelics because although they allowed me to enter into mystical states many times, when the trip was over, I was back in my old, disconnected reality, and more importantly, I was back being my old, disconnected self. I then understood that the chemical or plant agent gave me the experience. It was not mine; it was borrowed. I needed to learn to access it using my spiritual practices (*sadhana*), rather than relying on drugs. I then entered into a to-date four-decade-long and ongoing quest into higher yoga (I'm using this somewhat awkward term higher yoga only because many Westerners erroneously identify yoga exclusively with postures). With every decade gone past, I understood the significance of my experiences more, remembered more of them and, importantly, learned how to integrate them. Integration means that the vehicle, your surface personality, partakes of, and is changed by, the experience. There is a beautiful anecdote about this featuring the Indian 14th-century mystic Kabir. Kabir was told by his students he could not expect of them what he expected of himself because he had seen God and they hadn't. To this, Kabir said, "I have seen God for one second and the rest of my life was in service to that". That's integration. If integration is done well, one second of revelation is enough. If integration is dysfunctional an entire life spent in revelation on psychedelics will not be enough.

To give you an example, there is no point in stating that we experienced unconditional and divine love and then continue to treat people arrogantly or condescendingly. An integrated psychedelic experience or mystical experience brought about by traditional means, teaches us humility because it shows us a reality of ourselves beyond ego. The problem is that on the humility-scale psychedelic users are not on par with non-drug-induced mystics, but exactly on the same level as non-mystics and users of opiates and cocaine. This was confirmed in a study conducted by Michael Lerner and Michael Lyvers (Values and beliefs of psychedelic drug users: a cross-cultural study, 2006). This means that on a humility-scale, psychedelic mystics perform as if they hadn't had a mystical experience. What's the point then of having had a mystical experience if it doesn't change who you are? Shouldn't the value of an experience be measured by the extent to which it transforms us?

In some people, psychedelic experiences can actually inflate and boost their egos, confirming to them they are special and superior to others. In Mullumbimby, I bumped into a man, who had only recently been released from the mental ward after a psychotic episode. He was now chewing on my ear he was about to start a worldwide spiritual movement via Facebook! On another incident, I received an email from an exotically dressed gentleman complete with a brocade silk robe, sitting on some form of peacock throne. The email informed me this man would liberate the entire of humanity by sending orgasmic Kundalini-shockwaves around the planet. I could receive the shakti of the guru simply by paying money into his account. No login details or anything else required. I'm sure the shakti just follows the money trail. God help us!

A few more magic mushroom loose-ends to tie up before we go on to DMT and ayahuasca. Brotherhood of Eternal Love-founder John Griggs died young and mysteriously on a psilocyn trip. Psilocyn is the compound that psilocybin transforms into when ingested. The Brotherhood were the world's largest supplier of psychedelics, and it's unlikely this was a botched street drug. John Griggs's close friend Michael Randall was so gutted that he decided to take the very same batch of psilocyn and die if necessary. Randall's experience turned out to be completely fine. John Griggs was considered by all around him an advanced spiritual being, and his wife Carol was with him throughout the trip. That means we can probably rule out death because of a psychotic episode, or an accident caused by delusion. We are then left with the hypothesis that Griggs died from a heart attack or aneurism in the brain. This drives the point home those using psychedelics should be screened for serious health conditions. For those interested, there is an interesting movie about Griggs, the Brotherhood and the early psychedelic movement, called *Orange Sunshine*.

Terrence McKenna, the leading plant hallucinogenic proponent of the 80s and 90s and author of *The Invisible Landscape, True Hallucinations, Food or the Gods* and *The Archaic Revival*, believed that magic mushrooms propelled the evolution of the human brain. In this "stoned-ape-theory", McKenna proposed that when looking for food in the African savannah, our hominid ancestors came across magic mushrooms, and their psychedelic content enlarged our brains in a short time. This idea would be appealing to users of psychedelics, but it still makes our evolution accidental. According to this theory, had those jungles not dried out, we'd be still sitting up in the trees happily throwing bananas at each other. I instead propose that matter and the cosmos are crystallized cosmic intelligence, which is animated by infinite consciousness. We and all life are their interface, the interface of cosmic intelligence and infinite consciousness. According to this view, there was no way life could not have evolved towards more complexity and intelligence because the cosmos itself is not only intelligent and complex, but it is undergoing a process towards more complexity and greater intelligence. Hence by law, more intelligent species evolve.

Another word on indigenous cultures and plant agents. When I moved to Australia, I began a systematic study of Aboriginal culture. I found it uncanny how little, despite my history with plant agents, I could understand Aboriginal culture and spirituality. It was only years later, through yogic *sadhana*, that I could activate the throat chakra, and understand the states of consciousness of indigenous shamans. The interesting thing about Aboriginal culture is that it is purely animistic and pre-shamanic. Shamanism represents a later phase of animistic culture in which the majority of the tribal population had already become separated from the mystery of nature. Because of this, the use of plant agents was introduced, and with it, a specialist caste, the shamans, which by themselves already are the foreboding of a priestly elite. Australian Aboriginal culture does probably represent the original animistic human culture, in which all individuals are still completely embedded in the earth-based spirituality, without substance use.

A discussion of magic mushrooms cannot be complete without honouring the disruption that their discovery by Westerners caused to indigenous communities that used them as a sacrament. Magic Mushrooms entered Western conscious attention when in 1955, the investment banker R. Gordon Wasson with an entourage visited the Mexican Mazatec *curandera* (healer) Maria Sabina, who was a traditional keeper of the sacred mushroom ceremony. R. Gordon Wasson subsequently wrote a book about her and the mushrooms and disclosed her location. This brought an ongoing stream of anthropologists, hippies and artists and, so it is rumoured, even Bob Dylan, Keith Richards and John Lennon, to the doorstep of her humble home. Sabina, who was initially hospitable to the strangers, began to look at them more and more like a curse. Mazatec community life was so interrupted that Sabina was eventually ostracized for having brought in the foreigners and her house was burned down. Eventually, the Mexican army blocked off the tribal lands and prevented foreigners from entering so normal community life could resume.

Ayahuasca and DMT: Dimethyltryptamine is the active ingredient in the brew Ayahuasca, used by Amazonian shamanic tribes. DMT can be smoked, but when ingested, it needs to be combined with other substances so it can be absorbed by the gastric tract, rather than broken down. Of all psychedelics, DMT has the most rapid onset of symptoms, but they are also quickly over. The whole experience can be over in five minutes and even a megadose DMT experience will have you back to normal in 15 minutes. It used to be called the businessman's psychedelic, as you could take it in your lunchtime break. Terrence McKenna contributed a lot to popularizing DMT, especially his description of non-human intelligences that one may typically encounter while under its influence, which he called "self-transforming machine elves". Dr Strassman, in *DMT and The Soul of Prophecy*, likens these non-human intelligences to the angels in the Hebrew Bible. My take on them is that they are what the indigenous people call spirits. When I studied Comparative Religion in my 20s, belief in spirits was a sign of a primitive, pagan and native mind. It was not something that academics seriously considered in those days. Comparative religion back then accepted that there were two different types of spirituality. On the one hand, the devotional attitude that the Abrahamic religions express towards an anthropomorphic (having human characteristics)

God that speaks human languages (Sanskrit, Hebrew, Greek, Latin or according to the King James Bible, even English) and wants devotees to follow these given instructions word-by-word. This devotional, anthropomorphic spirituality is also common in India, represented through Gods like Krishna and Shiva. In the next chapter, I will show this form of spirituality is third-eye chakra informed.

On the other hand, scholars and academics accepted a spirituality in which the Divine did not have the quality of a being, but more of a state. This state was typically called Nirvana (in Buddhism), the formless absolute or nirguna-Brahman (in the Advaita Vedanta school of Hinduism) or the Dao (by Chinese sages like Lao-tzu or Chuang-tzu). To make things a bit more complex, this generally far-eastern state-spirituality was also acknowledged by Christian mystics like Dionysius the Areopagite, John van Ruysbroeck and Eckhart von Hohenheim. It was, however, never formally acknowledged by the Christian churches. In the seventh chapter of this book, I will show these strata of spiritual experiences to be powered by the crown chakra.

But when looking at indigenous spirits and what McKenna calls self-transforming machine elves, we are looking at a completely independent, third category of spirituality. This third category of spirituality, although in the past neglected by Western academics and scholars, stands in equal rights and importance to the two categories of states reported by Abrahamic and Asian mystics. These states informed by Earth-based spirituality have been lost to the majority of the world's non-indigenous population, after our metaphorical self-ejection from the Garden of Eden. In the last few millennia, we have tragically completely lost access to an essential third of humanity's spirituality, and we have paid for it with a complete disconnect from nature, which now, after centuries of accelerated destruction of the biosphere, lets us look into the yawning abyss of environmental holocaust, ecocide and the mass extermination of as much as 90% of the world's species, humanity included.

When taking these shamanic substances, it becomes very obvious that the spirits are real, and that the material world and other-than-human lifeforms have important messages to convey to humanity. These messages we should heed, but for centuries and even millennia, we have been too busy conquering, coercing and dominating the natural world. I remember really scratching my head when I first heard Aborigines saying things like, "these hills over there are our ancestors, by performing such and such acts they created us in the dreamtime". In a process in which plant agents originally may have been a catalyst, and decades of yogic sadhana provided the transformation and integration, I can now see and hear these indigenous people are right, and if we moderners can't see what they see, then this is only due to our complete blindness to animistic spirituality.

The 'hills over there", the oceans, the forests, the rivers and mountains are indeed ancient spirit-beings that are our ancestors, and they deserve our respect, worship and protection, similar to all the animals and plants around us. If you go to Bali, an animistic culture, and you ask the people there why they are engaged in ritual offering day-in, day-out, they will tell you they are feeding the spirits. Our modern Western culture has stopped feeding the spirits because we are too haughty, self-important and ignorant to do so. Indigenous people believe that the deterioration in mental health of modern industrial people is taking place because we have broken the covenant with the spirit world. The first step towards healing would be to see indigenous people, who have been the guardians of this planet for tens of thousands of years, not as backward and ignorant, but as people who can help us to make amends. Whether plant-agent-using like the Amazonians, or those without hallucinogenic drugs like the Aborigines, indigenous people can help us to heal the natural world and return to a relationship with it that comes from giving instead of taking. A ritualistic use of substances (rather than a recreational use) may have a role to play herewith those for whom they are suitable, but caveats must be in place.

My personal impression with DMT was that its effect was over much too quickly. I'm a slow learner and like lots of time to ponder things, for this reason, the long-active hallucinogens like LSD worked much better for me. DMT compresses an eight-hour psilocybin or Ayahuasca experience into 10 minutes. It is over in a flash, which comes at a price. With those who take strong psychedelics over the long-term, especially DMT, I have noticed holes in their auras that make their *prana* leak out and seems to make them too non-committal, scattered and confused to practice serious *sadhana*. It seems this effect can already take place with very few doses of DMT. Due to its strength, it does scatter prana easily. William S. Burroughs, Beat Generation writer and author of over 20 books including *Junkie*, *Naked Lunch* and *The Soft Machine*, said about DMT, that it plunges you into demoniac latitudes. I think a lot of uncritical glorification of the DMT experience abounds.

Ayahuasca is a different story, which was incidentally also confirmed by William S. Burroughs in his book *The Yage Letters* (Ayahuasca is in some areas called Yage). There are probably as many Ayahuasca recipes as there are tribes, and possibly even different shamans in the same tribe use different ones. Some shamans dose very lightly and some dose severely, hence the vastly differing accounts of the effects. Like other psychedelics, Ayahuasca has shown to be helpful with depression and addiction. Dr Gabor Maté, one of the leading experts on addiction, ran a successful Ayahuasca-retreat, that returned great results. For another enthusiastic appraisal of Ayahuasca, please read Jeremy Narby's, *The Cosmic Serpent*.

There is a new burgeoning Ayahuasca-tourism industry in Peru, Colombia and other countries. Some of the shamans advertising are not shamans at all but have only recently set up shop. Some of the traditional healers have stepped forth accusing those "shamans", of being only sorcerers, who are siphoning not only money but also psychic force from their hapless clients. It is worth repeating that in traditional indigenous culture, clients or patients do not take hallucinogens. It is only the shamans who take them to enter the astral plane, and to expel spirits that cause physical or mental disease or other misfortunes in the lives of the clients. The new recreational wave of Ayahuasca-tourism often amounts only to pop-shamanism. But Daniel Pinchbeck reports in *Breaking Open The Head*, that for many indigenous communities selling Ayahuasca-services to foreigners provides the necessary income to support the maintenance of their traditions. A nuanced approach is needed when assessing this complex problem.

There were several widely reported deaths of ayahuasca-tourists while under shamanic guidance. The most notorious of those was the death of Canadian Sebastian Woodroffe. Woodroffe procured a gun and shot his shaman, the revered 81-year-old Olivia Arevalo Lomas of the Shipibo-Conibo tribe. Woodroffe was lynched and killed by members of the tribe, for whom Lomas was one of the bearers of their culture. The double-murder attracted an 800-strong police force, descending onto the tribe, which again sparked protests. Lomas was one of the leading indigenous rights activists, who all face threats for trying to protect their lands. The investigations revealed that Woodroffe was in a long-term tutelage under Lomas, studying indigenous healing arts and plant medicine, which also involved Ayahuasca. It appears that Woodroffe was on bipolar medication and reacted adversely to the Ayahuasca. His relationship with Lomas gradually disintegrated and after several altercations, he eventually shot her multiple times with a gun he purchased solely for this purpose.

This unfortunate story again drives home the much-needed screening for mental conditions before using psychedelics, but it also highlights another important issue. The Amazon area has the world's highest incidence of killing of indigenous activists and nature protectors. Lomas' tribe called her "the mother that protects the earth in the jungle". After her death, indigenous people accused the state authorities of double standards. They said that "foreigners can come here and kill us like dogs and the state does nothing". It is easy to identify the ongoing colonialist process in Ayahuasca tourism, although we cannot reduce it to that. While indigenous people initially accede to the wishes of foreigners to supplement their meagre income, they soon find out that their culture is being sold and often bastardized. This episode sadly is very similar in structure (although with a less dramatic ending) to the life of the Mexican Mazatec *curandera* Maria Sabina, already described in the magic mushrooms section.

With every story of success and glory of psychedelics, there seems one of downfall, which do not make the current psychedelics-as-panacea-for-all news. Just the other day, I participated in an information evening staged by a group of psychologists and attended by hundreds of visitors in which psilocybin and MDMA were promoted as fixing depression, PTSD, headaches, end-of-death anxiety, lack of creativity and spiritual thirst. I was glad nobody suggested they would fix mould and rust, too. There is a frantic psychedelic-revival that is reminding me of the Dutch tulip-mania of the 17th century. I see it as my duty to offer a comprehensive view of the subject from all sides, rather than just the enthusiastic psychedelics-can-do-no-harm rant of late. In that vein, a friend, Bob, recently met again an old high-school mate, Joe (both names changed for privacy). Joe told Bob that in the previous years, he had taken Ayahuasca and DMT 1500 times. Shortly thereafter, Bob heard of Joe's sudden demise by means of suicide. Joe had a wife, two kids and a successful business, and although he seemed to be on an intense inquisition, he appeared bright, and not depressed. Bob, therefore, inquired further to discover what so suddenly could have changed Joe's outlook on life. It turned out that not that long ago, a third friend of theirs, Ken, had gone missing. After several months, his remains eventually were found in the outback and the coroner's report showed suicide as a mode of death. Joe volunteered to identify his badly decomposed remains and took his own life shortly thereafter.

    I cannot speculate here whether Joe visited the morgue while on hallucinogens, but with 1500 trips under your belt, there is not a lot of time left to not be under the influence. As a young seeker, I spent some time with Indian ascetics and one thing they taught me is to spend time at the burning ghats, and to watch burning funeral pyres while meditating on impermanence. The point is to accept that it will be your body up there in the flames in a theatre near you soon. I have to admit to my doing that on a couple of occasions with psychedelic help to drive home the point with more urgency. This was not something unusual but was common practice among hippies in the 1970s. You had to have come back from the Mekong in your underwear (because of being robbed), and you had to have spent a few nights at Manikarnika Ghat in Varanasi (India's biggest burning ghat) on psychedelics, to name a few things. Back then, I thought of myself as incredibly robust, as being capable of taking and stomaching anything. Today, I consider that maybe I was just lucky.

My hypothesis about Joe is that when he saw the body of his friend in a semi-decomposed state, his subconscious accepted a general imprint of morbidity. Seeing that his friend Ken had brought about this state with suicide, Joe's subconscious accepted this program and followed suit. In psychedelic language, we used to call this "getting stuck on a trip". I'm not sure how popular that term still is today, but it's similar to what is today called, "going down a rabbit hole". This also tallies with the finding of the CIA, that psychedelics made you more open to suggestions, a tendency that the cult leader Charles Manson masterly exploited, as we will learn in the section on LSD.

The phenomenon of "getting stuck on a trip" is important when dealing with psychedelics and I will delve into it at some depth. Here a more benevolent example: Decades ago, I had scored a whole set of Tibetan Tangkas and hung them on my wall. While on a high dose of a psychedelic, I inadvertently gazed at them. I remember that I had a recording of Tibetan monks chanting and put that on, too. I spent the entire journey listening to that music and gazing on these tangkas. The next day I joined pretty much every Tibetan Buddhist sect in the state and practised their disciplines (Ngöndro and later the Six Yogas of Naropa) ten hours a day as if I was some reborn ancient Buddhist. It took me about 18 months until I woke up and asked myself what I thought I was doing. I carefully backtracked my steps and realized that 18 months earlier, by means of a powerful psychedelic combined with visual and acoustic imagery I had hypnotized myself into the belief I was a Tibetan monk. I'm not saying here there is anything wrong with Tibetan Buddhism. I'm just saying that when I realized that I had brainwashed myself using a psychedelic, that the trip finally ended. Such is the power of psychedelics. A minute change in what we coincidentally come across while under the influence, can profoundly influence our life, or as in the case of Joe, it may even end it. Caution needs to be exercised. The Beat generation writer Jack Kerouac, author of *On The Road* and many other books, compared psychedelics to communist brainwashing (as quoted by Jay Stevens in *Storming Heaven – LSD And The American Dream*). The reason the CIA gave up on their psychedelic experimentation was not that the substances did not lend themselves to brainwashing but because the outcome was too unpredictable.

A few years back, I was contacted by a student, let's call him Tim, who had developed a serious psychosis after a single dose of Ayahuasca. Because no psychological treatment nor antipsychotic medication seemed to help much, Tim approached me with the request to help him through yoga. After initial attempts focusing on inversions and pranayama techniques, I concluded that Tim's heart chakra was closed and his throat chakra overloaded, a typical case for psychedelic-induced psychosis. I recommended him to visualize the heart chakra in the centre of his chest (and supplied him with a traditional fire-red image), while pronouncing the syllable of fire, YAM, and at regular intervals to mentally repeat resolutions (*sankalpas*), such as, "I am pure love", "I am an embodiment of divine love", and "I love and accept myself"".

According to his own statements, Tim rapidly improved, and after being locked up in his apartment for almost two years, he could finally resume a normal life. I am no psychologist, nor do I claim to have found the cure for psychosis and, to make it clear, I have no desire at all to work on such cases and suggest you visit your local psychologist instead. The evidence supplied here is completely anecdotal or as the saying goes, "the sample size is one" (the point being that the statistical value is almost zero. The point I am making here is that Tim's rapid deterioration from a single Ayahuasca-experience probably was due to the openness of his subconscious to negative suggestions taking place during the experience. In his case, he was given the psychedelic by a person that appeared to have a manipulative agenda.

Similarly, Tim's recovery was probably to a significant part due to his readiness to accept the mantra and the visualization, to deeply embed the resolutions in his subconscious, and to accept that they were an authentic reflection of his state of being. And this shows us exactly the crux with psychedelics: we are in an open and vulnerable state, in which an at other times insignificant observation or notion can now penetrate us deeply and change the direction of our life. If you do understand that, though, you can also decide to reverse the damaging direction. The question is, how deeply can we accept a healing resolution to be true about ourselves? And the overarching question is can't we do all this work without psychedelics and therefore with less risk? It is this position I am arguing for, and I am attempting to gradually present the arguments and tools for such work.

You may be surprised to find here repeated negative stories about psychedelics side-by-side with positive ones. Why don't you find a lot of cautionary tales elsewhere? Writers on psychedelics regularly fall for positive-story-bias, similarly to writers who report on those who made stock-exchange- or financial-derivative-fortunes. Those who got lucky are happy to tell their heroic tales. But you hardly ever hear stories such as, "How I got taken to the cleaners and lost ten million dollars at the stock exchange". Such a story has no hero and those subject to those wipe-outs usually just silently hobble home and lick their wounds. Similarly with psychedelics. Those in whose case the trip backfired rarely stand on the marketplace shouting about their misfortunes. Instead of that they often spend a long time recovering from drug-induced psychosis away from the limelight. Knowing many of these tales, I regard it my duty to report them as well.

The substances in this category are all produced by the brain. Their purpose is to be emitted by the brain at the moment of death or after significant spiritual practice and discipline. They seriously expand our sense of self to eventually, if sufficiently high doses are ingested, activate the evolutionary brain circuitry that would be typical for a shaman, i.e. the throat chakra. If the person using the substance has previously existing psychopathology, or in yogic parlance if any chakra beneath the throat chakra (typically the heart or navel chakra) are blocked, then they will experience strongly magnified psychotic states. That's why these substances used to be called psychotomimetics, i.e. mimicking a psychosis, before the labels psychedelics (soul-revealing), hallucinogens (bringing about hallucinations), or even entheogens (God-inducing) became en vogue.

CHAPTER 5.

Many substances in this category are used by shamans in a sacred and ritualistic setting. They have also shown to alleviate depression, oppressive compulsive disorder, addiction and anxiety due to terminal cancer in a therapeutic setting. These arguments are often used to justify recreational use. But recreational hallucinogen use is a far cry from a shamanic or therapeutic setting. Ecstatic revelation on the one hand, and excruciating horror trips on the other, are both the daily bread of the recreational user, with often only moments between both. Any usage should be approached with great caution, respect and in the spirit of sacrament.

The already quoted R. Gordon Wasson proposed that the soma of the Vedas was a psychoactive mushroom. I do not believe that to be the case but hold the position that the term soma is a metaphor for lunar *prana, prana* stored in the moon. Moon here is a metaphor for the lunar *pranic* battery, which is within the centre of the cranium. Lunar *prana,* or shall we say a lunar (psychic) tendency, can be increased simply by practising a pranayama technique called Chandra Bhedana (moon piercing), which I have described in great detail in my book *Pranayama the Breath of Yoga*. This technique has a reputation to make one lunatic if overdone, a reputation it shares with psychedelics. The difference between both is that the breathing technique enables you to daily dial it up or down exactly how much more or less psychic (lunar) you want to be. With the psychedelic, once you have ingested it, you are more or less at its mercy, and the mercy of the diatribes that your subconscious may throw your way.

Gabor Maté, in his aforementioned book, quotes the Dalai Lama, who when being asked whether he thought drugs might be a shortcut to enlightenment, responded, "I sure hope so".

CHAKRAS, DRUGS AND EVOLUTION

This attitude closely reflects mine. I took copious amounts of psychedelics when I was young and because of that, I am not in a situation to tell anybody they can't or shouldn't use them. Are they a shortcut? There isn't really a lot of evidence for that. I did experience a lot of unusual things, but generally, I could not embody them, I could not make them mine, and especially not when I needed them. Psychedelic use created a lot of spiritual confusion for me. The Dalai Lama's response of focussing on hope is probably an acknowledgment that the spiritual path is long and windy, and therefore hope for a shortcut represents an understandable human sentiment.

THE SPECIAL CASE OF MARIJUANA

Under marijuana, I treat all tetrahydrocannabinol (THC) containing drugs, which include marijuana (the buds of the cannabis indica plant), hashish (the pollen), hashish oil (compressed extract) and synthetic THC. Marijuana is, in some regard, a special case similar to that of the already covered ecstasy. Most drugs described here can be relatively easily allocated to a single chakra. Ecstasy, marijuana and ketamine cannot. Marijuana has a mild positive effect on the throat chakra, while having a mild negative effect on the heart and power chakra. The above-described plant hallucinogens do not affect the heart and navel chakra at all.

Marijuana's positive effect on the throat chakra consists of a modified perception of space and time. Marijuana is often consumed by artists. The extreme sensitivity to rhythm in eastern- and Reggae music is due to Marijuana drawing time units long, and percussionists and drummers, or for example, Indian table players, becoming much more sensitive to intricacies

CHAPTER 5.

of rhythms. Similarly, Middle Eastern geometrical sacred paintings are clearly influenced by an increased sensitivity to space produced by the activation of the throat chakra.

At the same time marijuana mildly impedes the heart chakra, which if smoked daily and especially in large quantities, impedes the processing of emotions and eventually contributes to their bottling up. Marijuana-addicts often surprise through their emotional immaturity, even if at the same time they may be intellectually well endowed. There are always exceptions to the rule, and one may as well be the Rastafarian leader Bob Marley (with the Rastafarian religion likely to play a role here). But as we see with all drugs, a few exceptions who, through strong, already existing tendencies in their personality, overcome the tendency of a particular drug, do not disprove the general assessment of that drug. Marijuana also mildly impedes the navel chakra. Generally, marijuana-smoking communities (such as the hippies), are marginalized and disempowered, as marijuana mellows one's drive to leadership, domination and success. This, however, does not have to be only a negative thing, as we will explore later on.

In India, *charas* (a form of hashish), used to be widely smoked or ingested as *bhang* lassi, for sacral purposes. Especially the worshippers of Lord Shiva (the destroyer of the ego), and amongst them more so the ascetics, smoke *charas* as a form of worship of their god and to be close to him. One variant of the Shiva mythology, related to me by Hindu ascetics, states that Shiva conjured up the world into existence when sitting in the jungle, smoking *charas*. We humans then are his stoned dreams and phantasies, and smoking *charas* is used to wake up from that dream. Especially this last phrase does not immediately make sense, but maybe it would if smoking *charas* long enough and in sufficient quantities.

Also in India, pot-smoking Shiva-ascetics become more and more marginalized. The author has witnessed scenes where ascetics, although officially seen as a hoary adjunct to Hindu culture, were beaten up by the police, and driven away from town centres, where their mingling with foreigners was seen by the authorities as disturbing.

Marijuana used to be legal for most of history in many countries worldwide, but the influence of Western governments during the Reagan-Thatcher era made most countries reverse their traditional laws, and install draconian punishments, including the death penalty for rather insignificant quantities. This absurdity takes place against the backdrop that a large portion of humanity smokes pot as a form of self-medication, to cope with the unreasonable stresses of modern, fast-paced life, including the breakdown of social structures and urban uprooting. To make it absolutely clear, I do not smoke pot and I do prefer yogic techniques to any drug, including marijuana, but pot-smoking for many people seems to be a reasonable strategy (as long as one keeps frequency and dosage under control) to decrease mental breakdown in a global society in which economy, ecology, political systems and social fabric are increasingly exposed to an epidemic of mental health disorders. On the one hand our society forces many people to smoke marijuana as a form of stress-release and decompression and on the other hand, it criminalizes people for doing so. Makes no sense at all.

So, why do people smoke pot? People self-medicate with marijuana because it helps them become more relaxed and laid-back (reflecting a stretched sense of time). It can also make people more aware of their bodies or unconsciously held tension, and makes many people more sensual, reflected in an increased libido in some, and an improved appreciation for music or taste in others.

Marijuana makes many people more lunar, which is a yogic way of saying it activates the holistic right brain hemisphere (increased sensitivity for nature, art and the views of others), the parasympathetic nervous system (rest and relaxation) and introversion. Pot-smokers are often happy to just be by themselves and potter around (!) doing nothing in particular. It can improve lateral, non-linear thinking in some, and I've seen it stop people from going over the cliff into burn-out. There are obvious benefits to pot, which would lead a holistic and wise society to keep it available as a self-medication and mental-health option.

Another important point is that on the relativistic-fundamentalist scale of the mind, marijuana will take you out of the fundamentalist side and further over to the relativistic side. That means you become more open to the viewpoints of others and less certain that your own views are right. You can even descend into relativistic confusion, where you are questioning whether any position held, may have intrinsic values at all. This would indicate that one smokes too much for one's own good.

So, why have many societies, besides political allegiances, have made it illegal? It's illegal because it makes people less driven and therefore contributes to lowering GDP, with GDP's constant elevation considered the holy grail by our economists. Remember the saying behind coffee, the most legal of all drugs, "do more stupid things faster with more energy"? Pot-smoking makes you consider the opposite, "do less things slower with hardly any energy spent".

Hmm... maybe that doesn't actually sound as stupid as first thought. Pot-smokers can look lethargic. They may sit around and think about doing things for such a long time, that eventually they figure out that they are not worth doing at all. You know the saying, "why put off until tomorrow what you can do today". The marijuana equivalent is, "why put off until tomorrow what you can avoid altogether". Could there be value in marijuana for a society that has in 400 years displaced 100 million through slavery and colonialism, has another 100 million indigenous people, and destroyed their cultures, has poisoned the atmosphere with CO^2 and methane, killed two-thirds of all wild mammals in the last 60 years, has depleted the world's fish stocks by 80% and in many places has killed 75% of all insects including our pollinators, has acidified and heated the oceans and filled them with plastic waste so marine fauna is choking, has brought about the bleaching of reefs and the melting of glaciers and pole caps, has depleted its topsoils and aquifers and poisoned them with ridiculous practices like fracking? The bill of worshipping for centuries so-called progress, which is only our hubris to think that we can outsmart nature, is about to be presented. Marijuana can actually decrease that hubris and certainty. It makes one realize that we aren't actually that smart, that nature is always smarter, that we should respect it and are only a small part within it.

But our consumerist-capitalist society doesn't want to see that. It wants us to be driven by a desire for profit and for consumption. Consumption of what in hindsight often presents itself as useless. Our economic model runs on stoking unreasonable desires, only to sell more unreasonable, unnecessary, further polluting objects. In making the money to fulfil our steroid-fuelled material desires, we are turning ourselves into industrial wage slaves, often producing the very useless things then sold back to us and other industrial wage slaves. In doing so we are raising GDP, which is a sanitized way of saying we are making the already obscenely wealthy even richer.

The war on drugs wants us to believe that pot-smokers are dangerous people. But they are gentle creatures, who if they pose a danger at all, are so then to themselves, rather than to society. People on cocaine, with their unhealthy ambitions, are more likely to be a danger to society. Personally, though, I have to admit there are things about pot-smokers that I find annoying. In the already mentioned little town called Mullumbimby they have a particularly strong strain of marijuana called Mullumbimby Madness. Driving into Mullumbimby used to make me crazy as there was always a stoner in front of me driving 35 in a 50 km/h zone. Most speedometers, as you can check with your GPS, need to display 55km/h to replicate a real-life speed of 50 km/h. But people on Mullumbimby Madness, with their increased sensitivity to time and space, find even driving at 50km/h an unbearable strong and scary sensation, so they have to slow down to 35km/h. I sometimes had phantasies of calling the cops, "Please, officer, there is another stoner in front of me doing 35. Can you please come and stop them from impeding my accelerated progress?"

While a lot of this article sounds positive, Marijuana is addictive and I have witnessed incidences of marijuana-induced paranoia and psychosis. Again, studies claim these incidences can be avoided by previously screening people, but I'm dubious about the effectiveness of such screening. There will always be cases of people who react sensitively to marijuana and whose life then enters a downward spiral. Marijuana is a mild drug and in that regard is in the same category as coffee and alcohol, although in any other regard it has nothing in common with these substances. Mild here means that for many people, it is possible to have days without usage and on other days to keep dosage low. Mild also means that for a deterioration of the situation, usually large and consistent doses have to be taken, which is again opposite to drugs like cocaine, heroin or crystal meth, where a deterioration can occur quickly.

But reggae musicians like Bob Marley or Peter Tosh reported smoking an average of 200g per day. That's a staggering 6kg per month and to all that I know, they remained functioning. A good part of that may be due to the spiritual character of Rastafarian culture, but for me, it's still inconceivable. I smoked hashish and, to a lesser degree, marijuana for a couple of years during my late teens, but I mainly did it for social reasons because all my friends did it. Ultimately, I did not like nor enjoy how my mind worked on cannabis. I was always more interested in meditation and pranayama, and after watching my mind going down rabbit holes for a while, I quit from one day to the next with no withdrawal symptoms. If anything, then boredom got me to quit.

Chapter 6.
THE THIRD-EYE CHAKRA AND LSD

THE THIRD-EYE CHAKRA

While at the navel chakra, our sense of self includes nations, corporations, cults, tribes, religions, movements, ideologies and even football teams, of which we see ourselves part of, at the heart chakra it expands to include the whole of humanity. Other people then are not anymore seen as belonging to the category of "other". There is no human other anymore. However, other species and the environment are still seen as somebody or something else. With the activation of the throat chakra now, our sense of self again expands, to include all the aforementioned. We have the visceral experience that the entire material cosmos and all beings are a crystallization of one common intelligence. However, we are relating to this intelligence only through its many crystallizations, emanations, manifestations, permutations and computations. It is only with the activation of the third-eye chakra that we experience revelation of, and communication with, this cosmic intelligence directly. Before third-eye chakra activation, we only deducted this intelligence from its workings.

Both experiences, the one of the throat and the third-eye chakra, are unique. Neither of them can replace the other, nor are they reducible to each other. Unfortunately, that's what our culture has done and when thousands of years ago the first individuals activated the third-eye chakra (leading to sky-based religions), the throat chakra activation (representing indigenous and Earth-based spirituality) was discarded as being unnecessary, or even in conflict with the capacities of the third-eye chakra. They are not, and both are essential for what we could, in common parlance, call an enlightened culture and civilization.

The third-eye chakra is not really a single chakra but a constellation of about half a dozen energy centres in the cranium. It is called the third-eye chakra not because it is on the forehead but because of its position in the middle of the cranium, behind the "third-eye" location. Similarly, the navel chakra is not in the actual navel but at the same level and height, as is also the case with the heart and throat chakras.

The location of the third-eye chakra is the third ventricle of the brain. This ventricle is very significant, as it is surrounded by the main endocrine and neurological switchboards of the brain – the pituitary and pineal glands, the thalamus and the hypothalamus. The ventricles are hollows filled with cerebrospinal fluid. They directly connect to the sacrum. The sacrum floats in the sacroiliac joints (if they function properly) and it performs a constant bowing movement called nutation and counternutation. This movement acts as a pump for cerebrospinal fluid (CSF), which is moved by the sacrum up the spinal cord into the brain. Here the pumping is enhanced by the movement of the cranial bones. CSF is linked to the phenomenon of Kundalini. The sacrum and the sacral chakra play an important role in moving Kundalini up to the third-eye chakra in the third ventricle. It is important to convert the sacral chakra into a motor for our spiritual evolution.

The third-eye chakra is also the lunar storehouse of *prana*, or lunar *pranic* battery, and as such is directly linked to the navel chakra. The navel chakra is the storehouse of solar *prana*, and its function is male and catabolic. This was described in more detail in the chapter on the navel chakra. The third-eye chakra is the lunar storehouse, and its function is female, nurturing and anabolic. Both chakras are linked and harmonized through *Nadi Shodhana pranayama*, which is described in my book *Pranayama: The Breath of Yoga*. The lunar pranic battery powers these functions:

- Right holistic brain hemisphere
- Left lunar nostril
- Relativistic mind
- Parasympathetic nervous system
- Introversion
- Afferent (incoming) nerve currents
- Sensory-neurons
- Anabolism (building up tissue)

The navel chakra dominates today's society, while the heart chakra is at this point, only a vision and promise of the future. This is reflected in the fact that production facilities are male dominated, and, while everybody in a position of power believes that we need to dissect the world, extract minerals, build factories and make profit (all male catabolic concepts), the idea that the whole planet is one living organism that needs to be nurtured (an anabolic concept linked to feminine spirituality) –

a process that may impinge on profitability – is still considered too intuitive and right-brained by many.

Whereas the throat chakra is legislative, making you understand and see sacred law, the third-eye chakra is divinitive, that is, this chakra shows you the intelligence according to which the cosmic master plan of creation unfolds. This intelligence is the intelligence of the Divine; it *is* the Divine. The third-eye chakra shows you the Divine with form (in India called *saguna* Brahman), whereas the formless Absolute, the *nirguna Brahman*, can be attained only in the crown chakra. The third-eye chakra represents the need to commune with the Divine itself and pass the experience of communion on to others.

However, it is important to go from the heart chakra to the throat chakra and then onwards via the third-eye chakra, and not straight to the crown chakra. At the level of the crown chakra, there is no more relating to others because there is no longer an individual identity. The crown chakra represents the dissolution of the individual. Particularly if one goes straight from the heart chakra to the crown chakra, one may not only develop the erroneous philosophy that the world is an illusion but also that God, the Divine with form (*saguna* Brahman), is non-existent or just a reinterpretation of the formless Absolute (*nirguna* Brahman), and is suitable only for those of slight intellect.

Doctrines that propound that the individual self is identical with the divine self, result from a lack of emphasis on the third-eye chakra. The omnipotence, omnipresence and omniscience of the Divine can only be seen when the third-eye chakra is opened, and not when one goes straight to the crown chakra. The third-eye chakra confirms the accuracy of Ramanuja's (an Indian theologian) *beda-abeda* doctrine (identity-in-difference). Contrary to Shankara (another Indian theologian), who stated that *atman* (individual self) and Brahman (cosmic self) are identical, Ramanuja correctly said that they are both identical (in the regard they are both consciousness), and yet different (the cosmic self is omniscient, omnipotent and omnipresent whereas the individual self is not, the body of the cosmic self is the entire universe, whereas the body of the individual self is only five to six feet tall). This important realization ceases to be theory once both, the third-eye- and the crown chakra, are activated. Activation of only one of them, especially with exclusion of the throat chakra, leads one into a theologian trap.

The quality of the third-eye chakra is *sattvic*, as was that of the throat chakra. *Sattva* means intelligence particle and the third-eye chakra shows you cosmic intelligence. This chakra has only two petals, which is significant. The number of petals indicates the number of major *pranic* channels (*nadis*) that terminate at a chakra (excluding the central energy channel, Sushumna, on which all chakras are strung like a thread). The third-eye chakra has the lowest number of *pranic* channels, but they are the two most important ones. They are Ida and Pingala, the lunar and solar pranic channels, which power the right and left brain hemispheres, the parasympathetic and sympathetic nervous systems, afferent and efferent nerve currents, lunar and solar mind, relativism and fundamentalism, anabolism and catabolism and mind and body, respectively. The place where Ida and Pingala meet Sushumna is also called *Mukti Triveni*, the liberating triple confluence. It has this name because, if *prana* is placed into the third-eye chakra, Ida and Pingala are both suspended, and the mystical state (revelation of cosmic intelligence) takes place.

The third-eye chakra, where the three *nadi*s meet, is the termination point of Ida and Pingala. Whoever reaches this point goes beyond these two *pranic* channels. Ida and Pingala are essential for our functioning, but they prevent the mystical state by making us fall for one of the two extremes of the mind. They make us fall prey to duality. Duality means to fall for either of the two extremes of solar or lunar mind. The solar mind believes that only one truth exists and fails to recognize the many other truths. This mind develops into the direction of fundamentalism. The lunar mind falls into the trap of relativism, which means one recognizes the many truths but fails to see the one truth. If both *pranic* channels are suspended, for the time of their suspension, one can see reality as such without using the categorising and dichotomising mind. During that time, one is beyond time and beyond death, as the *Hatha Yoga Pradipika* confirms (IV.17).

During the mystical state (revelation of cosmic intelligence), the sound OM is heard. To hear this sound emitted by the Supreme Being, *prana* (life force) has to be placed into the third-eye chakra. This is the yogic meaning of taking a bath in the triple confluence, *Mukti Triveni*. However, although *prana* is to be placed into the third-eye chakra, the mystical syllable itself is heard in the heart chakra, also these two chakras being intricately linked. If one remains absorbed in the ecstasy of the third-eye chakra, however, it is near impossible to pass on one's experience and to be understood. For a life of divine service and divine love, one needs to step back down and place *prana* into the heart chakra.

Related to the third-eye chakra are two of Patanjali's ethical guidelines (*niyamas*), self-study (*svadhyaya*) and placing oneself into the service of cosmic intelligence (*Ishvara pranidhana*). Let us look first at the importance of self-study, which according to tradition is nothing but the study of sacred texts. The corruption visible in religion today should not keep us from looking for the sacred in the written tradition. People like to point their finger at corruption within religion and I can't blame them but we need to remember that corruption is not limited to this realm: people have done exactly the same within social movements, political and economic systems, sports, science and entertainment. Wherever there is power, corruption appears. Lord Acton (1750CE) eloquently expressed this by saying, "Great men in almost all cases are not good men. Because power corrupts and absolute power corrupts absolutely". Studying sacred books afresh, with no preconceived and confused ideas, try to reconnect to the original vision of the ancient seers, may it be the Vedic *rishis*, Gautama Buddha, Lao-Tzu or Jesus Christ. Such study is called self-study (*svadhyaya*) and, as Patanjali says (*Yoga Sutra* II.44), it will reveal to you the appropriate form of the Divine to meditate on (in Sanskrit called your *ishta devata*).

Once this revelation has taken place, the second observance of Patanjali relating to this *chakra* comes into force. It is that of placing oneself into the service of cosmic intelligence (*Ishvara pranidhana*). For traditional practitioners this means serving your chosen form of the Divine, but for contemporary practitioners serving the cosmic intelligence as represented in nature might be easier. Such surrender has again several phases or stages. In an early stage we simply pray and ask cosmic intelligence for guidance. When asking for divine guidance, we ask the Divine to point us in the direction we should take. Eventually, we step aside more and more and let the Divine act through us, we let the Divine perform its will through us. I have pointed out this process in great detail in *How to Find Your Life's Divine Purpose*

– *Brain Software for a New Civilization*. In this volume I have also attempted to create a new theology, which takes clues not only from sky-based religions such as Hinduism and Christianity, but also from different branches of Western Science such as quantum physics, astrophysics and evolutionary biology, and finally the important teachings of indigenous cultures. It is time that we evolve to a new spirituality informed by both reason and mystical experiences rather than just superstition.

To place ourselves into the service of cosmic intelligence, activating the third-eye chakra (which reveals to us the Divine with form, also called the God immanent), is much more important than activating the crown chakra (revealing the formless absolute or God transcendent). This is so because the formless Absolute/God transcendent/infinite consciousness neither acts nor performs, it only witnesses. It also does not confer instruction, which the Divine with form, the God immanent, does. While recognizing ourselves as consciousness is an important part of one's spiritual development (as will later be covered in great detail), what matters most is *dharma* (duty, righteousness), the question of what is right action. If we are to lead a divine life, we must first seek the Divine with form, cosmic intelligence, of which the world, human society, and all life, are a manifestation and expression. If we go straight to the crown chakra, we cannot get much inspiration towards bringing divine love into this society and world, as the crown chakra leads to the formless Absolute and the great dissolution (*nirvana*). These are noble aims in their own right but they cannot tell us how to live our life here in this body. Any dissolution should only be desired after each one of us has completed their own personal sacred duty (called *svadharma* in the Bhagavad Gita); that is, one has made one's individual contribution to divine life and divine love on Earth. The revelation of what exactly that is for each individual comes with activation of the third-eye chakra, but it should be accessed as early as possible by a technique called vision-practice, described in *How to Find Your Life's Divine Purpose*.

At the level of the first chakra, if asked about God one might say 'I don't know what you're talking about'. At the level of the second chakra, tribal allegiance will determine one's beliefs. At the third chakra one may portray oneself as a rationalist or atheist on the one hand, or a believer on the other, but the decision is made based on advantages that come with it – thus politicians often bash the holy book of their electorate to get re-elected rather than out of true love for the Divine.

At the level of the fourth chakra, one recognizes the existence of the Divine in people one meets and develops trust, and here the spiritual path truly starts. A feeling of trust is something personal, whereas belief ordered by one's superiors or society is impersonal. At the fifth chakra one understands divine law and can use it for the furtherment of all. At the sixth chakra one realizes the Divine as that cosmic intelligence that expresses itself in all and through all, but maintain one's individuality. At this level we become one humanity within the one Divine. Although we may worship it in different ways, we realize its and our essential unity. At the seventh chakra one merges into infinite consciousness, and eventually one's individual identity will be extinguished, like a drop merging into the ocean. At this point, all activity falls away.

It is so important that we do not rush ahead but first realize what this current chakra has to teach us. In the Yoga Sutra, eight classical samadhis (ecstatic trances or revelations) are listed, which I have described in great detail in my text *Samadhi The*

Great Freedom. Of these the first four are didactic, that is they are training-*samadhis*. The fifth, called ananda samadhi, is a *samadhi* on the throat chakra, it shows us the entire world as a crystallization of cosmic intelligence. The sixth *samadhi* is called *asmita samadhi*. It gives us an experience that cosmic intelligence expresses and computes itself through us by individuating through us. This means that not only the pure consciousness (*atman, purusha*) within us is sacred, but also our individuality is a permutation of cosmic intelligence. At this level we have an experience of stepping aside and letting the Divine perform actions through us. In common parlance this state is called *being-in-the-zone*. Jesus called it, "it is not me but the Father in me that doeth the works". Krishna said about it in the Bhagavad Gita, "Surrender the fruit of all actions to Me, and be free, oh Arjuna". But for this to take place, for cosmic intelligence to act through us, we need to become conscious of that possibility. The law here says that cosmic intelligence can do through us only what we can comprehend it doing. Before third-eye chakra activation we can only unconsciously co-create with cosmic intelligence. With this chakra activated, this becomes conscious co-creation.

If we look at our history during the last few thousand years, only a select few activated this chakra and often they became religions leaders. Unfortunately, usually, the followers of these leaders did not understand the significance of working on the heart- and throat chakras. A third-eye chakra religion that forgets about the heart chakra may believe that only the form of the Divine accepted in that very religion is real, and its adherents may kill individuals of other movements as infidels. In this process they completely overlook that even those "infidels" are children and expressions of the very Divine they worship but do not truly understand.

But third-eye chakra religions that by-pass the throat chakra awakening, may become a tool of environmental destruction because its followers don't realize this entire biosphere and all of life is only the crystallized body of the very Divine they worship. If we do get a third-eye chakra religion that ignores both the heart and the throat chakra we have a perfect tool of manipulation, suppression and domination in the hands of a cynical, self-serving priesthood. It is important to not rush ahead in one's realization and activate the chakras, evolutionary brain-centres, in order. Even after we have had epiphanies based on some, we need to continue to perform formal practices that emphasize all higher chakras, especially the heart and throat chakra. Our painful history of the last few millennia is a powerful reminder what happens if we don't. With this in mind, let's now go to a drug that, at least theoretically, can activate the third-eye chakra, LSD. It must, however, be already apparent how important in this context traditional spiritual practice is, and if such a drug is not harnessed by such practices and not taken in a sacred context, is likely to do more damage than good. As usual, use of this substance comes with many caveats as it is just as likely to set one back spiritually, rather than provide progress.

THE THIRD-EYE CHAKRA DRUG: LSD

LSD (lysergic acid diethylamide) occurs naturally in the ergot fungus (mother corn) that grows on rye, and I believe it is also naturally produced by the brain (but to my knowledge it has not been found yet). The latter I believe because, with extensive training and practice, I replicated all of LSD's effects with yogic methods. The effects are sometimes so similar that it feels as if yogic techniques trigger endogenous LSD, i.e. LSD that the body itself produces in the brain.

LSD has a long and chequered history. It was most likely, in its ergot form, used as a sacrament in the Mysteries of Eleusis cult in ancient Greece. The Greeks had the knowledge of how to neutralize the extreme toxicity of the mother corn and used it as a sacral brew in their initiation ritual for upper class boys. Socrates, Plato and Aristotle all went through this initiation and with all three it can be noticed how the mother corn influenced the development of their intellects. This is noticeable in Plato's writings, *The Last Days of Socrates* and *Republic*. The other great influence, which combined with the Eleusis cult to bring about ancient Greek's remarkable explosion of intellect, is its import of Indian schools of thought via trade routes. So has Plato's philosophy remarkable similarities with Patanjali's.

The European witches also knew how to neutralize the toxicity of the mother corn. They gave it as a potion to women about to give birth to make this process easy and pain free. This gave the ergot drink the name mother corn. On a spiritual level, for a skilled person a high-dose LSD trip teaches exactly the same capacity at the other end of life. LSD can, at the time of death, make partition from the body easy and pain free and is therefore also here a mother corn for a birth into a next and higher life. For this reason Aldous Huxley ingested LSD on his deathbed.

Working for Sandoz in Basel, the Swiss chemist Albert Hofmann was given the job to isolate mother corn alkaloids with the goal to find a drug that would make giving birth easier. None of the isolated substances showed promise, so he shelved them, including one called LSD25. Years later Hofmann had the intuition to have another look at this substance. He discovered its psychoactive effect only accidentally, when handling some vials and afterwards noticing strange effects. He deducted that a drop of the new substance, which had fallen on his skin, must have penetrated it and brought on the effects. He then looked up the potency of mescaline, which at the time was the strongest known psychoactive drug. Hojmann took a fraction of the quantity needed to bring on such symptoms, had the drug been mescaline. But he still significantly overdosed. Hoffman realized that the experience would be strong, jumped on his bicycle and drove home through the countryside. On the way home he hallucinated, such as the grain fields rolling in wavelike patterns. This marked the first LSD trip ever experienced, an occasion still celebrated in the subculture today as "bicycle day".

Sandoz marketed LSD as a psychiatric drug, treating all sort of mental disorders and it became popular during the 1950s and 60s. Cary Grant took LSD under the tutelage of his psychologist 100 times and afterwards stated that he was "truly, deeply and honestly happy". The CIA tested LSD on a great number of people and often without their knowledge. One of the CIA's assessments was that LSD made people more open to suggestion, which is a tendency we will delve into later.

In 1963 the US senate gave the Harvard Psychology professor Timothy Leary the assignment to research potential usage or dangers of LSD. However, when Leary reported enthusiastically to the senate that LSD presented a unique chance for humanity, the senators had already made up their minds to declare it illegal, which took place in 1968. But by then Leary, his colleague Richard Alpert (later Ram Dass), Aldous Huxley, Alan Watts, Alan Ginsberg and Ken Kesey's Merry Pranksters had turned on an entire generation to LSD, and the counterculture was born.

Since entire volumes have been written on LSD's influence on John Lennon, Jimi Hendrix, the Grateful Dead, Keith Richards, the Cream, Pink Floyd, etc., there is no need for me to recite this here. This is a book on the spiritual impact of drugs, not their cultural.

LSD appears to be non-toxic, you can take enormous amounts (as we will later discover) without major physiological symptoms, and it is non-addictive. I would say the latter mainly because it is much too much work to take it. It can, however, have adverse psychological effects and it can provoke you to do dangerous things, as we will soon find out. Some people report visual and auditory hallucinations, but I have hardly ever noticed any. One of the main problems with LSD is its potency. You need only about 100 micrograms to have a significant experience. A microgram is a millionth of a gram (0.000001g) and a working dosage of 100 microgram is only just a ten thousandth of a gram (0.0001g). LSD trips do not come with the dosage printed on them so there is rather little one can do to find out, besides trying it out. A lot of so-called LSD on the black market used to be amphetamine laced with strychnine (rat poison). Another problem is the Hallucinogenic-persisting-perception-disorder, in common parlance called flashbacks. Especially if people had a strongly negative experience, repercussions and reverberations can be felt for a long time.

LSD's main effect, as far as I could see, is that it is a giant magnifying glass that brings any personal issues one may have to the fore. If you have major psychological issues, LSD, like other psychedelics may magnify these, but it also can be used creatively if one is taken to introspection, self-reflection and self-analysis. Let me give you a few examples: In my family there was a lot of intergenerational trauma passed down, and

CHAPTER 6.

during my teens I had significant conflicts with my parents. Since neither party involved displayed great communication skills, these often ended in altercations. I remember this particular day, I must have been around 16, when I came home a bit too late after a long night on LSD. I would usually time it so I disappeared into my room before my parents got up. When I approached our house my mum opened the door, handed me a broom and said, "Here, sweep the footpath". Had I been my usual teenage self I would have had an outburst accusing her of being an imperialistic agent of the bourgeoisie (we were a socialist family), attempting to manipulate me into being her slave for menial tasks, followed by an exclamation like, "stop hassling me" or "stop badgering me all day long". My poor mum! I was a real handful. Anyway, on this day, while up to my eyeballs on LSD, I looked at her and just saw this person trying to do her best. She didn't do what I felt I needed, but also not out of any feeling of malice, but more because, like me, she was descended from a long lineage of ancestors who carried with them a real lot of baggage and was just trying to get by. I grabbed the broom out of her hand and while looking at it I thought, "Why not! After all, she has wiped my backside (well, arguable she whipped it a fair bit, too), fed me, clothed me and if I think today, that I'm dysfunctional, I better get over it and take responsibility for my own feelings and stop blaming her." A notable breakthrough for the person I used to be! That morning for the first time I swept that pathway in complete peace and acceptance, rather than seeing myself akin to one of the slaves building Pharaoh Cheops' pyramid, in dire need to be liberated from my Pharaoh-mum through a Soviet-style revolution.

Another incident taking place shortly afterwards involved me riding my bicycle while on LSD. I suddenly dissociated and watched myself from the outside, from some distance away. To my great shock, visible sitting on the bicycle was not I, but my father. At the time I had a really difficult relationship with him, and he represented everything in authority that was wrong, in hindsight an obvious psychological projection undertaking in an attempt to carve out who I was, independent from him. When I suddenly saw him in the physical space taken up by me, I was initially in total shock, that strong was the rejection I felt towards him. Then it dawned upon me that my rejection of him was only an inner conflict and rejection of who I was. I also could see myself as an extension of my dad's, and his ancestors' karma. I was not just a completely autonomous person, but in many ways a karmic result set in motion by his and his ancestors' intentions, in some way a fulfilment of their intentions and aspirations. I could see for the first time that rather than being completely independent and different from him, I was actually painfully similar to him. From that day onwards, when I saw him do things I didn't like, I didn't just judge and condemn him, but inwardly thanked him for making me alert to aspects of myself that seemed unhelpful, so I could then consciously counteract them or let them go.

The following memory is from my first ever LSD trip. One thing really important when using LSD and plant hallucinogens is to remove or cover up all mirrors in the house, although according to Daniel Pinchbeck the Bwiti in Gabon apparently start their ibogaine rituals before a mirror. It's one thing to choose to have a mirror-session and an entirely different one to get accidentally trapped in front of one. I didn't know that and on one of my first trips I happened to walk past the mirror and just glanced at myself from the corner of my eyes. There I was, glued to the spot for the seemingly next few hours. My face

CHAPTER 6.

transformed into endless permutations of human and animal faces. I remember seeing myself as wolf-like with barred teeth, snarling at myself. I could see all the suppressed anger and aggression within me, barely concealed under a thin veneer ready to break out at the slightest threat. Up to that point, I was considered a troubled, angry, and even dangerous young man. I had a history of violence, getting into fights and I had seriously beaten up quite a few opponents. A long string of attempts to punish and discipline me, had not only failed but made me more angry and mistrusting. My basic life feeling was that of a rabid dog, desperately fighting to survive and the only way I knew to do that was to attack pre-emptively with great viciousness. I could see all that history in that image of this wolf, that I carried in myself. I realized that I was that wolf to myself and to all those around me, externalizing all those raging inner conflicts. I never got into another fight after that. I spent the better part of the next 18 months all by myself in a forest, meditating myself out of my aggression and letting it go on the exhalation. I realized that I had never consciously chosen to be that way, but it was the existential state of being of my ancestors and the social field around me. Now, having woken up to it, it was necessary that I took responsibility and let go of all this negative programming.

But the journey in front of that mirror continued, and the wolf had only been the first image. I don't know how long I spent looking into that mirror, but it seemed aeons. The faces projected onto my face went all the way back in our evolutionary history to single-cell organisms, and then again, in more rapid form, forward to today. I remember having almost arrived at today with a rapid succession of images, when my eye suddenly glimpsed something disturbing. "Wait a second. Can we please fast rewind, no stop! Forward again, stop. There! What's that?"

CHAKRAS, DRUGS AND EVOLUTION

And there it was, Gregor Maehle on LSD at 3 am in the morning wearing a shiny black SS uniform, complete with Skull Brigade beret. For those of you not in the know, the SS Skull Brigades were ideologically trained Nazi elite forces who, besides other nasty things, also manned concentration camps. They were not your regular armed forces servicemen, but soldiers systematically trained and brainwashed with the objective to commit war crimes. That was really hard to stomach for me. The wolf was one thing, but now a Skull? Well, I'm born around 18 years after WW2 and on my dad's side, our family were commies. On my mum's side, we were peasants and supposedly not party-members (but that's what they all say, don't they). So, theoretically, I shouldn't have seen a Skull, but there he was. I quickly made a note to myself, "Couldn't have been me. If I had lived back then, I would have been a ninja-assassin and single-handedly killed all the Nazi top brass and changed the history of our country (being 16-years old, you still have such heroic ideas about yourself). The good thing about LSD is that it makes it harder to get away with such bullshit. Was I really that much better than those people? Or was I just lucky to be born a bit later? Could I not, if born in worse circumstances, with less opportunity to be free and myself, saddled with just a bit more trauma and painful experiences, possibly angry and violated in childhood, have done similar things? I was not so sure anymore.

I asked myself (on LSD), what would it take to do such things, such as war crimes or mass murder on an industrial scale? I realized that what was required to perform such an atrocity was to be in an intense state of pain, a pain that contracts us so much we become totally unsensitised to the pain of others. Buddhist philosophy has six realms of beings: gods, who are encapsulated in pride, animals bound by fear, demons dominated by anger, hungry ghosts, being slaves to desire, hell-beings, overcome by pain, and finally humans, who are subject to a mix of all those. Out of those six categories, only humans, says Buddhist philosophy, have the potential to be liberated because their state is in a constant flux. The model is to be understood metaphorically, not literally, so all six categories describe states of being experienced by humans. To hand out pain to others, such as mass murder on an industrial scale, we need ourselves to be in such a painful and a contracted state we cannot feel ourselves and others anymore. That's what the Buddhists call the realm of hell-beings, the realm of enormous, constant and overwhelming pain. The performance of such atrocities, although in the short term offer a way of processing one's own pain, in the long-term leads to further pain and contraction. It is not a workable method of compensation.

It is difficult and ultimately impossible to come to terms with collective memories of that kind, which involve collective trauma and karma, too. Continuing to stare into that mirror, collective memories of the Holocaust soon combined with those of 400-years of slavery and on to the wholesale slaughter of indigenous people around the world, to form one collective ocean of pain. Realizing how traumatized everybody around me was, I could only resolve to be as kind as I could, and to be an agent for healing in a desperate, apocalyptic world, as much as my limited capabilities allowed. And this was just my first trip of 150. Did anybody think LSD was about nice colours and optical hallucinations?

It's not. It's about shedding light on any unseen aspects of our psyche, which need looking at and which need acknowledging. If that works well, one can let go of conditioning. If it doesn't, you only further traumatize yourself. The difference is often just a razor's edge apart and I would be a fool if I would claim to know what exactly parts the two. In my late teens, I was a frantic reader of Freud and Jung, and I may owe it to both, that I came out of psychedelics in one piece. Let me give you an example that powerfully drives this home: right from the very dawning of my intellect I was fascinated by history and religion, and they should become the first two subjects I studied at university level. Before my psychedelic career, I had looked into the crusades, the inquisition, the witch burnings and the role religion played in colonialism. I wondered whether a god in whose name this was performed could really be the good guy? And if he wasn't, then could the one they call the bad guy possibly be the good guy? In my questionable, juvenile innocence, I decided to find out for myself and, for this purpose, fixed an image on my wall of the Beelzebub to meditate on. The particular image in question was created by the Swiss artist H.R. Giger, the creator of the alien in the horror film of the same name.

Murphy's law becomes even truer when on LSD. I noticed this image on my wall with a cursory glance and who would have thought, the Prince of Darkness suddenly not only came alive, but broke through the wall and lunged at me. Years later, I saw a scene in *Lord of the Rings*, where the magician Gandalf is accosted by an entity called the Great Balrog of Morgoth, and after a hefty fight, both fall into the bowels of the Earth. When watching that scene, I was surprised how close the animation artists came to what I saw on that day. With the Balrog, fuelled by a significant dose of LSD, hot on my tail, I had to first figure out how to manage my extreme fear, lest the Antichrist should devour me. I used deep breathing combined with Tibetan Buddhist protection mantras, which created a bit of distance between me and the Great Beast 666, but he still continued to chase me from one end of the galaxy to the other. Eventually, I recognized the influence that the Catholic brainwashing, which I was subjected to in kindergarten, had on my present predicament. With that realization, the Beelzebub finally shrank to a size of six feet, at which point I thought I could handle him. But it was the memory of my great-grandmother calling me "spawn of Satan" (she was a cranky old person who compensated for her extremely painful life with cursing many in her path) that I finally realized this Balrog was only but a representation of my ancestors' judgments on themselves, and the resulting layers of self-hatred, self-loathing and self-condemnation that now caused me to hate myself.

It is a neat sentence to write, "the Great Beast dissolved once I realized him to be a projection of the self-hatred conducted by my own ego". But I had to reason, rationalize, contemplate and meditate myself into this realization over several hours on a journey on which each second subjectively stretched to aeons in the evolutionary scale. Subconscious and collective fears, especially when built up in ancestral lineages over a period of centuries, don't just suddenly disappear only because you thought a clever thought. And if they do, then only in children's books and Hollywood movies.

This story was sort of heavy and the reader by now would look forward to some light entertainment, right? Here it comes! Due to its non-toxicity, there do not seem any deaths directly caused by overdosing on LSD, but people have died from doing silly things while under the influence. I came pretty close, too. On one of my last LSD-journeys, I took a morning ride on my beautiful Royal Enfield Bullet motorcycle through Goa, India, when suddenly "the acid kicked in" as the saying goes. Stopping the motorcycle to enjoy the surge and looking around to figure out what stupidity I could perform next, I suddenly noticed a few hundred metres away to my right a chain of hills. I had scaled those hills on foot before and remembered they were steep, strewn with huge, serrated boulders and definitely required the work of all fours to get up and down. What better idea than to do it on an Enfield Bullet, a magnificent example of classic, 1950s British motorcycle engineering, but it's clumsy and heavy off-road, particularly when lacking off-road tires and with my ancient specimen, properly functioning brakes. What happened next was that somehow my body, the LSD, the Enfield Bullet and the hillside coalesced to produce a mountain goat-like forward-movement, during which the Enfield leapt from boulder to boulder, as if it was indeed alive. I don't consider myself a particularly talented off-road rider at the best of times, but here every neuron in my brain and every muscle fibre in my body were conscripted in service of heavy-hoeing this archaic, 200kg, totally under-motorised road bike up this mountain. I still don't know how I managed and I know I didn't actually manage it at all. It was as if an intelligence greater than me that day took delight to enact itself through me, the bike, and the mountain. And just as well because otherwise, I'd be dead today. I remember making it to the top with a boiling, crackling, overheated engine. I took a deep breath and thought, "okay, now the same thing in reverse" and headed downhill, which was even more dangerous. I came with squealing tyres to a halt at exactly the same position on the road from which I had originally assessed the situation. I looked back to the hills with a braindead mission-accomplished-type gaze and, spinning the bike 180 degrees, I took off in a cloud of burned rubber towards the next stupidity, which I gladly don't remember. What I did was absolutely dangerous and tempting fate. While I was certainly slightly crazed in those days, the LSD sometimes made me even more so. I leave it to the reader to determine the morale of this story. Definitely one shouldn't drive motorcycles when on LSD or, better don't drive vehicles or operate machinery at all (although in Mullumbimby, apparently, it's very common). Furthermore, it is questionable whether LSD is suitable for unsupervised young males, and since young females are doing stupid things, too, equally so for them. But what about everybody else? Hallucinogens do necessitate a great deal of maturity. How exactly the presence or absence of such maturity in individuals can be determined and their suitability to take LSD, is beyond my understanding.

Let's go back to some of the psychological effects of LSD. If used with great skill (which I often lacked), it's used to cleanse the mind from conditioning and to make it open and receptive like the mind of a child, or even newborn. Again here the connection to the mother corn. But with that comes great danger and opportunity. Every new idea seeded into the mind now becomes powerful and the mind attaches itself strongly to it. I mentioned this already as "getting stuck on a trip", and it is an ongoing problem on psychedelics. Even when not on psychedelics, we constantly get "stuck on trips", but it's generally less of an issue. While under the influence of hallucinogens, the mind is much more open to imprint, and if the imprint is destructive, its result can be much more damaging. When taking LSD with friends, I've noted frequently that my mind would take on a sentence uttered by somebody and mull over it (as if it was some great revelation) and possibly enact on it, too. I also remember some of my friends coming back days later and mentioning a sentence I had said in passing and forgotten, and they attached incredible import to it. This is what is meant with the CIA statement that LSD makes the mind more open to suggestions. It is a very dubious quality of LSD and I quickly figured out that the only way of safely taking it was to take it alone (which on the other side requires the ability to step out of oneself and babysit oneself during a psychedelic journey, an ability only learned through a lot of experience).

Let's have a close look now at what it means to "get stuck on a trip". This first example involves the already mentioned disgraced Harvard professor of psychology and self-styled LSD-prophet Dr Timothy Leary. Leary had a great influence on me in my teens, but when later on two occasions I had the opportunity to talk to him one-on-one, I was thoroughly disappointed to find somebody who was simply swept away by the Zeitgeist of his historical period. He was preoccupied with breaking away from convention, without himself being aware of where he was going, or where he was leading people. He also seemed more concerned with manufacturing his own public persona, than with possessing any true mystical insight, although much of the hippie-generation considered him an evolved spiritual being. To my eye, he was simply a showman.

Leary was introduced to the chakra model by a Tantric yogi who frequented Leary's Millbrook community during the 1960s. With his knowledge of brain-physiology, derived from his psychology studies, it was easy for Leary to recognize in the three lower chakras the three tiers of the brain as represented in the neuroscientist Paul D. MacLean's triune brain theory (more on that in Paul D. MacLean - *The Triune Brain in Evolution*). Leary was now looking for a contemporary way to integrate the chakra-doctrine and the triune brain theory into a model that describes our current and future evolution. According to his own statements, while doing so, he once watched Star Trek while under the influence of LSD. He suddenly "understood" that the commanding officers of the USS Enterprise, Scotty, McCoy, Spock and Captain Kirk were nothing but representations of the first four chakras. I suppose we should be open to the fact that theoretically, you could have a divine insight into the machinations of the cosmos pretty much from watching anything. But already here we learn of a problem with psychedelics. To some extent, especially when using high doses regularly, the nervous system is scrubbed clean like that of an infant and becomes receptive to primary imprint. Whatever you then perceive may become so deeply embedded in your subconscious it may take years, sometimes the rest of your life, to play out that dynamic. This is quite similar to the fact that it often takes us decades to realize that most of our life is only a re-enactment of the constellations of our nuclear family during early childhood.

Leary, watching Star Trek on LSD, got stuck on the idea that the main characters of the series depicted the lower four chakras of the human past, and that the extra-terrestrial races they encountered in space represented our future evolution. For the rest of his life then, Leary looked at William Shattner's depiction of Captain James T. Kirk as the embodiment of the fourth chakra (the heart chakra) or as Leary called it, "the socio-sexual brain circuit". We may savour the irony of that fact for a moment: A former Harvard professor of psychology, while reflecting on the meaning of the chakras, takes LSD and watches Star Trek. He then projects his desire to understand the chakras on a random happening, the fleeting images of the four main protagonists of an, at the time popular, science-fiction TV-series and we witness the birth of a lifelong-held claptrap-philosophy.

Ironically, Leary as an academic psychologist, would have taught in his classes the power of projection, which includes seeing meaning where there is none. However, the power of the psychedelic made him see Star Trek as the equivalent of a divine revelation, similar in status to the Tao Te King and the Tibetan Book of the Dead (both of which Leary also consulted on LSD but which unfortunately did not inform his evolutionary theory). I'm sure the scriptwriters of Star Trek would have had a good chuckle, had they known.

Leary's thought and philosophy never recovered from brainwashing himself into the belief that Captain Kirk was the embodiment of the heart chakra. With that, he never understood the heart chakra, nor the higher chakras. True awakening of the heart chakra does not represent our socio-sexual conditioning, as Leary called it, but it gives you the experience that the world and all beings are only a manifestation of divine love. True examples of an active heart chakra are Jesus Christ, Mahatma Gandhi, Martin Luther King and Nelson Mandela, but not Captain James T. Kirk. I'm sorry.

Getting stuck on a trip, example two: this example involves a contemporary American spiritual teacher. Let's call him John. John took significant doses of LSD while studying the Bhagavad Gita. Because in the Gita the Lord Krishna talks in the first person, John took the constant "I" in the text personal and came to think of himself as an avatar of the Lord. It's a typical example of LSD's capacity to make your mind malleable, that when reading a text written in the first person, you would think it talks about you. That's why LSD in the old days was called psychotomimetic, i.e. mimicking a psychosis. Most people realize the mistake and discontinue the psychosis-like equation when the effect of

CHAPTER 6.

the hallucinogen wears off, but John did not. He got stuck on this trip and proclaimed that devotional worship of him would be the only proper means of spiritual awakening for anybody else. He proclaimed himself to be "the divine lord in human form" and lectured from a raised dais surrounded by full regalia, such as staffs, garlands, flowers and oriental carpets, while everybody else had to be seated on the floor. He eventually went even further by stating that his followers only needed to meditate on his image or body in order to "participate in his enlightened state". A tall story and it shows that if you proclaim a tall story with great conviction for long enough, somebody will always buy it.

John frequently instructed his followers to have public and group sex, to produce pornographic movies, and to perform all sorts of sexual practices, with drug use also being encouraged. Disgruntled followers and media reports listed ongoing sexually, physically and psychologically abusive and humiliating behaviour, while others reported having profound metaphysical experiences in John's presence, attributing these phenomena to his spiritual power. Various controversies, playing themselves out in multiple lawsuits, continued until John's death, but so did tales of his spiritual grandeur. What should concern us here is the capacity of a person to talk themselves into believing they are an avatar of God. It is normal that one has profound realizations when studying scriptures like the Bhagavad Gita. That's what they are for. It is also foreseeable that when studying them while on psychedelics, these insights appear magnified. So far, so good. What is worrisome is the capacity of psychedelics-induced mystics to fall for their own story, the capacity to be tricked by their own mind to believe into their own mystery. If I have not made myself absolutely clear, an expletive might help. On psychedelics, you are more likely to "fall for your own bullshit"!

Falling for your own story is a staple problem of mysticism. In the life stories of Jesus Christ and Buddha, they are represented by the Prince of Darkness tempting both, right after their awakening. The Devil, or Mara as he is called in Buddhist philosophy, promised both freshly awakened mystics cities, armies, kingdoms and as many women as they wanted, if only they identified the newfound realization with themselves, their personage and physical form, their phenomenal self, or surface-self. Now, all spiritual awakening is really only a disconnect from the surface-self, and instead an identification with the deep self, the *atman* or consciousness. This abiding in consciousness is brought about by a temporary shutdown of the ego. After the mystical state is over, the ego again arises and says, "You have attained spiritual liberation, now go and identify it with me, the surface-self and this body".

A skilled mystic, such as the Buddha or Christ, will simply say, "go behind me Satan", and refuse to identify the *atman/* consciousness with their surface-self, i.e. the egoic body/mind. The terms Devil, Satan or Mara are metaphors for the ego, the program that identifies our consciousness with our body and mind. This is an important program without which we could not function in the embodied state and yet be infinite consciousness. Calling the ego "Devil" or "Satan" when you just came out of divine revelation and the insecure ego wants you now to identify the revelation as egoic, i.e. as pertaining to the ego, is understandable and even apt because the egos ploy does constitute a defilement and desecration of the beauty just experienced. An inexperienced mystic can fall for the trickery of the ego and permanently believe that henceforth worship of

CHAPTER 6.

their personage and physical frame can lead to liberation. This makes them a failed mystic, or to use a less favourable term, a charlatan. As we have seen with John's example above, the dissociation from the ego after a successful mystical experience is not made any easier by psychedelics. I actually believe it is made more difficult. There is some data on the fact that psychedelic mystics do not share the importance of humility that natural mystics emphasize.

Getting stuck on a trip, example three: The next story took place again over 40-years ago and involves a friend, let's call him Dave. Dave apparently took a single dose of LSD and saw himself as Jesus Christ. He then undressed and naked, hugged everybody around him telling them their sins were forgiven. I don't think Dave meant anybody harm. There is a beautiful innocence to that story. His nakedness symbolized for him purity and that, indeed for the time being, he saw the inner sinlessness of the *atman* in those around him. The problem was that he performed these actions, not in a circle of friends, but on the main intersection of our little town (wasn't Mullumbimby but could have easily been). He quickly attracted the attention of the local constabulary.

Now if in Dave's shoes, I would have switched the narrative. You need to come up with something like, "Sorry officer, my belt broke, and I lost my pants, and then the wind tore my shirt off". Something, anything, would do, but don't stick to the Jesus Christ story, as beautiful as it is. But my friend was stuck on his trip. He stuck to his story and was deemed a threat to the community and to decency. I'm sure he wasn't, but I'm not at all surprised at that assessment. He was admitted to the mental ward and put on Haloperidol (often sold as Haldol), a very strong anti-schizophrenic/anti-psychotic medication, with severe side effects. Staying in the mental institution for years, he eventually got hold of heroin and became addicted to it. Injecting, he contracted aids. It was still the early 80s and no treatment was available. He died soon thereafter. It still saddens me, but it highlights the unpredictability of psychedelics. This took place after a single dose of LSD and is not the only one of this type of story that I encountered.

I should mention here that LSD is not the only psychedelic that encourages one to take one's clothes off and channel the Nazarene. Jay Stevens in *Storming Heaven* describes Timothy Leary introducing Beat poet Allen Ginsberg and his boyfriend Peter Orlovsky to psilocybin. Instead of entering an introspective state, Ginsberg danced naked through the house, proclaiming to be the Messiah, saying he had come down to preach love to the world and they would walk through the streets, telling people to stop hating. Very similar to my friend, but Leary deterred the two poets from leaving the house. Instead, they then attempted to phone John F Kennedy and Nikita Khrushchev (it was the time of the Cuban Missile Crisis) to talk them out of using the bomb once and for all. Unfortunately, on that fateful day, neither Kennedy nor Khrushchev was available by phone!

Getting stuck on a trip, example four: Charles Manson and the Manson family. I realize I'm not doing much here for the great reboot of the psychedelic revolution currently gathering steam. I promise to narrate a few more positive stories, after we have made it through this present inquiry. When histories of LSD are written, they often focus on Timothy Leary, the Grateful Dead, and the summer of love in San Francisco. And that is a nice thing to do, but to discuss LSD comprehensively and to understand it, we need to also look at the Manson family. Then we understand that LSD doesn't have a lot of inbuilt characteristics but works like a giant magnifying glass that brings to the fore already existing tendencies of our psyche. If one does have a handle on Freudian and Jungian analysis, and practices spiritual disciplines to improve oneself, psychedelics can be a powerful tool. If you are functioning more akin to an unconscious robot, driven by your programmed imprints, then LSD can, and probably will, seriously backfire.

By the time Charles Manson formed his cult in 1967, the Manson Family, he had already spent more than half of his life in prison for a long string of offences. At his boy school, he was raped by other students, constantly beaten, and ran away from school 18 times. From then on, Manson's life was one long quest for survival and pre-emptively manipulating others, to prevent their attacks. Manson came to believe in an imminent apocalyptic race war between America's black and white populations. A white supremacist, Manson believed that all white people would be killed, apart from the members of his cult. His cult would eventually rise and rule the world, with Manson as their master. To provoke the outbreak of this race-war, Manson caused his followers to commit nine murders in July and August 1969, including the highly pregnant Hollywood actor Sharon Tate married to film director Roman Polanski.

Manson was initially sentenced to death, but with the death sentence abolished in California, he served a life sentence and died at age 83 in late 2017. There is no point here in analysing the bizarreness of Manson's belief system, but what should interest us is how he brainwashed his group of followers, mostly young women. The youngest member of the cult, Dianne Lake, who was 14 later reported that at the old ranch, which housed Manson's community, the whole group would regularly take LSD and perform orgies, which were "Very methodically done.

LSD was given out like a sacrament. We took turns taking each other's clothes off, in a circle... He orchestrated all of it. He even arranged the partners." Two of Manson's female followers were later charged with poisoning a prosecution witness with a burger laced with ten LSD trips, and three of Mason's followers were allegedly under the influence of LSD during the Tate – Labianca murders.

It is uncomfortable and inconvenient looking at these scenarios, but if we want to have an informed discussion on psychedelics, excesses like the Manson family must be included. Manson seems to have understood that on LSD, people are extremely sensitive to imprint. In his session, he is said to have used music and suggestions, until his gullible followers accepted the reality he imprinted in them. LSD brings to the fore and enhances already existing tendencies. If somebody desires, and is ready for, deep spiritual experiences, LSD seems to bring them about. If somebody has an existing psychopathology, LSD seems to enhance that, too. If there is a criminal tendency, it might also be increased. For example, before the Brotherhood of Eternal Love cornering the American LSD market, LSD's main distributors used to be the notorious Hell's Angels. I can't think that the Hell's Angels liked LSD because they wanted to turn on the world to love and peace.

I would like to further explore the CIA's assessment of LSD making you open to suggestions. During my own psychedelic experiments, I quickly noticed that I often picked up ideas from friends who I was journeying with. Sometimes these ideas continued in my mind like programs on autopilot. I also needed to make sure that I didn't just run into somebody, who would send me on a confusing tangent. I even noticed that anything I ate on or before the day of using psychedelics, would profoundly influence my experience. For this reason I would fast for 24 hours, not watch any movies or listen to music, and go into social isolation to prepare for an experience. I also learned that if in the night before a journey I had a negative dream, I would take this as a sign to postpone it. All of this seems excessive, but in the Indian Puranas, you find the idea that the very last thought before you die will determine your rebirth. There are numerous stories in the Puranas of seriously horrible people, who accidently murmured the name of a particular Hindu god when they died and were then saved by that god. I think we need to understand that psychologically, rather than literally. Whatever you do, speak, think or feel in a key situation, whether that be your death or a psychedelic experience, can leave a subconscious imprint so powerful that it immediately asks for its own consummation. This means this imprint needs to act itself out now, and any other imprints must wait. This concept is also in line with Patanjali's teaching on karma, where acts performed with great intention and intensity, ask for immediate karmic results. While that does not mean that other karmic acts are deleted, they are delayed and, for a while put on hold.

In terms of psychedelics this means we need to take extreme caution to avoid any negative imprints coming our way. The *Hatha Yoga Pradipika* (a medieval, tantric yoga text) states that, "It is always through bad company that they lose all their yogic merit". LSD being a giant magnifying glass on our psyche, we need to make sure that we have the chance to work through some of our negative programs, rather than picking up more by exposing ourselves to random contacts. LSD can, if handled properly, lead to great revelations. So said, for example, Steve Jobs, CEO of Apple, that taking LSD was a profound experience and one of the most important things in his life (Huffington Post

October 22, 201). The philosopher and postmodernist Michel Focault said that LSD was the greatest experience of his life and that it profoundly changed his life and work (Open Culture September 1975). Francis Cricks saw the DNA double-helix on LSD and received the Nobel prize for it (Strassman, *Inner Spaces*). Karl Mullis, who received the Nobel prize for his DNA amplification technology credited LSD for helping him develop it (Harrison A., LSD - The Geeks Wonder Drug, 2006). None of these four characters was in any way inherently hip or spiritual. It again drives home the point that LSD does not have by itself any particular characteristics. What these four people have in common is their extreme sense of purpose and concentration, and LSD may have provided them with a catalyst to enhance this tendency.

One thing that forms a common thread through LSD experiences is the unpredictability of the drug, a quality notably confirmed by Jerry Garcia, the lead guitar player of the Grateful Dead. I found this out myself when I was once on a forest walk with a few friends. I have to firstly mention that as a boy and teenager, I was very impulsive, violent and constantly got into fights. When I was 16, I so savaged an opponent in a fight that afterwards I realized that I had to stop fighting, as I could now extend serious harm. The particular incident I am describing here, was the last time in my life when I was involved in any form of violence, in this instance, ritualized violence. While I was walking along on LSD, I noticed one of my friends, an athletic 18-year-old, let's call him Steve, looking at me. We both suddenly stopped and stared into each other's eyes. I felt that same, strange glare in my eye, that I later had during the Royal Enfield Bullet motorcycle episode. Something came over me, and over him, too. Within a split second, we were at each other's throats and performed on the forest floor the most brutal wrestling match I have ever witnessed. The strange thing was that something else seemed to move both of us. There was a bizarre, choreographed quality to all our movements. This went on for quite some time with both of us covered in mud and our friends looking on silently. Eventually, we just separated and with no words spoken, we had figured out the fight was to be continued with sticks. We broke some suitable branches off the surrounding trees and again attacked each other with a vengeance. I always marvelled later that none of us got seriously hurt. While we both seemed to be intent on killing each other, miraculously we were completely matched and moved around each other in some weird war-dance choreography. Tired after a long fight, we eventually stood across from each other with sticks raised for the next attack, like two samurais. I noticed then that I had such huge gashes in my arms that blood was flowing down from them onto my stick. As if directed by one thought, we threw our sticks away, gave each other a hug and bloody, muddy, and with torn clothes, we continued our walk, and never, ever talked about the incident. Looking back it seemed like some weird archaic initiation, and it shows that on LSD anything can happen from one moment to the next.

Albert Hoffmann, the Swiss chemist who discovered LSD, suggested in *LSD: My Problem Child* that a responsible sacral use of the drug would be to ingest it only four times in one's life, at the culmination of each of the four major life-crises, i.e. puberty, adolesence, midlife crisis and death crisis. He suggested that a guide was necessary and that the guide should be a qualified psychologist/psychotherapist who at the same time doubled up as a shaman. Hoffmann was right that both these qualifications would be a much-needed resource. However, both of these modalities take in the vicinity of 10 years to qualify in, with the shaman qualification likely to take even longer. I am not aware of anybody in the world currently holding both of these qualifications, and the shamanic culture is rapidly dying out, with humanity losing its shamanic knowledge at an ever-accelerating pace.

The greatest danger for psychedelic users is complacency. Users pop a trip and if they are lucky, they see God. The vast majority, as Dr. Rick Strassman discovered, don't feel inspired to engage in formal spiritual practice to integrate the experience. My feeling is that because the experience is initially had so cheaply (you pay a handful of dollars for a psychedelic) that most people don't see the point to afterwards perform decades of spiritual practice to integrate their experience. They would rather pay another handful of dollars for the next trip, which again is not integrated. In some ways the ease with which the hallucinogen is obtained, compared to the effort of decades of *sadhana*, creates an obstacle. Think how many hours you have to work to pay for a trip (let's say half an hour give or take) and put that into perspective with the expense you incur to integrate the experience (probably thousands of hours of spiritual practice time, which could also be spent making money, taking drugs or having fun), then you see the discrepancy. This very fact is the reason most people can't be bothered to do the integration work. Most psychedelic-induced spiritual experiences remain unintegrated and, therefore, to a large extent, a wasted opportunity. This contrasts with one of my students who recently told me she had a single Ayahuasca-experience on which the solution to all her problems were revealed to her. She vowed to not take it again, until all of her solutions were integrated and embodied. A laudable attitude.

CHAPTER 6.

So, what did I get out of LSD, if anything? Let me first place a caveat: I do not recommend the use of psychedelics because the risk/reward ratio is much less favourable than the current, renewed enthusiasm suggests. There are safer alternatives such as yoga, which in the long term proves to be much more sustainable and easier to integrate. However people will always use psychedelics, narcotics and stimulants and the more high-quality information they have, the safer they are and the more high-quality decisions they can make. A case in point is the refusal of the Australian government to accept drug testing kits for music festivals. Young people die because they inadvertently buy botched street drugs, although considering how many people use them, these cases are rare. The government argues from a moral high horse that allowing drug testing kits would be supporting drug use. It's not supporting drug use, it's keeping young people alive. They deserve to know that what they are putting into their brains and this right is not waived by the fact that they are using a substance that the government has declared illegal.

THE FOUR PHASES OF SUCCESSFUL PSYCHEDELIC EXPERIENCES

Looking back, there were four phases to my encounter with LSD and they can be understood only in context. I developed and isolated them after some trial and error, but eventually, I followed this system more or less successfully. I call these phases, Phase 1 preparation, phase 2 purification, phase 3 revelation and phase 4 integration. Let's start with phase 1 preparation: initially, one needs to be really clear what one wants out of this experience and what one's intentions are. As with many other areas of life so also here, "if you don't know where you are going, you will end up somewhere else". As I have shown in this article on LSD, anything can happen. It's not wise to just pop a couple of pills with a few friends and see how it pans out. Some carelessly entertained notions that spontaneously come to the surface, could under the influence, become deeply imprinted in our subconscious, and we could spend years of our life trying to undo them. We need to ask ourselves, what do we need to learn and acquire, what skills should we possess to achieve our outcome? This is much in line with the approach a shaman would take. For example, when studying Carlos Castaneda, you will see that the greatest part of his training under the shaman Don Juan is not the actual intake of entheogens, but is devoted to acquiring the skills needed when under the influence. Make no mistake. This is not something to toy with. This is a sacred discipline.

In my case, I was undergoing extensive study of the sacred scriptures of various wisdom traditions. Some friends told me that psychedelics were some form of shortcut to divine revelation and that's what my firm expectation was. Perhaps with my expectations I had prepped and conditioned myself that my experiences would go in that direction. I knew which questions I wanted to ask when I got there. I had studied meditation and various limbs of yoga, but due to my youth felt I just needed booster. At the same time I had an understanding that psychological problems can hinder spiritual realization and since I could not afford a shrink, I had myself aquired a good working knowledge of Freudian and Jungian psychology. Reading one or two books is not enough here. One has to be sure that even under pressure one could analyse oneself, even during the onslaught of a panic attack. It is a certain maturity, or should we say distance to oneself and one's own issues, that is required. In this phase, one would also need to get assessed for any bipolar, psychotic or schizophrenic tendencies in one's own history and that of one's family lineage. If such disorders are present now, or existed in the past, psychedelics are a no-go. I have previously expressed doubt that all of those conditions can be sufficiently screened, but I have read papers from psychologists who claim it is possible. It is beyond my understanding and expertise.

Phase 2 purification: during this phase the actual entheogenic *sadhana* (spiritual discipline) would start. Knowing we have to eliminate everything that could send us into a tailspin, a setting is created that completely protects us from any unexpected negative influences (is that actually possible?). The psychiatrist and medical doctors who have undertaken psychedelic research, introduced their test subject to very low doses. During those initial low doses, I practised a simple method of becoming aware of sensations coming up from my subconscious, acknowledging them and then consciously letting them go on the exhalation. Sometimes these sensations and perceptions were lingering, or I would become aware that they are based on a deeper program of self-rejection, built on some particular early-childhood trauma that now caused self-hatred, etc. Gradually, as I went deeper into the states, I excavated deeper layers of my subconscious and ancestral and collective programming came into the foreground. The process shifted naturally from Freudian to Jungian analysis. I will not go into any details here. I don't want to talk excessively about myself and also don't want to bore the reader with my own story, nor that of my ancestors. Important to understand is this path is not about taking a substance, which will do the work for you. There is lots of work to be done, hard work. The mystery is covered and buried under layers or conditioning and programming. These need to be gradually excavated and removed. Some of that is always tedious, confronting and uncomfortable.

Phase 3 revelation: As the work in the previous phases set the direction and removed the obstacles, I now went to medium doses and used the same associative meditation technique and letting go with the breath method as above. Please note, that I simply describe here what I did. I don't think that any of that is suitable for emulation as, in hindsight, I seemed to possess an unusual resilience regarding psychedelics. I have seen people go psychotic and schizophrenic from much less than 500mg. Even Albert Hofmann, who discovered LSD, thought he would either die or go insane simply from ingesting 250mg. It is also important to notice that none of the methods described in my *Pranayama* and *Yoga Meditation* books can be used in conjunct with psychedelics. The neuroscience researcher Dr. Robin Carhart-Harris (Head of Psychedelic Research Centre at Imperial College London) describes taking psychedelics as an increase of entropy (disorder) in the brain. That means that psychedelics enable you to let go of old, encrusted pathways in your mind and enable you to have a fresh look at things. The practices I have described in the above books are creating order (neg-entropy). While both can be done sequentially (as I have done during different decades), if done simultaneously, they present conflicting forces that will destabilize the psyche. While we are talking about entropy, Michael Pollan, who used psychedelics when he was in his 60s, in *How to Change your Mind* muses that increasing entropy in one's brain might be an interesting thing to pursue when old, but whether a young brain needs more entropy, is questionable. I think that's a reasonable train of thought. However, I want to add that mere age does not protect you from harm incurred through psychedelics.

With eyes closed and with awareness directed inwards, I could now dive inwards through consecutive layers of my being. There were outer layers such as body, mind and ego, which I purified (from past trauma and conditioning) through self-analysis and letting go. Once this had occurred, I found beneath them two layers of experience, which I call cosmic intelligence and infinite consciousness. I will describe the cosmic intelligence experience here (because it is associated with the third-eye chakra) and the infinite consciousness experience in Chapter 7 (because of its relation to the crown chakra). When reaching the cosmic-intelligence-level I saw that I was not an isolated being, I was not a six-foot-tall biomechanoid trying to survive in a physical world, but I was a minute spec of awareness within a cosmic network of appearances all created, powered and eventually reabsorbed by one common cosmic intelligence that expressed itself simultaneiously through an infinity of beings and all matter. Things on this level were not what they seemed to be. Especially matter, stones, air, water, trees, were all luminous, crystallized thought. Thought that was, however, not thought by me. Not even my body and my mind were powered by me. There was one cosmic intelligence with infinite creative potential creating the world by thinking it into existence. There was nothing not thought into existence by this cosmic intelligence. This intelligence was what the scriptures called God, but also that most concepts of God were flawed because they were anthropomorphic, i.e. having human characteristics.

For us humans, it is very difficult to understand God; maybe we never will. God was not a giant, irate, bearded, white male, sitting in the sky alternatingly throwing lightning, locust, floods or plagues from the sky. God was a cosmic intelligence so vast, that it required the sum total of all universes as its hardware and harddrive. I'm not wishing to say that God is a machine, insentient, or a computer program, but the IT metaphor seems helpful to some extent. I could only grasp the significance of an infinite and infinitely intelligent object with metaphor. This object was simultaneously the subject because I was not separate from it, but it was also the awareness in me. It had also thought my body and mind into existence and everybody else's. This object was simultaneously beyond time and space, but also time and space were within it. It had given birth to time and space.

There was nothing in me or outside of me that was not part of this object (God or cosmic intelligence), but I was given the opportunity to think "I", to identify myself with something and disidentify with something else. I could see this cosmic intelligence had an intricate interest in me and all other beings. I could see it was computing and permutating itself through me and all other beings, that it was individuating through me. I also noticed this object, the cosmic intelligence, wanted me to do something, it wanted to do something through me. It wanted me to grow, evolve, mature and develop, so it could express and compute itself to greater and greater extents through and as me. I realized this object wanted to co-create through me and all of my brother- and sister-creatures, which included all life forms. I also saw this intelligence wanted me to notice that wherever I was, whatever I did, I was in that object. I realized the truth of the Bible's statment, "in Him we live, move and have our being". I saw there was nothing but it and that past, present and future were all contained in that cosmic intelligence.

Phase 4 integration: this is the crucial phase without which all the other phases are wasted. How do I understand what happened and to what extent does my vehicle, my surface-self, partake of my experience? To what extent does my surface-self and my behaviour transform? To what extent do I become a changed person after a revelation? I'm assumng that we all agree that if I consider I have had some form of divine revelation, my behavior must change. My ability to treat others with respect must increase, a certain inner nobility must shine through, otherwise, all that I'm saying is just flowery talk, I'm just blowing hot air. It is exactly this what the Hatha Yoga Pradipika means when in IV.113 it says, "as long as the prana is not conducted into the central energy channel, all this talk of self-realization is just the jabber of madmen".

Self-realization or divine revelation is not something that we watch in a movie and then go home and nothing changes. It is valid only then when it has transformed our relation to *dharma*. *Dharma* is a complex term in Indian philosophy, but simplified, it means right action, to do the right thing. A revelation is valid only to that degree to which we show that our sense of self has increased, to the extent that service to others becomes increasingly important, and now comes naturally to us. *Others* here means the people around us, the family of humanity, the greater community of all life, the entire nature around us and cosmic intelligence. We must ask ourselves, to what extent are we not just driven by our own satisfaction, but by placing ourselves into the service of this cosmic intelligence that permeates and processes everything around us?

Integration took place through a daily sadhana of chanting and contemplating texts like the Yoga Sutra, the Bhagavad Gita, the Upanishads, etc., and a systematic practice of postures, pranayama, chakra/Kundalini meditation, kriyas and later samadhis. I have to admit that when I started, I did not know this was integration work. After more or less 3 years of intense psychedelic experiences, I simply stop using the substances because I was annoyed that I could still fall out of the experience, and feel and behave as if nothing had ever happened. However, after many years and decades of intense practice of all yogic limbs, I could suddenly recall more psychedelic experiences, and finally understood their significance. Suprisingly, often only then could I remember them and integrate them in detail. Integration, again, must be measured by our ability to more place our daily life into the service of revelation and understanding of that cosmic intelligence that expresses itself through the entire material cosmos and all beings.

How long did integration take? In the first decade after the psychedelic experiences not much integration happened at all. This was due to my being busy with my latest distraction, gurus. Because of my infatuation with various cult leaders (I was still just living through my 20s) I practised a ragtag, hodgepodge, mumbo-jumbo-like cocktail of contemporary meditation techniques that did little. It was only once serious scriptural study set in, and with it a systematic practice of classical yogic methods, that integration seriously took off in the second and third decade after discontinuing entheogens. I am now nearing the end of the 4th decade of integration and the process is still going on.

The big question I am asking myself, would all of my realizations have taken place, had I never taken psychedelics and instead only done my yogic techniques. I do believe so! And if so, then there wouldn't be such a strong argument pro psychedelics because yoga is so much safer. However, I know

I cannot prove this point because I cannot go back and run a simulation of my life without psychedelics. It is a feasible that the psychedelics provided fuel for my spiritual *sadhana* and that without them, I would have been more complacent in my subsequent practice. I shall never know.

The next big question is asked from the opposite vantage point and that is whether psychedelics actually did do the opposite, meaning, did they possibly slow me down? I cannot be sure, but there is a lot of evidence in my life for that. After psychedelics, I basically spent 10 years in spiritual confusion. I wouldn't say crisis, but it would be fair to say I was spinning across the planetary surface like a headless chicken in search of a spiritual saviour. This was a common pattern in the 1960s and 70s psychedelic generation and I see it replicated today in many young students who come to me, especially in those who have consumed the DMT-variants of psychedelics. The DMT-flash is too fast and too powerful to be meaningfully integrated. There seems to be an enormous spiritual thirst but a lack of resolve and commitment to see the challenge through by means of *sadhana*. I do think that psychedelics also slowed me down spiritually because they confused me and scattered my intention and resolve.

I've also noted another problem with psychedelic-inspired mystics. Mysticism is said to induce humility because you realize that you are only a minute emanation of an intelligence of cosmic proportions. There is nothing better to put you into your place than a true divine revelation. If things go right, you come out with a feeling of not taking yourself that seriously anymore, but that the only thing that makes you worthy of living is service extended to others in pursuing making them evolve and grow. However, in a study mentioned (M. Lerner and M. Lyvers), psychedelic mystics scored lower on a humility scale than non-psychedelic mystics. It was even found that psychedelic experiences could actually inflate egos leading to grandiose beliefs about one's superiority to others. My gut feeling is that it boils down to our only paying little for a psychedelic agent. The experience is cheap to come by (at least if measured by its monetary expenditure), meaning when a revelation occurs, our ego may decide that the revelation must be due to the greatness of our personage (rather than the our spiritual practice) and that therefore we are entitled to it. I have to admit that egomania resulting from (failed) mystical experiences is a complex problem, that can occur even in non-psychedelic mystics. This so-called guru-syndrome requires an in-depth analysis of its own, which is beyond the scope of this study.

Rather than on the serious note of the previous paragraphs, I want to finish this chapter on a light note. This tale, in which I literally make an ass of myself, is from one of my last LSD-experiences, which took place in Goa, India. At the time I enjoyed watching sunsets from the Chapora Fort, an abandoned, haunted, former Portuguese fortification overlooking the Indian Ocean and the Chapora river. On this day I had done so aided by LSD. Not long after I sat down on my favourite spot, I noticed a stinging pain in my right buttock. Being on LSD, I ascribed it to my unsteady mind and breathed through it. The pain got worse, but with help of the psychedelic I sequestrated it away in my mind, and soon enjoyed the clear, starry night to which the sunset gave way. I remember thinking several times during that night, "Why is that pain still there and why the hell is it so strong?", but the psychedelic kept me engaged and distracted. It was only, when after sunrise, I finally rose from my seat, that

CHAPTER 6.

I discovered a small squashed scorpion exactly where my right buttock was positioned. The Buddha once said that our mind jumps from branch to branch like a monkey that first drank a bottle of liquor and then got stung by a scorpion. Because of my experience, this saying took on a new meaning.

THE CASE OF KETAMINE

To be complete in my exposition I also want to quickly discuss the case of ketamine (ketamine-hexachloride), sometimes called Vitamin K, or just K. Ketamine is actually an anaesthetic with strange, some say kinky, side effects. Ketamine was widely used as a horse tranquilizer and is now finding application against depression in humans, especially in the 50% of patients in whom conventional anti-depressants, such as selective serotonin-reuptake-inhibitors SSRI's), don't work. Ketamine has the disadvantage that it is addictive. At some point, there has been a huge ketamine epidemic in the UK. As a mind-altering agent ketamine was popularized by the neurologist, delphinologist and inventor of the isolation tank, Dr John C. Lilly. Lilly wrote the 1960s LSD classic *The Centre of the Cyclone* and he believed that ketamine could take you further than LSD. My personal impression was that ketamine didn't do Lilly much good.

Ketamine is known for its out-of-body experiences and feeling of floating in space. I remember a high-profile case of a veterinarian, who had injected several young people with ketamine and while they were anesthetized and had out-of-body experiences, he performed sexual acts on them. Such cases were possible because you literally leave your body on K. I took ketamine twice and each time, the experience was the same, and so blatantly suggestive that it's almost embarrassing to narrate it. In my experiences with my astral body, I entered an elevator, which took me above the clouds to a stratospheric world. When exiting the elevator, I was greeted by an angelic person, who identified themselves as my heavenly guide. They (gender could not be ascertained) lead me across a wide plane, which rested upon clouds, and which was replete with legions of angels arranged in what appeared to be battle formations of the Roman legion (the study of ancient warfare technology was one of my pastimes when young). They all wore the typical long white robes, had two white wings on their backs and played bombastic, glorifying music on harps and Roman trumpets. There would have probably been a few 100.000 of these angels and they were ordered around a massive central throne, made from clouds, on top of which a giant pyramid of light, at least two kilometres in diameter, hovered. The pyramid in the middle was adorned with a single, giant, eye and my heavenly guide alerted me to the obvious, i.e. the eye in the pyramid was YHVH. In front of YHVH was some form of gargantuan reception desk, operated by a large number of angels. I was made to stand in a cue of people and wait. Eventually, I came to the front and was given an envelope with instructions for my earthly life. After that, I was rather unceremoniously ushered back to the elevator and driven back down. The experience repeated itself almost verbatim during my second ketamine episode, only this time the envelope said "update". On each occasion the letter contained in the envelope described something rather insignificant, halfway between the obvious and the banal.

    I have to admit to being unable to fully appreciate these experiences. Had I not been such a self-critical, analytically minded cynic, I could have probably started some fundamentalist doomsday-cult, with me as the prophet at the centre. But to me, it was all put on a bit too thick, almost corny, clichéd, and certainly stereotyped. I remember being up there and thinking, "Wow, dude, this is really like a celestial 1937 Nuremberg Nazi rally for the good guys". It seemed to be a return to pre-critical childhood phantasies about religion, the sort I entertained as a four-year-old. But my readers may interpret these experiences differently, or on a deeper level, and for this purpose I have included them here.

Chapter 7.
THE CROWN CHAKRA AND MEGA-DOSES OF LSD

THE CROWN CHAKRA

This chapter discusses the seventh *chakra*, called the *Sahasrara* (thousand-petalled lotus), which is supra-cranial and, therefore, in English, aptly called the crown chakra. At this point, any identification with being human or even being limited in space and time, ceases. There is an erroneous understanding and over-emphasizing of this chakra in some eastern philosophies and religions, which seem bent on leaving everything behind and reducing all experience to this chakra alone. This has to some extent marred the evolution of religion and society, and to understand this we have to deeply understand all implications of this complex chakra.

The function of the crown chakra is absorptive, if you do place your life force in the crown chakra for longer terms (such as several days), your individuality is likely to be permanently reabsorbed into the formless, infinite transcendental aspect of the Divine. As a drop falling into the ocean becomes one with it, so the yogi will dissolve into the Divine by becoming absorbed into it. The form of yoga that deals with this is called Jnana Yoga. In Jnana Yoga, it is not devotion to the Divine with form (*saguna*

Brahman) that is sought, but absorption into the formless absolute (*nirguna* Brahman), what physicists call the unified field. This absorption is referred to by Buddhists as *nirvana*. There is a discussion among yogis whether this absorption should take place either at all, or at the very end of one's life/lives, when all sacred duties towards the Divine and humanity are fulfilled. This will be discussed at the end of the chapter.

Meditating on the crown chakra is not appropriate until activation of all other chakras is achieved, as it otherwise could backfire. So was the nowadays popular genre of Kundalini-accidents introduced to the general public by Gopi Krishna's 1971 book *Kundalini – Evolutionary Energy in Man*. Without undertaking any other yogic preparation, the Indian civil servant Gopi Krishna sustained concentration on the crown chakra daily for 1 – 2 hours over 17 years until a sudden Kundalini-surge took place. For the next 12 years, this put him into a state between madness and death before his condition stabilized and morphed into spiritual liberation. Yogic practitioners need not be concerned that any of this will happen if they practice systematically and stay away from undue extremes. A yogi following due course would first practice asana, kriyas, pranayama, yogic chakra-Kundalini meditation and samadhis. There is no virtue in activating the crown chakra unless the heart-, throat-, and third-eye chakras are all activated. The effects of rushing ahead and opening the crown chakra out of context, would be overwhelmingly negative. Besides performing extreme one-sided practices akin to that performed by Gopi Krishna, ingesting mega-doses of psychedelics, particularly LSD, are the other major avenue to open this chakra out of context.

An important aspect of the crown chakra is that it is beyond the three *gunas*. The *gunas* are the three elementary particles of

Indian philosophy called *tamas* (mass particle), *rajas* (energy particle) and *sattva* (intelligence particle). The term *gunas* is sometimes translated as "qualities", but this leaves the depth of the Sanskrit term extremely truncated. But if we accept this translation here for a moment, then the term beyond-the-three-gunas means beyond quality or quality-less. It is called quality-less because the crown chakra can reveal only one thing and that is pure consciousness (strictly speaking, it's not really a thing, but "entity" or "category" sounds awkward). The term consciousness in yoga is not defined as what we are conscious of, but as the entity itself that is conscious. That means that awareness is the function of consciousness and consciousness is the seat of awareness.

Consciousness is that within you that never changes. Even as you get old, the pure consciousness within you does not age because it has no quality. Time and space occur within consciousness, rather than consciousness within time and space. This means that consciousness is eternal and infinite. The number one huge benefit (the only benefit) of realizing yourself as consciousness, is that after this realization, all fear of death is gone. This is because you now know yourself to be infinite and eternal. If you spend too much time focussing on the crown chakra, you become somewhat too otherworldly, meaning your interest in your physical life is lessened. This would be a real shame because the material world in which you live, including your mortal shell, is God's crystallized body. What you do here and how you live your life matters to God. After you have tasted the oceanic ecstasy of infinite consciousness, however, worldly life then all seems a bit of a bother. It is nevertheless important to fulfil one's own duty (*svadharma*) first, before dissolving into infinite consciousness. The purpose of our life is to firstly fulfil our duty and only then attain liberation. That's why the sage Yajnavalkya says, "Yoga can only succeed conjointly with fulfilling one's duty towards society".

Because it is supra-cranial, the crown chakra can usually only be accessed outside of the breathing cycle, sometimes called the breathless state (*kevala kumbhaka*). The breathless state is a state in which there is no agitation of the life force whatsoever. There is disagreement amongst yogis whether this means actual breath retention or whether extreme long, slow and barely noticeable breathing also counts. The yogic science of pranayama deals with bringing about the breathless state and those interested should realize that it is similar to learning a new language or learning to play an instrument. It will not happen on a weekend or even in a year.

The crown chakra can be understood as the summit of a mighty mountain. To reach this summit, you have to decide on an angle of approach – whether you approach over the north or south face, etc. All the paths leading to the top represent particular schools of thought, philosophies, sciences, religions or schools of yoga. While you are on your way up you only have a very limited view of the mountain. You see only one side. Because the other approaches are out of your sight, it might appear to you as if your path, the path of the school you follow, is the only feasible one.

Once you are up on the mountain, which Abraham Maslow called the peak experience, the scenery changes. While initially you are so overwhelmed by the lofty heights that you look into infinity, after a while, you become accustomed to it and become curious about what is happening on the other slopes previously hidden to your view. You walk around the edge and look down, only to find to your great surprise other paths are leading up;

people are coming up along all the slopes. Among those on top of the mountain, there is great peace and no squabbling. Although they stem from many cultures, nobody claims that theirs is the only way up. Up here, all are united in the peak experience, which is beyond mind and words. Whatever can be expressed in words is only of relative, limited value, even of dubious worth. It can never be the complete and exclusive truth. Up here on the summit of the crown chakra, all our words and views reveal themselves as relative. What really matters up here is not what you believe and hold true, it is the visceral knowledge of the divine origin of all beings and therefore their shared sacredness. It is the realization that the God transcendent (the infinite consciousness) expresses itself through all beings and all beings are therefore sacred.

A similar message is encrypted in the invocation to the Nagaraj, the one-thousand-headed serpent of infinity, which goes like this:

> OM, I bow to the king of the serpents,
> who embodies infinity, who carries the universe
> and simultaneously blazes forth all knowledge
> with one thousand hooded, bejewelled heads.

The thousand-headed king of the serpents is also called Ananta, meaning infinity. This is reflected in the fact that sometimes he is depicted as a snake biting into its own tail thus forming a circle. Another of his names not mentioned in this chant is Adishesha, which means residue. Adishesha is the combined residue of all universes that became unmanifest.

Through his thousand bejewelled heads, the Nagaraj propounds a thousand versions, views or interpretations of the one underlying truth. These views or interpretations of the truth include all religions, all schools of philosophy, all sciences, all branches of knowledge, all schools of yoga, all cultures and all languages. The thousand heads are a concession to the fact that as soon as you use words, as soon as you attempt to filter the one underlying truth through a linguistic code, your words must be an interpretation of that truth and not the truth itself. The truth itself can only be conveyed through the luminous silence of the formless absolute, the infinite consciousness. This is the deeper meaning of Jacques Derrida's saying, "there is no meaning outside of the context". Derrida, a philosopher of postmodernism and poststructuralism, held that words can be understood only against the background of the person that used them, that is the enculturation, personal and ancestral history, that formed the meaning they allocate to words. The sum total of this field of knowledge is called semiotics. Yoga holds that within the semiotic field, i.e. as soon as mind and language are used, knowledge is relative and subject to interpretation. But according to yoga, reality can be perceived directly by suspending the mind (and ego) in the breathless state, the revelation of the oceanic ecstasy of infinite consciousness. Here there is total freedom, which can never be had in the realm of manifestation and meaning.

The peculiar anatomy of the thousand-headed serpent includes the fact that all heads are attached to a single tail. The tail is silent. It does not have a mouth to express itself, as no single mouth, no view of the truth, could claim to be its sole representation. The tail represents the formless Absolute, the *nirguna* Brahman, the infinite consciousness, the unified field, the God transcendent. The tail is the silent, inexpressible origin and base of the many heads. The important law expressed in this metaphor is there are many ways the same truth can be expressed, but none is the truth. The one tail has many heads attached to it. But it is impossible to reduce the tail to a single head. This means that no verbal truth, however elegant and eloquent it may be, has a monopoly on the tail. While all religions, philosophies, schools of thought and sciences may project to you they have the exclusive access to the tail of Brahman, they all only share joint access to the same truth without representing it.

The tail of the thousand-headed serpent is a metaphor for the experience obtained when *prana* is placed into the crown chakra. While *prana* is suspended in the crown chakra, it is impossible to describe one's vision in words because the mind and ego are suspended. There is, therefore, no true crown chakra religion, science, philosophy or teaching. When mystics come down from these heights, they grapple for words to describe what they have seen to convey it to others. In doing so, they inevitably use conditioning, mind, linguistic codes and their past, to cast into words what is unsayable, what is eternally beyond conditioning, mind and words. Thus, sages and mystics of all ages have had to come down to the heart-, throat-, or third-eye chakras to describe an experience that, while it is not contained in these chakras, cannot be taught either if one remains in crown chakra because then there is only silence. Whenever the Buddha insisted on answering through silence, he wished to remain in his crown chakra experience. However, the entire Buddhist cannon is an effort of the intellect (third-eye chakra) to interpret and express teachings of the crown chakra.

There is no mantra to activate the crown chakra as it is beyond the reach of sound. Quantum physicists are trying to define the state before the Big Bang that brought forth the known universe. Time is measured by change, and since no change occurred before the Big Bang, some say that this state is beyond time or is timeless. Space can only be measured as a distance between two points, but since no points existed prior to the Big Bang, this state is also beyond space. However, in the next moment, the Big Bang brought forth time, space and the known universe. Therefore, the state before the Big Bang is described as having infinite potential. Since time did not exist before the Big Bang, this seed state of the universe, called deep reality/unified field or infinite consciousness, is eternal. That means it does not only exist right now, but permanently and all the time in a timeless and eternal state, outside of our known world. That's why it's called transcendental, beyond. William Blake said, "There are things that are known and there are things that are unknown. In between there are doors." While the chakras all represent such doors, the primordial door to the Great Unknown is the crown chakra.

The main problem associated with the crown chakra is that people believe they have to go there straight away, without attending to the chakras below it. However, if we could collectively open only even just the heart chakra, we could overcome conflict, ambition, competition, greed, fear, crime, violence and war. Further, if enough of us were to open the throat chakra, we could overcome hunger, disease, global warming, pollution and destruction of the environment. If many of us opened our third-eye chakras, we would realize the Divine with form, first within and then outside of us. The most important part of that is to recognize the Divine in every other being that we encounter. If we did that, humanity could return to life in harmony with all around us. Somewhere in each of us is the knowledge that one has a role to play in this.

CHAPTER 7.

Decades ago, when I was still with my tongue hanging out, chasing after the nirvana (nirvana means "extinguishing of the flame" or colloquially said "being snuffed out", both to some extent apt representations of the crown chakra purpose), a good friend told me, "Why are you so keen to get into that silly nirvana. It's completely boring there. There are only elderly Asian males hovering in lotus posture and nobody says or does anything". Although a seemingly funny and silly comment, today, I think it is much to the point. Why not become first truly alive, why not first love all beings and be of service to them, why not fall in love with life, nature, the Divine and understand and contribute to Its incredible work of art, the universe and all beings in it, with the ability to become conscious of the ecstasy, freedom, intelligence, harmony, beauty and love of the Divine? If we do that first, nirvana will eventually come on its own accord, in due time and not prematurely. When the chakras are activated in order, we realize that each being has a divine purpose and that the Divine is thrilled to co-create through each of us. The term *thrilled* is a verbatim quote from the Bhagavata Purana, where Krishna says, "There is no greater thrill to me than seeing the devotee realize me and turn towards me. I then cannot but rush to that place and embrace the devotee". We shouldn't understand that quote in an anthropomorphic way and therefore imagine a blue-skinned god, complete with yellow silk, peacock feather and flute, popping out of thin air in front of us. The quote is to be understood metaphorically, as the thrill of cosmic intelligence realizing that one of its creatures and children has now become conscious of It and is ready to actively channel It and thus co-create.

THE CROWN CHAKRA DRUG: MEGA-DOSES OF LSD

There is a distinction to the experiences available on different doses of LSD. One hundred micrograms of LSD give a robust person a significant experience, but they can push a sensitive person with pre-existing conditions over the edge into serious psychological destabilization. At around 400-600 micrograms, even a robust person will have intense experiences, but this dosage can have significant negative results if unintegrated and unacknowledged subconscious content surfaces and is not properly dealt with. In this chapter, I am talking about doses from 1000 micrograms upwards, which I attempted after several 100 microgram experiences and about 30 midrange experiences of 400-600 micrograms. A 1000 microgram dose does sound extreme, and for most people, it will be. However, such doses and higher ones have been used in psychotherapy on patients with oppressive-compulsive disorder (OCD). OCD patients are able to resist even 500 microgram doses. Resisting here means that even hours after the dose has been applied, the patient does not appear to display any symptoms whatsoever. In *LSD Pathways to the Numinous*, the psychiatrist Stanislav Grof describes the case of a 22-year-old OCD-patient who, even after given 1500 micrograms, resists the experience and suppress it completely. While I do not recommend anybody to take psychedelics, to take megadoses is downright playing with fire and courting calamity. Looking back, it seems like the spiritual equivalent of Russian roulette. In Russian roulette, which prominently featured in the Vietnam war movie *Deer Hunter*, one places a single round of ammunition in one of the six chambers of a revolver and leaves the others empty. One then spins the cylinder and, holding the pointy end against one's temple, pulls the trigger, hoping that one doesn't hit the loaded chamber. It seems an apt metaphorical representation of mega-dose psychedelic experiments. You never really know whether you come out the other end in one piece, and as we will see later, there are safer methods available, which may take a bit longer but will still get you there.

In my case, certainly at 1000 micrograms, initially, all hell broke loose. What I found fascinating about LSD was the length of the experience, which gets longer as the dosage is increased. It allowed me to work out my resistances, and once I let go of them, to then access deeper levels of the psychedelic experience. This is juxtaposed to a DMT experience that unfolds so fast and is over so quickly, that skill plays a subordinate role. I remember LSD experiences where it took me several hours to figure out the cause of a subconscious tension that prevented the potential of the experience to unfold. On the downside, if one cannot figure out why one is stuck in a negative mental vortex or maelstrom, the length of an LSD experience can appear soul-crushing.

I stayed at the 1000 microgram level for a while and eventually significantly increased the dose. Looking back, I have nothing to say in my defence, apart from that I was 19 years old and really curious, crazed really. Some of the things I saw were extremely frightening, but some others so revealing that I kept going. I then took a single dose for which I again increased the dosage several times over. I now think that 40 years ago, I took this dose to stay in those realms, which obviously did not work. Please note, although no lethal dose of LSD has ever been established, some scientists opine that one could die from as little as 12,000 micrograms, although no such cases have ever been reported. I also may have been lucky because I was desensitized after regular use. After taking LSD, it takes up to

14 days to again build up one's full sensitivity and during the peak of my activity, I took it twice a week.

After this final trip, I largely retired from psychedelics (just as well). I felt I had seen it all and the substances did not lead to a permanent realization. During this final experience, I took around 72 hours to reconstruct who I was, I simply couldn't remember, while under the influence. This includes being unable to remember my name, my personality, character traits, anything related to the surface-self. After the experience, I gradually reconstructed my personality from reading my friend's and family's response to my presence. I closely observed them and gathered from their expectations who I was supposed to be or had been. In the early days after that final experiment, it seemed that I had deleted a good part of my psychological hard drive, but it seemed to all come back, eventually (at least so I think).

I would think that the likelihood to go psychotic from such extreme doses is very high, but I never came close to that. A part of that resilience was the realization that LSD is a profoundly psychological drug. The psychiatrist Stanislav Grof, for whom I have great respect, said that what the microscope is to biology and the telescope is to astronomy, LSD is to psychology and psychiatry. I always reminded myself that whatever took place on LSD is only my psyche's interpretation of reality. With that, I do not mean to say there is no reality independent from my psyche. What I mean to say is that the version of reality I see is created by my psyche. For example, I once looked up at the night sky and watched the milky way. The spiral galaxy soon enough turned into a giant kraken that reached into my direction and threatened to not only devour me but the entire planet on which I sat. After watching the approaching kraken, and my impending ingestion by it for a while with interest, I realized that it was a projection of my basic belief I was living in a hostile or at least indifferent cosmos, in which I am subject to incredibly powerful forces that do whatever they want. With that realization, the kraken dissolved and the spiral galaxy again appeared in its place. The kraken was really just a projection of my negative psychological beliefs onto reality, and the resulting fear and tension.

Before I relate some of my experiences on mega- and extreme doses, I want to caution anybody to imitate what I did. The main reason I sustained little harm was that at the best of times I find it rather difficult to identify with emotions. When they do come, they come delayed and distant as if I'm walking through a zoo and looking at strange beasts behind bars. I'm seldomly in the grip of, let's say, intense fear, pain, shame, humiliation or anger but watch them from far away, looking at them rather interested. This can be rather frustrating for those interacting with me, not the least my poor wife, but in extreme situations like this, emotional distance to oneself is an important asset. During an adverse psychedelic experience, this personality trait gave me extra time to analyse and assess why an experience would have gone pear-shaped.

After I had ingested the final megadose, I sat in a meditation posture and awaited the onset. When it came, it felt like a mixture of somebody dropping a large building on my head, while an extremely powerful explosive device inside of my head was ignited. Within a split second I was gone. The only thing I remember was that for a long time I was looking into this explosion taking place inside of me, an extremely bright light that filled out everything, and there was nothing else. I think I was in that state for a really long time, but I never found out exactly how long. Initially I didn't even realize there was something like time. There was just this incredibly bright light and nothing else.

Eventually, there occurred this feeling I was watching this intensely bright light. When that phase commenced, the idea of an I, of a perceiving entity, was not yet attached to any memory of my previously existing personality. What I perceived as "I" was only pure awareness of the bright light. At some point, then I concluded that this light was awareness too, but there were the first signs of a split, that is, I could separate my own consciousness from the bright light, which was cosmic consciousness. I also realized this immensely bright light of cosmic consciousness was at the centre of this immense Big Bang-like explosion that had started everything. No memories of a life before that Big Bang had returned yet.

At some point, I sensed that a deep relationship of love connected the observing individual consciousness to the cosmic consciousness in the centre. Then gradually started the realization I was a being separate from this transcendental object in the centre, and that I had some form of mission, a job to do. Visions appeared, and the cosmic consciousness was surrounded by a layer of intelligence, that enabled itself to embody as everything.

Up to this point, everything I had seen was incredibly beautiful and clear. But now I moved away more and more from the centre and the light and as I did, I became aware of the fact that I had a long and chequered history as an embodied being. I saw that I comprised elements, such as minerals, compounds and molecules. Eventually, they combined to form life, and with that, for the first time, I became distinctly aware of space and time. I saw myself travelling through a long ancestry of single-cell organisms and eventually eukaryotes (multi-cellular organisms). At some point, I saw myself lying as a primitive vertebrate first under water, then in the mud. These transformations kept going until I saw myself evolving through various life-forms. Eventually, I became mammalian. I had experiences of giving birth and the experience of great pain at seeing my children die or being eaten. I was given birth to, gave birth, was being eaten and ate others, countless times. Eventually, I became human. I saw myself travelling through prehistory and history and being a participant in pretty much every culture and civilization that ever took place. I was the sum total of all these experiences. Not just a body here and now, but I was all bodies, all lifeforms, all experiences that ever took place.

Eventually, I arrived in what before the explosion, I regarded as the present moment. I became aware of my body but didn't know what to do with it. I tried to understand what it was good for and looked at it more closely. It had a surface, its skin, and wanting to discover what was beneath it, with my awareness I did dive into its depth. Here I found peculiar organic molecules. Wanting to see what held them together, I entered a molecule and found atoms within it. My awareness drew close to an atomic nucleus and upon entering I could see the elementary particles within. My curiosity was not yet stilled, and upon penetrating an elementary particle, I saw photons and eventually quarks. When I did enter a quark, I found inside of the quark an infinite space that contained an entire universe. At this point, my awareness had enlarged to the point that this entire universe was contained in it. It was a universe that contained billions of galaxies and black holes.

I was happy and content with my sense of self expanded so that an entire universe was inside of my consciousness. At this point, I noticed a thin silvery thread that I was dragging behind me. I looked along this thread and saw it traversing the depths of the universe. Finally, I understood that it would lead me back to a human body, that in a far-away world and in a long-ago life, I had considered mine. I decided this body was not necessary anymore, like a chrysalis I had hatched from, and my true nature, an infinite being, had now become apparent. I decided to tear the thread and not return into my body again.

I was just about to tear it when a strange memory occurred. I realized this body had a mother. I saw that my mother would find my dead body and the autopsy would reveal "died from a drug overdose, possible suicide". I saw my mother going through pain, doubt, self-questioning, stigma and all that comes with such a diagnosis. I remembered the pain I experienced when those I had given birth to, died before me. I could not do it.

My problem now was that I had been outside of my body for such a long time I had expanded to the size of a universe. I travelled through this universe towards my physical body, gradually reducing my size, but even when I saw Earth, I was still the size of the solar system. I saw my body and as if using a sky-wide funnel, I had to squash and compress myself into my body by force. I lived with compression symptoms for about a year. During that time, I often asked myself, "Why in a body?"

When I was finally becoming embodied again, my body was still sitting in the forest in a seating position where I had left it behind what seemed several days earlier. I'm assuming my body sat there for about 48 – 72 hours. When I stood up from the ground, I moved my cold, numb and stiff limbs so clumsily and unconsciously that I tore the quadriceps muscle of my right thigh lengthwise. I felt a strong surge of pain and was limping for the next few weeks. I can still point to the source of that pain today, four decades later.

I went through a protracted period of having to guess my personality, as I had forgotten most. People looked at me questioningly, if I acted out in a strange way. I didn't want to attract any attention, so using my old personality was a good cloak. The whole experience took place in the forest, which was where most of my psychedelic experiences happened. I was very much used to sitting at night in the forest and simply blending in. When moving around, I had developed a sixth sense like an animal that could move around very lightly. On several occasions, I would come very close to deer or boar, which did not seem too bothered by my presence.

The situation was right the opposite when going back to town and to my room. I remember wanting to sit down on a chair, but upon seeing the grid-like, molecular structure of the chair and the molecules of my body, the atomic nuclei of my body and those of the chair were too far apart. When trying to sit down on it, I was apprehensive of sliding through the atomic gaps in the chair and falling into oblivion. I took quite a while to look at the atoms of the floor under my feet and trusting that my feet were not sinking in, although again the spaces between the atoms were too far apart to actually touch. Eventually, I accepted that the inability of the surfaces to penetrate each other was not due to solidity or lack thereof, but due to a magnetic field at the surface. I realized that I had to relearn a lot of premises I used to take for granted, but which had dissolved under the analytical gaze of the psychedelic agent.

The avid reader may have noticed that the first part of my experience largely tallies with the *Tibetan Book of the Dead*, which I had been studying for years. One hypothesis would be that reading the *Book of the Dead* guided my experiences into this direction, and there may be some truth in that. Another explanation would be that the teachings of the *Book of the Dead* are simply true, and that's what I think. The *Book of the Dead* is attributed to the siddha Padmasambhava, who the Tibetans call Guru Rinpoche. If half of what is told about him is true, he was one of the most evolved yogis ever to grace this planet. Padmasambhava taught that the *Book of the Dead* is an authentic map of the phases between death and rebirth. LSD, in high enough doses, lets you simulate this process and along with the *Book of the Dead*, we have a roadmap in our hands.

One mystery of LSD is there are pre-existing ports in the brain and only a handful (or in my case bucket-full) of LSD molecules are needed to dock into those ports and bring about the most miraculous things. And yes, the happiness hormone serotonin uses the same ports, but the effects of serotonin are negligible relative to those of LSD. The sometimes-aired hypothesis that those ports are only designed for serotonin and that LSD somehow accidentally hijacks them to bring about fancy, psychosis-like phantasies does not make sense. What are the chances of a biomechanoid evolving with random mutation and natural selection, in a senseless, mechanical, entropic universe, destined to collapse into a giant black hole, to have ports in his brain which, when accidentally stimulated by a mischievous substance, produce a coherent vision of the projection forth of the universe, the evolution of life therein, and the role of the individual in that evolution? The chances are zero. Stanislav Grof once said those chances are similar to a tornado going through a junkyard and randomly assembling a fully functioning Boeing 747.

CHAPTER 7.

The deeper reason those ports exist and why the brain naturally can produce psychedelics (through yoga and other ecstatic techniques) to bring about these effects, is because the purpose of mystical states is the renewal of society. The purpose of these states is to bring humanity back in line with the transcendental object, the infinite consciousness at the core of the mystical experience. This will be explored in a later chapter.

Another experience on mega-doses of LSD involved me becoming aware of permutations, alternate paths, of my own life. I encountered quite frequently permutations of my own self that would have played out had I made slightly different choices. Every time when you make a choice, you are moving something akin to a karmic number-lock. Every new number combination on the lock is the basis for future decisions. In each situation, you do have a certain number of choices, but the variety of choices you have is also predetermined by choices that brought you to this point. On LSD, I could look backwards into my life and see how much the last 10 or 100 choices I made affected the variety of new choices, and degree of freedom, at my disposal right now.

I realized that some traumatic choices during my childhood haunted me my entire life. They did so because they had long-lasting repercussions by influencing all decisions downstream. Had my conditions been slightly worse, involving more pain, and were choices made earlier in my life slightly less advantageous, my life could have gone seriously wrong. I realized for example, that a few times in my teens, I decided to dissociate from peers who later down the track got themselves into serious trouble. I did not do that because I am an essentially virtuous and good person, but because in those moments, literally by the breadth of a cat's whisker, I had enough freedom and choice to give those offers a miss. What I saw on LSD was not only a confirmation of the law of karma, that all thoughts and actions have results that influence us in the future, but it was also a confirmation of the psychological theory of situationism, which states we are not inherently this way or another, but rather that our psyche results from decisions made according to situations. For example, if somebody is subjected to sexual abuse in their childhood or is growing up in a warzone, however heroic and resilient their psyche originally is, they will end up with large emotional scaring that will play itself out in more negative reactions later in their life.

One way this played itself out in my psychedelic use was horror trips. A horror trip was the term we used back then for a psychedelic experience, during which some form of trauma comes to the fore in which one is caught in an emotional and mental tailspin. The term tailspin is a helpful metaphor here. Tailspins were a problem occurring in early aviation, where an aeroplane was caught in a self-enforcing downward spiral. The only escape action is a counter-intuitive manoeuvre that needs to be practised beforehand because, once the tailspin takes hold, the pilot is likely to be caught in a fear reaction and will have difficulties acting rationally.

In my case, 40 of my roughly 150 LSD experiences turned into so-called horror trips. During them, I encountered profound negative emotional and mental states, from which I could not extract myself while under the influence. Some were extremely scary and frightening, others involved being bogged down in shame, self-depreciation and guilt. Why did I continue? A lot of that was curiosity, a hard chin and the belief I could figure out, eventually, how to get out of these psychedelic tailspins. When I did come out the other side, I had to admit to myself that it was not so much due to me being a smart or wise or morally high-standing person. It was more a result of the fact that although a large part of my childhood and youth was subjectively quite painful, I was lucky enough to be thrown into situations where my choices gave me just enough wiggle-room to exert the emotional freedom necessary to extricate myself from some serious hallucinogenic messes I had entangled myself in. I have known others who were less fortunate. You may think that I am unnecessarily dramatizing adverse reactions to psychedelics. Most regular psychedelic users I knew had these types of experiences. Jay Stevens in *Storming Heaven – LSD and the American Dream* confirms that the hippies in San Francisco's Haight Ashbury district in 1967 believed that sustained and regular LSD use would at some point led to a phase of adverse and negative experiences through which one had to work through. I have seen too many people that did not emerge intact on the other side.

FINAL THOUGHTS ON USING PSYCHOACTIVE SUBSTANCES

There is currently a new enthusiasm for psychedelics, with a definite buzz in Silicon Valley, among psychologists and in spiritual circles. I don't quite understand how we got back here, as for me it's such an old hat. Back in the 70s I was on some rock festivals where up to 100,000 people were tripping together on LSD and similar substances. In those days, we believed that psychedelics would fix all of humanity's problems. On at least one occasion, the Brotherhood of Eternal Love dropped free LSD from an aeroplane onto a rock festival ground. The Brotherhood's biggest single LSD-production run was 160 million doses. That's a lot of

LSD and it did not change the world for the better. In the late 60s and 70s tens of millions of people worldwide took psychedelics. If it was all so great, why did the hippie movement fail like it did? Do we have to go there all over again? It seems as if we haven't learned the lessons from back then or maybe the old people are dying off and the youngsters have to do it all over again. If we do have pre-existing negative tendencies, psychedelics will not change that. Daniel Pinchbeck points out in *Breaking Open The Head* that the Mayas and Aztecs, although using psychedelics, still were enamoured with human sacrifices.

The neuroscientist Sam Harris on his blog page, expresses the belief that psychedelics may be indispensable for some people, especially those who, like him, initially need convincing that profound changes in consciousness are possible. Harris suggests, though, to afterwards continue one's development with practices that do not present the same risks as psychedelics. If we follow that rationale, I probably didn't need psychedelics in the first place, as I didn't need convincing that changes in consciousness are possible. Right through my childhood and up to my early teenage years my main interest was mysticism, devouring any texts on the subject I could find. I only got sucked into psychedelics because at the time everybody said they were a shortcut. How would they have known? Now almost sixty years old, I can vouch for the fact that psychedelics are definitely not a shortcut. I would also like to challenge the notion that psychedelic experiences, by themselves, are truly life changing. I know that's exactly what many people say, but are they really? My observation is these experiences truly changed my life only once I had integrated them through years and decades of spiritual *sadhana*. Had I not practiced the many methods of yoga, I believe I would have remained an unchanged person. What could a yardstick be for us to determine whether a psychedelic experience has changed somebody's life? The yardstick that yoga uses is the increase of one's level of independence from external stimulus to sustain one's (mental, emotional and spiritual) equilibrium. It is my long-term spiritual practice, in my case yoga, that has increased this independence, not psychedelic usage. The psychologist Bill McGlothlin (as quoted by Jay Stevens) in 1966 conducted a study that included personality tests, measuring levels of anxiety and creativity, and changes in values, before and after a course of LSD. He found that personality changes were minimal, although test subjects claimed that enormous changes had taken place.

I want to offer an explanation, already alluded to, why psychedelic experiences by themselves cannot truly transform you. The world is an endless chain of cause and effect. On a psychological level, this plays itself out as the law of karma. The transformative power of a psychedelic journey is limited to what you had to do, to obtain the substance. Usually, this is the effort and the associated karma that you had to undergo to obtain the purchase price. A karmic investment of $10–30 cannot get you very far. An entry ticket costing a few bucks won't get you through the Pearly Gates (but decades of sadhana will). To give you another example, a happy and fulfilled death doesn't just consist of an ecstatic death-experience on the spot. It is earned through an expansion of self, brought about by a life in service of others. Simply taking a psychedelic and hoping to come out a changed person is like trying to get into the Kingdom of Heaven without changing yourself. The problem is that the Kingdom of Heaven *is* your changed self.

Having used psychedelics, we are then faced with integrative work, our spiritual discipline and practice (*sadhana*). This practice we anyway have to do, whether we have taken psychedelics or not. The big question is why take them in the first place? Yes, they do open a window, but if we don't heed the call and start the work to integrate what we have seen, nothing is gained. And in many people using psychoactive substances confuses them and scatters their resolve and concentration.

I would like to allay any concerns of those who have not taken psychedelics that there may be something out there that you cannot get, that you are missing out on, if you don't use drugs. There isn't! Whether we have used entheogens or not, we are still all sitting in the same boat. What gets the boat across the river is spiritual practice, *sadhana,* not drugs.

But I hear already the interjection, "What about the Amazonian tribes, of which so many use entheogens?" The answer to that is that on an evolutionary scale, those tribes are relatively modern, they are only a few thousand years old. The original, animistic mother cultures of the planet, like the Australian Aborigines and many Native American and African cultures, did and do not require the stimulus of substances to see that the entire world and all beings are crystallized spirit! In the last few chapters, I have shown the Divine as having several distinct, different aspects, such as the material cosmos as the crystallized body of the Divine, cosmic intelligence as the God immanent, infinite consciousness as the God transcendent, and the totality of all beings as permutations, computations, individuations of the Divine. If all that is true, is then not the idea of God in a pill the ultimate materialistic pipedream? Is not psychedelic use simply a pharmaceutical approach to spirituality, similar to antidepressants being a pharmaceutical approach to mental wellbeing? And if so, wouldn't a natural, organic and wholistic *sadhana*-based approach be the preferred option?

Chapter 8.
A MAP OF TRANSFORMATIVE STATES

ALDOUS HUXLEY'S *THE PERENNIAL PHILOSOPHY*

The remaining four chapters of this book will integrate the findings of the first seven chapters into a systematic and cohesive philosophy and nomenclature of mysticism, a map of transformative states. This map is a tool of navigation for the mystical terrain. A mystical state is a transformative state, a state in which new knowledge for our society is revealed. A mystical state is to reveal something hidden, something yet unknown so it can be integrated into life and society. This occurs when a person experiences a deeper level of reality and meaning, including feelings of delight, joy, and rapture, which informs them about the work they need to do, to truly become themselves.

What initially started my work on this section was a discussion of the pros and cons of perennialism. Perennialism is a concept explored by Aldous Huxley in his book *The Perennial Philosophy*. In this book, Huxley proposes that all mystics down the ages, whether Daoist, Buddhist, Hindu, Christian, Islamic or else have essentially experienced and taught the same, or at least something very similar. The differences in their description are obvious but, says Huxley, merely the result of cultural and linguistic differences. By analysing the descriptions of mystics from a variety of backgrounds a clear superstructure of mysticism, the perennial philosophy, could be cognized.

In the wake of Huxley's publication, a discussion arose mainly amongst academics, about the pros and cons of this so-called perennialism, with most authors coming out in support of Huxley. Importantly, if Huxley could be shown to be completely off-track, if all or every mystic was experiencing something entirely individual and personal, then the value of mysticism and the experiencing of transformative and mystical states would be largely diminished. If mystical states were totally personal, then their cultural value would be peripheral. If, however, it could be shown that mystics repeatedly access the same, or very similar, phenomena, it could be extrapolated these phenomena have near-universal value and application. If it could be shown that Huxley's basic idea was correct (even if his execution was simplistic), then the total combined body of the wisdom traditions of humanity could be utilized as a canon for a new type of universal mystic and spiritual practitioner. One truly at home in all traditions and has no preference for a single one. A mystic that equally understands the ecstasies of Sufi poets, the mysteries of the Qabalah, the teachings of Daoist, Hindu and Buddhist sages, but also the shamanic and animistic teaching of the Indigenous nations.

This is what this book attempts to do. It will create a common map of all transformative states, and in doing so, will show the entire, combined mystical traditions of humanity as the expression, or the becoming-itself, of one common transcendental object (in this text called the Divine), which expresses itself in all cultures and ages. The term "transcendental object" here stands for what the Abrahamic religions variously called The Father,

CHAPTER 8.

Yahweh or Allah, what Lao-tzu calls the Dao, what Buddha calls Nirvana, what Hindu tantrics call The Mother, what Lakota medicine men call the Wakan Tanka, the Great Spirit, what Indian Vaishnavites call Krishna or Rama, and what Advaita Vedantins call the nirguna Brahman, the formless Absolute.

Huxley's idea was a very important one, but he fell behind in its execution. Huxley essentially accepted that the true, right and perennial mystical experience, that is at the base of every revelation, is the experience of pure consciousness, of the formless absolute, of a transcendental object that is eternal, infinite, formless and quality-less. This is obviously the experience behind the Buddhist concepts of nirvana (a term denoting the extinguishing of a flame) and shunyata (emptiness). We can also neatly trace this type of experience in the Hindu school of Advaita Vedanta, where the nirguna Brahman (formless Absolute) is the only true reality, whereas the world is seen as an illusion (*maya*), superimposed onto consciousness like a mirage. We can further trace this state from India westwards to the Christian mystics like Dionysios, the Areopagite (8th century), and Eckhart of Hohenheim (12th century), who both spoke of God as divine darkness, a state beyond the intellect that cannot be known. We can also follow the footsteps of the formless-Absolute-experience eastwards to China, where it surfaced as the Dao in Lao-tzu's and Chuang-tzu's teaching, an abstract principle that cannot be fathomed by the mind and that yet manifests and balances everything. Even further east, the formless Absolute also surfaces in the Japanese state religion, Shinto, and possibly here it is the most clearly visible in the profound stillness, simplicity and austerity of classical Japanese art, such as painting and music.

If we want to see the experience of pure consciousness and the formless Absolute at the heart of all mystical experience, then we can, with Huxley, weave a pretty good case around this experience having been accessed by a wide variety of mystics across the planet. However, we have to leave out a lot of data points, our exposition will be tendentious, to say the least. Let's start with India: while the formless Absolute/infinite consciousness is the stalwart of Hinduism's most popular school of philosophy, Shankara's Advaita Vedanta, it has been opposed down the ages by numerous other schools. The Vaishnavaites, the tantric Shaktaites, the Kashmir Shaivites, the Samkhyites, the devotees of Rama or Krishna, and the Patanjali yogis all agree there is much more to mysticism than the formless Absolute. Many of these schools hold that the world is real and not an illusion. All Hindu philosophies accept the Upanishads as their bedrock. George C. Adams Jr., in his book *Badarayana's Brahma Sutras* analysed the Upanishads and concluded that only 15% of their statements refer to the infinite consciousness/formless Absolute (*nirguna* Brahman), whereas the remainder refers to the Divine as with form (*saguna* Brahman). The Bhagavad Gita for example, is a text that predominantly explores how the Absolute expresses itself in the world, as the God immanent (*saguna* Brahman). To follow through with his argument, Huxley had to act as if Hinduism consisted exclusively of Advaita Vedanta.

If we look at the Abrahamic religions, the differences become more glaring. There were a few Christian mystics that admitted a pure-consciousness-type experience of the Divine, but they had a hard time staying alive because they were pursued as heretics. Studying Christian mysticism, it becomes obvious that a loving, Bhakti-type (yoga of love and surrender) relationship to a Divine-with-form, is the mainstay of this religion. This is also plainly obvious if we read the New Testament of the Bible.

The same is to be said of Judaism. Huxley's main critics actually came from the fold of the kabbalah, Jewish mystics, who did not recognize themselves in Huxley's preference of the pure-consciousness-experience. Both in the Kabbalah and Hassidism (another school of Jewish mysticism), the practitioner develops a passionate love-relationship with the Divine. This is not the cool, detached Nirvana-approach, but a method in which emotion and passion are used to transform the lower, outer, phenomenal self, the day-to-day personality of the practitioner. This starkly contrasts with the pure-consciousness-approach of the, by Huxley, favoured school of Advaita Vedanta, where according to its main proponent Shankara, the lower self (*jiva*) does not actually exist, but like the world is just an illusion, a mirage.

Similar to Judaism and Christianity, so also in Islam, devotees do not just mediate in stillness until they see the formless Absolute, but instead an emotional, devotional desire for the Divine is developed in which often intense yearning, passion and suffering are invoked to bring about personal transformation. This is apparent in the poetry of R'abia of Basra, Attar, Rumi and in its greatest perfection, in Hafiz of Shiraz.

At this point, we then have two strikingly different categories of mystical states. Firstly, those that Huxley gave voice to, the cool, detached, eyes-half closed, dissociate form of meditation of a Buddha, Shankara and Lao-tzu. But the ecstatic, devotional Bhakti-experience characteristic for the Abrahamic religions, but also for devotional Hinduism, such as the cult of Krishna.

But what about the shamanic and animistic experiences that form the Earth-based spirituality of Indigenous people? The two types of religion we have discussed so far are entirely portable. That means you can be a devotee (in India called a *bhakta*) or a follower of the consciousness-only school (in India called a *jnani*) wherever you are, and the location does not change your practice. In indigenous spirituality the location matters because here we experience ourselves as an emanation of the land on which we live. You are related to the local animals, which are your spirit guides. You are also related to the mountains, rocks, the land, the rivers, oceans and plants, located all around you. In earth-based spirituality, all these are the ancestors of humanity. Indigenous religion is a religion of many spirits with whom humanity negotiates an interdependent life, involving all lifeforms. A true perennial (meaning eternal) philosophy cannot exist without indigenous spirituality, the original and most ancient form of human spirituality.

As explained, if we want to give earth-based spirituality, the indigenous religion, a name, then it would be the term animism for the original form, and the term shamanism for the somewhat more contemporary form. The shamanic-animistic complex, however, does not always stand by itself but is sometimes integrated as an original stratum into more modern religions. A good example here is the Japanese Shinto religion, in which many shrines are dedicated to mountains, trees and spirits. Another example is Indian tantrism, in which offerings are often made to earth-spirits (nagas) and in which also tree spirits (the holy Banyan), and location spirits (for example, the Himalayas but also many lakes) are worshipped. Perhaps animism, the belief that all of creation is alive, found its way into Daoism. And the oldest form of Tibetan Buddhism, Nyingmapa, is a fusion of shamanism, tantric practices and Buddhist philosophy. In Bali, we find a fascinating synthesis in which knowledge-based Buddhism, devotional Hinduism and the original animistic indigenous religion have combined in a three-tiered complexity.

A system that explains mysticism in its entirety must then consider there are at least three separate categories of mystical experiences, which deal with three aspects of the Divine. Or is there even a fourth level? Are all the experiences in which we, powered by an activation of the heart chakra, recognize the Divine in the person across from us, contained in the categories outlines so far? This chapter will offer a map that attempts to answer these questions, acknowledging that there are different categories of mystical experiences that cannot, and should not, be reduced to each other. It will also show a way forward towards an integrated spirituality that avoids the pits into which Aldous Huxley fell, while yet saving his overarching premise, there is a perennial philosophy. The philosophy is of one the Divine, which expresses itself on four levels.

THE PYRAMID-MAP OF TRANSFORMATIVE STATES

The model I am using to explain mystical states is that of the pyramid, to be precise a four-layered-, or four-storeyed pyramid. The top storey of the pyramid culminates in the apex. At this point, the pyramid is narrowed down to a point, and correspondingly mystical states pertaining to this layer have the least amount of divergence. This is the layer that Huxley described, and he was attracted to its small amount of divergence. When analysing these states, reported by various cultures and ages, we are immediately struck by their similarity. Also, when we look at their interpretation, the philosophies that arose from them, we conclude that they indeed point towards a common source, a perennial philosophy. Huxley almost exclusively analysed reports from this layer, hence the conclusion to which he came. Rather than simply refuting Huxley, I am proposing that he wrote only about the apex of the pyramid, it's topmost tier. The complete pyramid model adds three more layers, coherently explaining and interpreting states he ignored. There is, after all, a perennial philosophy, but one much more complex, nuanced, multi-facetted and multi-layered than the one that Huxley proposed.

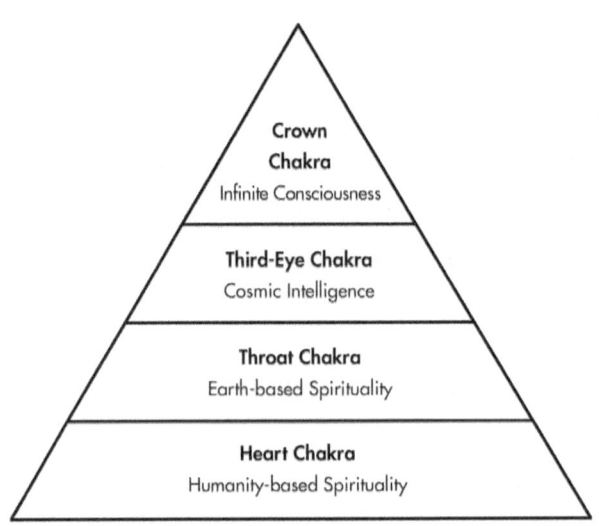

Drawing 1: Pyramid of Transformative States

THE TOP TIER: THE EXPERIENCE OF PURE
CONSCIOUSNESS, POWERED BY THE CROWN CHAKRA

The top-layer of the pyramid represents the experience of pure, content-free consciousness, *atman* or *nirguna* Brahman, as it is called in Sanskrit. Typical exponents and testimonies of this top-layer are the Jnana Yoga, Shankaracharya's non-dualist

CHAPTER 8.

Advaita Vedanta, Gautama Buddha's philosophy, Mahavira's Jainism, the Tibetan Dzogchen, and in China Lao-tzu and Chuang-tzu's teachings of Daoism. But even in Christian mysticism we find this school represented by Meister Eckhart von Hohenheim and his students, Dionysios the Areopagite (today by scholars often called pseudo-Dionysius) and the Belgium 14th century monk Johan Ruisbroek. In Patanjali's yoga we are referring to this state as objectless samadhi, in Sanskrit called *nirbija* or *asamprajnata* samadhi (super-cognitive samadhi). A prolonged remaining in this state according to Patanjali leads to *kaivalya* – spiritual liberation.

All these experiences are powered by the crown chakra and what we behold here is the God transcendent, the transcendental aspect of the Divine, the infinite consciousness. As the infinite consciousness is eternal, spatially unlimited, and without quality and form, it is not only everywhere the same but also in everybody the same. This is so because we share the same *atman*, the same consciousness. A person experiencing the *atman* in India four-thousand years ago, a person doing the same in Japan in the 12th century, and somebody experiencing this today anywhere in the world, are literally having exactly the same experience. Because all of time and space occur within the same consciousness, from wherever in space and whenever in time we access it, it will always be exactly the same. However, as we come out of the mystical state, our mind and ego will reboot. Ego and mind will then use our cultural background and context to describe the state; hence semiotics will create superficial differences in descriptions given by varied authors.

An interesting anecdote connects these types of states to the crown chakra, while pointing out there are other worthwhile states. The 18th-century Indian sage Ramakrishna was a devotional Tantric who worshipped the Hindu Goddess of destruction, Kali. He used to experience the category of mystical states typical for devotional Hinduism and the Abrahamic religions. After he had reached ecstatic states through this form of worship, he came under the tutelage of an Advaita Vedantic (i.e. dealing with the formless Absolute) master named Totapuri. Totapuri was a typical exponent of pure consciousness-driven states, as a non-dualist, he was not taken by Ramakrishna's worship. A pure Advaitin looks at a personified deity (such as Ramakrishna's Kali) as an artificial wedge driven between the consciousness of the practitioner and the infinite, universal consciousness. According to pure Advaita Vedanta there is no distinction between the two. A proposition of a personal deity, therefore, is presumably merely a diversion and, for advanced practitioners, supposedly a waste of time. Totapuri taught Ramakrishna to meditate on pure, formless and content-less consciousness, a practice which in Patanjali's parlance is called objectless samadhi. To Totapuri, Ramakrishna with no preparation went in a single sitting straight into objectless samadhi and remained therein motionless for over 12 hours, considered an incredible feat.

After 12 hours, Totapuri checked Ramakrishna's vital functions and found that his whole body had become cold and stiff and the only part of his body that showed normal body temperature was the crown of his head. Ramakrishna's experience at the time was powered by the fact that all his life force (*prana*) was absorbed in the very top of his head, the crown chakra. Yogis, who are highly technical meditators, long time ago discovered that you can access the state of pure consciousness not just by focusing directly on consciousness (which is difficult

CHAPTER 8.

because as a formless and infinite object, it eludes the mind), but also by fixing all vital force (*prana*) at the crown of the head.

When Ramakrishna, brought about by Totapuri's prodding, finally exited the state of pure consciousness, he made several baffling statements. Firstly, he said that the intrinsic value and meaning of the state of pure consciousness was no different, (and certainly not higher) than what he had experienced through devotional ecstasy. We need to remember that as we work through the following material. For not only do the followers of pure consciousness (we find them in most or all religions) believe that their states are higher and more significant than those experienced by other mystics (such as indigenous shamans or devotional bhaktas), but even within the actual schools of yoga we find the belief that states associated with the crown chakra are higher and more significant than those associated with the third-eye- or throat chakras. Ramakrishna certainly denied this with crown-chakra-induced states (experiences of pure consciousness) and third-eye-chakra-induced states (devotional ecstasy). He said both are one and of the same import. He did interject that crown-chakra-induced states give no information on how to live one's life. They confer an experience only of the transcendental, the formless Absolute and infinite consciousness, and therefore remove all fear of death.

But more baffling to Totapuri and more important, was Ramakrishna's second statement. He held that states of devotional ecstasy were more applicable to living in this world, as they are more conducive to interacting with other people and to leading an active life. There is amongst contemporary seekers and practitioners an over-emphasizing of crown chakra experiences. There is a general and misguided belief these states are a panacea for all problems, but they really only allay fear of death and fear of the unknown. The problem is that in many religions and spiritual movements there is not only an overemphasising of the transcendental aspect of the Divine, but also a reducing of all mystical states to those brought about by the crown chakra. In yoga, this demonstrates itself in the fact that practitioners only care about how they can, as quickly as possible, get to objectless samadhi, not realizing that this samadhi does not teach us how to live our current life. It does not teach us, for example, about right action (*dharma*), our life's divine purpose (*svadharma*) and service to others.

Unfortunately, this overemphasizing of the crown chakra, and the reducing of other important mystical states to that of pure consciousness has turned us away from life, the world, relationships and the body. The crown chakra cannot show us that all of these are the crystallized body of the Divine. Sincere yogis often succumb to the fallacy of wanting to quickly evolve up the chakra hierarchy, to ultimately get out of their bodies, and into nirvana. Regularly this is fuelled by the seeming complexity of modern life with all its frustrations and hopelessness. This wish is respective of what Sigmund Freud called Thanatos, the death urge, which includes the urge to die, to kill, and to become non-existent. This Thanatos, however, also fuels our destruction of life, the biosphere and all the beauty of nature. As a spiritual practitioner, firstly, we need to place ourselves into the service of life itself. Any tendency of wanting to escape its complexity, cannot be in service of life. An overemphasizing of the crown chakra also leads to solipsism, the belief that only one's mind or self exists. That other categories of mystical states are possibly more important and necessary than crown chakra states for a whole range of issues, we will explore next.

CHAPTER 8.

THE SECOND TIER: THE EXPERIENCE OF COSMIC INTELLIGENCE, POWERED BY THE THIRD-EYE CHAKRA

On this level, we directly experience the intelligence that out of itself makes quarks and photons, forming elementary particles, which again form atoms and elements, which form molecules and compounds, which form minerals, mountains, continents, ocean, planets, stars, star clusters, galaxies and universes. We directly experience this intelligence, which manifests itself as the natural evolution of life from the amoeba to the human and onwards, until life forms appear that can understand this cosmic intelligence, receive it and co-create reality with it.

Mystical experiences belonging to this level have a very different taste to those of the first level. In India, this level is called *saguna* Brahman, the Divine with form. A typical example would be Krishna in the Bhagavad Gita. Another example is Jesus Christ, of which the Bible says, "A child will be born and his name will be Emmanuel, meaning God-with-us." In philosophy, this form of the sacred is called the God immanent. The term immanent and Emmanuel are derived from the same root, it means "with us" or "perceptible". In the Indian Upanishads the divine with form is sometimes called the perceptible Brahman, which is opposed to the God transcendent (beyond perception), the formless Absolute. If the Divine could be perceived, we could derive much more information from it about how to live our lives than could be gained from the formless Absolute, the transcendental aspect of the Divine. The pure consciousness/God transcendent (although it forms our innermost core) is far removed from us in that regard that pure consciousness has little or no investment in us or even in the whole of humanity. The transcendental aspect of the Divine (pure consciousness) cannot actually experience grief, even if the whole of humanity commits murder of the biosphere (ecocide or omnicide, the murder of all) and then goes extinct with an environmental holocaust. Although most modern people would not intellectualize it in this precise way, there is a distinct collective feeling of, "Why should I care if not even God cares?" I have even heard pseudo-spiritual practitioners rationalize, "Environmental holocaust, mass extinction and ecocide are only notions occurring in the infinite ocean of consciousness." It is actually true and correct to say that the transcendental aspect of the Divine does not care because It is pure consciousness and therefore cannot judge right or wrong. It only simply is aware and conscious. What we should learn from this is that any theology or spiritual teaching that overemphasizes pure consciousness is flawed because it leaves out *dharma*, i.e. the search for what is right action. However, the immanent aspect of the Divine, cosmic intelligence, which has crystallized into the world and all beings, does care about creation and is intricately linked with it, and that's what will explore in this section.

When dealing with the immanent aspect of the Divine, a big obstacle for those analytically and intellectually inclined is that in most cases it has been anthropomorphized, it has been given human characteristics. We need to understand this has nothing to do with the God immanent but with the human tendency to project, and with our difficulty to understand the Divine without anthropomorphisation. As Sigmund Freud showed in convincing terms, as the infant grows up, she will project all her needs first on the mother and then later on the father. As we grow up then, this projection is transferred onto our romantic partners, superiors, political leaders, sports and military heroes, spiritual teachers and finally onto the Divine. While astute observers of human history may want to despair over our continued need to project a parent role on figures that ultimately have utilized and exploited this, it is simply a result of the human infant being born with no survival skills, and its need to learn these skills over a period of 20-30 years before maturing intellectually. To what degree maturity in us develops at all is a contentious issue. A 1948 psychiatrist convention in the USA concluded the United States harboured less than 1 million people to fulfil the definition of psychological maturity. This should give us at least an idea of how complex this issue is.

When understanding the immanent aspect of the Divine, it is indeed helpful to initially act as if She was a human being. In the history of religion the personal pronoun She for various reasons was often used to refer to the God immanent. In Indian tantrism the transcendental aspect of the Divine is often identified as the male god Shiva (the name Shiva being a metaphor for pure consciousness), whereas the immanent aspect of the Divine is identified with the goddess Shakti (a metaphor for the divine creative force, or procreatress). The Indian terms *prakrti, prana,* Uma, Parvati or Kundalini are likewise placeholders for the mother goddess. The term also exists in Hebrew, where She is called Shekinah, the feminine or energetic aspect of God. In the Greek New Testament, the term *pneuma* is used to describe the energy or breath of God. Notice that in India, the term *prana* (breath), which is etymologically related to the Greek *pneuma*, is also an epithet of the divine feminine. When the New Testament was translated into Latin the term *spiritu* was chosen to represent *pneuma* and again it is related to breathing. Same as the Sanskrit, Greek, and Latin sources, the English term 'inspiring' denotes both inhaling and revelation. The two meanings converge, and in the Gospel of Mark, we find that Jesus, after having been baptized by John, came up from the waters, inhaled the breath of God and was thus baptized by spirit, i.e. he attained revelation. The exact Bible wording is "when he came up the breath of God alighted on him like a dove and remained henceforth". Some yogic texts use similar words to describe Kundalini-awakenings.

While in Indian religions, the role of the divine feminine maintained its importance for somewhat longer, in the Middle East and Europe the Great Goddess quickly became replaced with ambiguous terms, such as the Holy Ghost or the Holy Spirit. Seeing that Jesus is the son, we must assume that the Father must have cohabitated with a Mother (the Great Goddess) to produce a child, but since the order of the day was to disempower women, the Mother was quickly replaced with the Holy Ghost, so that the oh-so-holy divine masculine was not contaminated and corrupted by any feminine and material influence.

However, when talking about the Father (transcendental aspect of the Divine) and the Mother (immanent aspect of the Divine) we have to remain clear about the fact that neither are humans. Anthropomorphisation (projecting human characteristics onto the Divine) can be helpful if we know that we are using a metaphor for something that is ultimately too difficult to describe otherwise. The God immanent, the Great Goddess, is humanlike in that regard that She is intelligent (notice that the term intelligence in many languages has a feminine gender, for example, in German - *die Intelligenz*), but Her intelligence encompasses the computing power of the entire cosmos. She is cosmic intelligence. A human on the other side has some form of intelligence, but it is largely limited to what is between his ears (I say *largely* here because, as described in *How To Find Your Life's Divine Purpose,* the human brain is capable of channelling a fair bit of cosmic intelligence). The God immanent is also humanlike in that regard She is embodied, but while Her body is the sum total of all universes, the body of a human takes up only a minuscule five- to seven-feet tall space, in an otherwise infinite multiverse.

But the main difference between a human and the God immanent is that the human has an ego, and the immanent aspect of the Divine hasn't. Ego is a piece of software that is a filter on our consciousness and enables the consciousness within us to identify for a limited time with a particular body and mind. We can therefore call this compound the egoic body-mind. Because the immanent aspect of the Divine does not have an ego (limiter in space and time), it is therefore everywhere and simultaneously in all timeframes. This is important for us to realize because there is no time and no place where we cannot access the Divine because there is nothing but the Divine. Additionally we need to understand that divine grace and divine love is bestowed on us all the time and cannot be withheld because the Divine does not have an ego from which to withhold grace. Lack of understanding of this has caused endless suffering, holy wars and much more.

The reason why human beings exist is that infinite consciousness (the Father, whom we experience in the crown chakra) can only be conscious of the material world (the Mother, whom we experience in the third-eye chakra) in a general sense because the God transcendent also does not have an ego to limit itself in time and space. The transcendental aspect of the Divine is simply an infinite ocean of consciousness that cannot limit itself in time and space. The God immanent (cosmic intelligence, the Mother) likewise can only express Herself in a general form by crystallizing Herself as an intelligent, material universe following intelligent laws. It does take the introduction of a piece of software called ego, which combines both the Father and the Mother in a single being, a so-called lifeform. In such a lifeform, both consciousness and intelligence are spatially and temporally limited, meaning a lifeform has a body and a span of life. A basic form of ego is common to all lifeforms, from the amoeba to the human. All lifeforms collectively form the divine child, referred to by the sexist term 'son of God' (it should be gender-neutrally called 'child of God'). Each lifeform is a conduit, a canal in which the infinite consciousness (the Father) and the cosmic intelligence (the Mother) permutate and compute themselves. Each being is truly divine as Jesus rightly said, "And have I not said Ye all are Gods. Ye all are children of the Most High."

The mystic at this level is not to sit like Buddha in objectless samadhi, still and motionless, with an empty mind, which is simply the function of the crown chakra. No, the function of the third-eye chakra is the renewal of society, the ability to bring, via mystical states, new information into society, information which it not yet possesses. All great progress in society from the ancient lawgivers like Manu, Moses and Muhammad, to poets like Valmiki, Sappho, Dante and Shakespeare, to composers like Bach, Beethoven and Hildegard von Bingen, to painters like Frida Kahlo, van Gogh and Dali, to scientists like Marie Curie, Einstein, Planck, to engineers like Stevenson, Edison and Tesla, has been caused by divine inspiration and revelation. Whether those inventors rationalized it in this way or not, a solution to a problem does not actually come from us thinking the solution into reality, but when the mind is receptive and intuitively aligned for an influx from cosmic intelligence. Our purpose in life is to facilitate this state so we can consciously co-create with the Divine. I have described this process in my earlier text *How To Find Your Life's Divine Purpose – Brain Software for a New Civilization*.

If the relationship with the Divine, powered by the activation of the third-eye chakra, is consciously experienced at this level, it then often engenders a devotional Bhakti spirituality. Devotees often feel a great love for the Divine, as typically expressed by the Persian mystic Hafiz of Shiraz. As seen from the chart, at this level, the pyramid is already much wider, which implies a significantly larger divergence in experiences, although similarities exist. The activation of the third-eye chakra (and the crown chakra, too) also gave us sky-based religions. This term implies that the Divine was projected into the sky, into heaven or even further away into nothingness or nirvana. But because we also lost access to the throat chakra, we lost earth-based spirituality and the understanding that Earth, all matter and all life (especially non-human life) is also sacred and crystallized spirit. This led to our estrangement from nature, to speciesism, and the human-made mass extermination of life on Earth. Because we lost access to the heart chakra, we looked at those who worshipped a different God as infidels. This became the cause of holy wars.

THE THIRD TIER: THE MATERIAL WORLD AS THE CRYSTALLIZED BODY OF THE DIVINE, POWERED BY THE THROAT CHAKRA

Whereas the second tier makes us realize cosmic intelligence directly, here we experience its results. We realize that the entire material world containing all beings, is not disjointed dumb and dead matter, but that the world is the crystallized body of God. It is like living inside a supercomputer of infinite intelligence, with the only difference this supercomputer is sentient, feeling and alive. We can understand the relationship of the second to the third layer by thinking of the second layer as the software and third layer as the hardware and hard drive of the second layer, cosmic intelligence.

But the IT metaphor is only suitable for describing the relationship of both of these layers to each other. The difference is that both layers are actually alive. The second layer is the source of all our intelligence and inspiration. We can say that the second layer is the superconscious mind of each individual, it is the part where the individual mind is linked into the cosmic mind. The third layer of the pyramid is where we learn that microbes, fungi, animals and plants are our brothers and sisters with whom we share the biosphere, with the purpose to create more life in a symbiotic process. But the knowledge here goes much deeper still. Everything we see is crystallized spirit and intelligence. That includes the mountains, oceans, forests, rivers, lakes and the atmosphere, which are only our mothers and fathers, our ancestors. Indigenous cultures still know this today, and worship these entities, but modern humanity has unfortunately lost this knowledge. Opening of this chakra lets us ultimately see that all matter is the crystallized body of God. All matter is sacred. This level is about falling in love again with nature and about a re-enchantment of the world. About seeing the beauty of nature in all its many manifestations. Our current philosophy, built on the subject-object split, lets us treat matter as if it is dumb dirt and is what has led to the host of problems we are facing today. There is no dumb dirt. It's all sacred and every place is a sacred site. Because of our misguided perception of matter as dumb dirt and our belief we accidentally sprung from dumb dirt, we are destroying this miraculous biosphere and are literally cutting off the branch on which we sit.

A complete activation of this throat chakra leads to an animistic understanding, that is the realization there is nothing dead in this universe, and that everything is spirit. Indigenous people do commune with rock spirits, wind spirits, fire spirits, and the spirits of mountains and rivers. For too long, in its hubris modern humanity has mocked indigenous people as primitive and savage. With a fully activated throat chakra we realize that it is us, who are primitive. We are the ones, who do not fully understand the world in which we live. It is us, modern, industrial humanity, who are the savages because via colonialism we are responsible for the death of tens of Millions of Indigenous people around the world and down the centuries. The exact number may actually exceed 100 million killed, but for obvious reasons documentation and research on this subject is sparse.

Throat-chakra-states prepare us to recognize the entire biosphere as an intelligent living being that deserves our love and veneration. It is our mother. The throat chakra is even more important for the evolution of humanity than the two higher layers of the pyramid. If we don't relate to the biosphere as our mother and lover, then in a few decades, there may not be humanity.

The pyramid model shows the throat chakra layer as being much wider than the two layers above. This illustrates that there is a much greater diversity among throat chakra states than at the higher levels. They vary extensively for different locations. The spirit is different everywhere. Another example is that all native medicine came about because indigenous people communed with plant spirits, animal spirits and mineral spirits, who taught them. The indigenous people of the Amazon know of 50,000 different healing plants. The anthropologists working with them must claim that the indigenous people got this knowledge by trial and error. This is laughable. Bands and small tribes of indigenous people usually have from around 2 dozen to sometimes a few hundred members. In such a setting, everybody in your world is your relative. You cannot experiment with a sick person because they are related to you. You also cannot risk to not heal them as you will live with their relatives for the rest of your life. It is ridiculous to assume that shamans had the freedom to make trial-and-error medical experiments with their own people, as if they were living, like Dr Mengele, in a moral vacuum.

If you ask the indigenous people how they arrived at their healing knowledge, they will say, "the plants told us". Unfortunately, modern humanity's hubris neither allows us to listen to plants, nor to take our indigenous ancestors seriously and to respect them. Since there is only one cosmic intelligence and everything is a crystallization of it, we are related to plants and rocks, too. Rock spirit is our oldest ancestor, which is confirmed by the mineral components of our body being its oldest parts. Science is now making tentative progress in describing these phenomena as we now know, for example, that humans and trees share 40% of the same DNA. Of course, we can understand them, if we only sincerely try.

Different to the two top tiers, throat-chakra-states are not portable, their differences depend on the land on which they occur. As an indigenous person, if you visit the area of another culture or tribe, you first negotiate with your hosts for them to introduce you to country. You don't approach the spirits of the land directly but through the people who have lived there for thousands, sometimes ten-thousands of years. The local indigenous people are the custodians and guardians of their country, the land on which they live. Coastal ceremonies in a certain area will completely differ from those in mountainous or desert areas.

Another difference is the approach of indigenous people to time. Australian Aborigines for example, are traveling through the vast empty continent along song lines and are using incantations and songs to "sing" the destination into the present. It is possible that whales use song lines in a similar navigator fashion. The different relationship that indigenous people have to time is highlighted in the following story. A group of anthropologists once wanted to introduce a tribe of Amazon hunter-gatherers to Jesus. When they told them that Jesus did live in Israel two thousand years ago, the indigenous people asked, "not here, not now?" They then lost interest and walked away. Because they do not share our concepts of time and space as involving separation, they are not interested in portable religions.

The Balinese people, also informed by throat-chakra-states and animism, constantly perform offerings to keep the spirit world going. This used to also be the case in the Indian Vedic culture, but is to a large extent lost, although some *yagyas* and *yajnas* (types of rituals) continue. The Vedas are largely animistic texts that describe the whole of the natural world as alive, and it is because of this that they appear so alien to us today. Nineteenth-century Western scholars described the Vedas as gibberish. They are the only animistic scriptures that humanity has ever produced, and it is because of that animistic nature we find it difficult to understand them. The Vedas say that abundance comes from an attitude of giving, whereas modern business philosophy has it that it is derived from taking. After the Vedic age, the Upanishads shifted attention away from animism and shamanism to third-eye-chakra and crown-chakra experiences.

Different to the two highest levels of the pyramid, which reflect an emptiness-based and sky-based spirituality, on the level of the throat chakra, we encounter earth-based animistic spirituality. Like all other levels, this one also is not immune to decay and corruption. In an original animistic society, every single member of a community is in contact with the spirit world. In some cultures, as time went on shamans, healers and medicine people derived more powers, a process that in in some places descended into constant tribal warfare, black magic and occultism. That a corruption of the throat chakra makes some indigenous cultures caught in a vicious cycle of sorcery has been reported by many anthropologists and shamans, including Carlos Castaneda, Jared Diamond, Martin Prechtel and Malidoma Patrice Somé.

In modern society, a corruption of the throat chakra (sometimes caused by DMT use) has us focus on conflicts between humanity and extra-terrestrial races, UFO abductions, or races that have previously come to Earth and are manipulating us. Western Science is also among the excesses of the throat chakra. We only need to remind ourselves of Rene Descartes vision of an angel who told him, "Control of nature is by means of measure and number". While science has brought numerous advantages, it has brought them only for humanity and often only for white males of the ruling class. Every year a greater amount of wealth is concentrated in the hands of fewer and fewer people. At the same time, people of colour, women, other species and the land are coerced, manipulated and exploited. The techno-utopia that was still promised in the 1950s and 60s is postponed further and further into an unknown future, and if it should ever come, then only for the super-wealthy elite. Western science today is often just a tool of domination, coercion and manipulation in the hands of those in power to further cement their position. A complete treatment of the subject how the philosophy of science is related to our alienation of and exploitation from nature is beyond the scope of this book. For more information, please consult Charles Eisenstein's epic *The Ascent of Humanity*. The subject-object split, a foundation of the philosophy of science has created our idea of *other*. *Othering* is the source of most of our society's problems. The split between observer-observed and mind and matter, once introduced, will re-create the dichotomy of me versus you and us versus them in humans vs nature, sedentary agriculturists vs nomadic herders, industrialists vs indigenous people, faithfuls vs infidels, whites vs blacks and men against women. All these conflicts are caused by a lack of seeing ourselves in the other and the other in us. This expanded sense of self is caused by mystical experiences and their banishment from the core of our culture has caused inconceivable harm down the centuries. It is time now for us to become agents for healing.

THE FOURTH TIER: TO SEE THE DIVINE IN EACH BEING, POWERED BY THE HEART CHAKRA

In the heart chakra we encounter humanity-based spirituality, the realization that the Divine is embodied in each individual, that we all are children of the Divine. The heart chakra teaches us we first need to come to a place of self-love, self-acceptance and self-esteem and from there, we can relate to others with a sense of dignity and freedom. This is gained after we give up any inner conflict with ourselves. The heart chakra teaches us we subconsciously initiate conflicts with others to externalize and outwardly project psychological conflicts we carry within us. We cannot obtain peace outside if we are still in a state of war within. We go out and compete with others, outdo them in sports and economy, invade their countries and colonize and exploit their lands because, deep within, we feel unworthy. We feel that if we have achieved something we will finally be worthy in the eyes of others and that will give us self-worth. But this self-worth never comes. No success and consumption inoculate us against depression, anxiety, trauma, panic attacks and a plethora of mental illnesses, which is a quagmire into which modern humanity will gradually descend unless it heals its spirituality and connection with nature.

That the world we experience reflects our inner world, was first popularized in the West by Carl Gustav Jung in his dream analysis. However, Jung learned this approach from studying yogic philosophy. In his *Transformation and Symbols of Libido* Jung quoted passages from the Vedas and Upanishads as early as 1912. He lectured in 1932 on Kundalini Yoga and in 1938 on the Yoga Sutra. In 1952 Jung published his book *The Psychology of Kundalini Yoga*. He is a true pioneer for introducing yoga to Western thought, however, yoga goes much further and is much more radical. In yoga, not only the dream state, but also the waking state is seen as an outward projection of subconscious forces. This does not mean that the outer world is an illusion, but it means that our subconscious draws into our presence factors and individuals that present particular deeply held traumas we previously incurred. These traumas are like archetypes that re-occur in our lives in new acquaintances we make, until they are recognized and healed. This teaches us to eventually give up the concept of otherness. We recognize that others are not adversaries in a rat race to demonstrate our fitness for survival by overcoming our foes, but they provide us with opportunities to consummate our karma, caused by our own previous actions.

In this context, forgiveness is important. We tend to go through life entertaining righteous anger (sometimes called holy anger) and holding grudges against people who have slighted or outsmarted us is a big part of that. We believe that we are entitled to hold those grudges and that somehow, they enrich us. We believe that if we let these grudges go, we would come up short, impoverished. We are afraid that letting go of grudges would mean we are letting others off the hook. But with these grudges, we are ultimately only hurting ourselves, for the subconscious cannot differentiate whether we metre out judgement towards others or towards ourselves. It always goes both ways. If we carry around a deep aversion against somebody, our subconscious cannot differentiate whether the aversion is against us or somebody else. It will apply it equally in both directions. For example, our conscious mind may say, "I hate so and so," but the subconscious mind will translate this into "I am hatred" and gradually poison us by doing so. Combine that with the fact that, at the moment of death, our mode of judging will turn around and be applied to us, then letting go of one's grudges and negative judgements is one of the healthiest decisions we ever make. It is basic mental hygiene. That's why Jesus said, "By the same metre by thou judgest, thou yourself shall be judged". The heart chakra informs us we must forgive. The root of all conflict is the contracted sense of self that we carry in us because as a society, a collective, we have not yet matured beyond the first three chakras. This expresses itself as the process of othering, which is only excluding somebody or something from our own sense of self. The beginning of the end of the process of othering takes places here in the heart chakra. Once fully activated, it includes the whole of humanity into our sense of self. This process is to be continued by activating the still higher chakras to prevent speciesism, exploitation of nature, etc.

The heart chakra also teaches us that each being has its own unique duty (*svadharma*) to perform here on Earth. That's why we should be cautious about recommending to others what their life path should be. Such an action is often just projecting onto them our own unlived and unacknowledged desires and traumas. Ultimately, as long as another person does not cause harm to other people, other species, or the land, their life's divine purpose is an affair between them and God only. At this fourth level of the pyramid, there is the greatest divergence of expressions. The pyramid of mystical states rests on the wide base of the heart chakra, its wideness reflecting the fact that it accommodates the unique divine purpose (*svadharma*) of each individual.

Chapter 9.
THE EVOLUTIONARY PYRAMID AND MASLOW'S HIERARCHY OF NEEDS

I regularly receive questions about the similarities and differences between my pyramid-map of transformative states and Abraham Maslow's pyramid or hierarchy of needs. As there are significant similarities (and differences, too), I will present them here in this chapter. To do so, we need to first add the evolutionary stages relative to the first three chakras back on to the map of mystical states, outlining our evolutionary future. Because the three lower chakras represent evolutionary stages of the past, i.e. reptile, mammal and primate, they are stages of the empirical and the known, rather than mystical states. The purpose of a mystical state is to reveal something hidden, something yet unknown so it can be integrated into life and society. The four mystical tiers of the pyramid represent four consecutive layers of future evolution. With the lower three chakras included, the map is not anymore one of mystical states, but now a map of evolutionary stages, past and future. Here is the complete pyramid with all seven evolutionary stages:

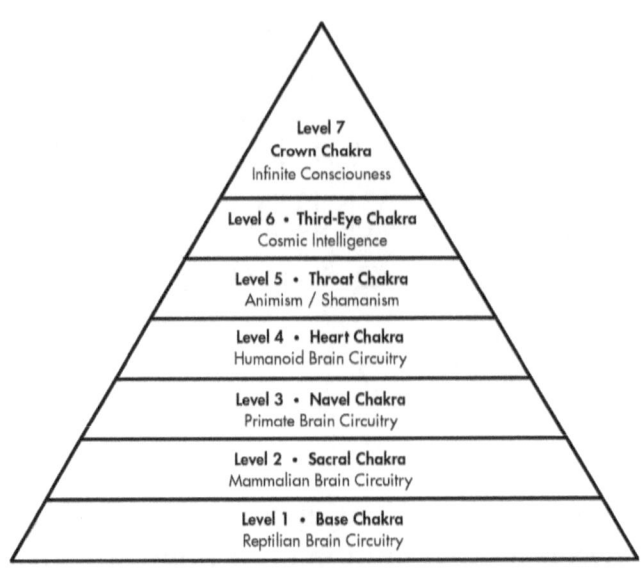

Drawing 2: Pyramid of Evolutionary Phases

Abraham Maslow shifted the focus in psychological research from the pathological to the healthy human psyche, thus creating humanistic psychology. He was interested in how people develop their highest potential and, in his terminology, become self-actualized. Maslow believed that the prime human motivation was seeking fulfillment and change through personal growth. Self-actualized people are those who are fulfilled and are doing all they are capable of. In self-actualization, a person comes to fulfil a higher purpose they find meaningful, a situation I call finding one's life's divine purpose.

Maslow acknowledged that each individual is unique; therefore self-actualization leads people into different directions. While for some, self-actualization is achieved through art, in others it will be science, entertainment, sports or entrepreneurship. Maslow believed self-actualization could be measured through the concept of peak experiences, which are what I label mystical or transformative states. This occurs when a person experiences a deeper level of reality and meaning, including feelings of delight, joy, and rapture, which informs them about the work they need to do, to truly become themselves. Self-actualization is a continual process of becoming rather than a solid state of perfection.

Maslow analysed cases of highly successful people to find out what drives them, including Abraham Lincoln, Albert Einstein, Ludwig van Beethoven and others. Maslow initially worked with a five-stage pyramid, but being himself a rapidly evolving mystic, he later in his life expanded the pyramid to an eight-stage model, including cognitive, aesthetic and most important, transcendence needs.

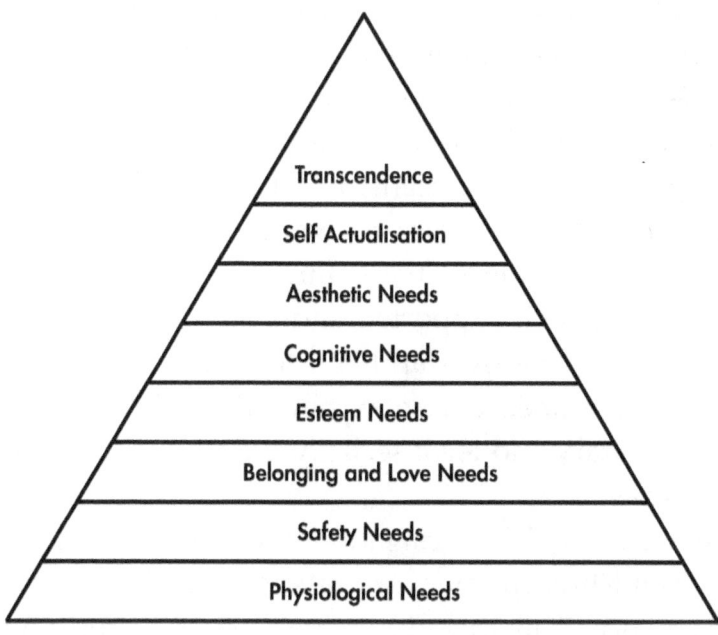

Drawing 3: Maslow's Complete Eight-Stage Hierarchy of Needs

Level 1. *Biological and Physiological Needs*: Here Maslow included food, shelter, warmth, sex and sleep, amongst others. This is very similar to the base chakra, which represents reptilian brain circuitry. The function of the base chakra is survival, and it directs the fight, flight and freeze reflex. Sex as a procreational and recreational activity, including to achieve pleasure and intimacy and the need for human warmth would not be included in the base chakra but rather under the sacral chakra.

Level 2. *Safety Needs*: Maslow includes here personal, emotional and financial security, a stable family situation, order, law, stability and well-being. Maslow believed that if one's familial security was threatened by domestic violence or childhood abuse, economic and law-and-order security were often sought as a substitute. In the evolutionary chakra model the second level is the mammalian chakra, that determines our family life, interaction with our spouse, children, parents, and our emotional life, security, but also our sense of belonging to small groups, such as clans, tribal bands and the need for territory. This chakra is also responsible for the limbic brain and its ability for non-verbal communication and the ability to be seen, accepted, supported and to feel loved. While there is a good amount of overlap here, the sacral chakra does not include religious or economic considerations. Striving for status, success, monetary and legal security are all included under the navel chakra.

Level 3. *Love and Belongingness Needs*: here Maslow includes family, friendship, intimacy, receiving and giving love, trust, and acceptance. This includes being part of a group, whether small, such as one's family, or large, such as online or religious communities. The navel or power chakra helped to create the primate brain, the neocortex. It regulates our status and position in complex societies, including economic and civic affairs and membership in religious communities. For somebody who's highest operational level is the navel chakra, this chakra empowers their ability to lead, coerce, manipulate and dominate others. Maslow's family and friendship complex are included in the sacral chakra, whereas to truly love, in the evolutionary model is included under the heart chakra.

Level 4. *Esteem Needs*: Maslow classified two categories, esteem for oneself (dignity, achievement, mastery, independence) and the desire for reputation or respect from others (e.g., status, prestige). The desire for reputation or respect from others in the evolutionary chakra system is associated with the navel chakra. Reputation or respect may also come from others fearing us or at least are concerned that we may outcompete them. Self-esteem in the chakra system has two sources, a psychological level (an inner attitude to ourselves) and a skills level (possessing skills that can be assessed from an external observer independent of whether we believe to possess them or not). On a psychological level, the heart chakra, when activated, reveals to us the unconditional love that the divine experiences for us and the fact that the divine, due to its lack of an ego, can only ever see us in divine perfection. This recognition of the divine in oneself also extends to all other beings and therefore heralds the end of conflict. On a skills level, the activating of the throat chakra lets us download skills directly from the intellect of the Divine. Such skills can be assessed independently from an external observer and will give us the esteem and recognition from the community around us.

Level 5. *Cognitive Needs*: knowledge and understanding, exploration and curiosity, the need for meaning, and Level

6. *Aesthetic Needs*: appreciation and the search for beauty and balance. These two levels, which Maslow added during the 1960s, are largely included in the 5th evolutionary chakra level, the throat chakra. This chakra enables us to see the whole cosmos as lawful and as the crystallized body of a higher intelligence. Animism, shamanism, science and art are all expressions of this chakra. This chakra, when activated, shows us that our purpose in life is to extend service to the community of life around us (including non-human life). Through such service, our life becomes meaningful and we are maintaining the incredible beauty and balance of the natural world around us.

Level 7. *Self-actualization Needs*: This is the level on which Maslow's work concentrated. It includes realizing one's personal potential, reaching self-fulfilment, seeking personal growth and peak experiences. Maslow called this "a desire to become everything one is capable of becoming". This level of Maslow closely tracks the 6th chakra, the third-eye chakra, which leads to a realization of cosmic intelligence. For the yogic mystic, this does not simply end in passively adoring this immanent aspect of the Divine. Rather than that, the yogic mystic learns from the Divine via vision-practice. She learns information pertaining to what the Divine wants to embody Itself through us. This is based on the realization that the Divine must individuate through us to become active on an embodied level.

8. *Transcendence Needs*: Maslow added this final level shortly before he died, reflecting what he found himself focussed on at the conclusion of his fulfilled life. He believed that a person that had achieved all the other levels, would now seek ego-transcendence. This means finding an expanded sense of self beyond one's limiting ego, and ultimately dissolution in the God transcendent via a mystical state. Maslow closely identifies

here the purpose of the 7th chakra, the crown chakra, which is the revelation of the transcendental aspect of the Divine, the infinite consciousness.

Summary: Maslow refined his hierarchy of needs throughout his life and the final version, which he published shortly before his death, achieves a great overlap with the pyramid of evolutionary steps, especially in the upper half. If we amalgamate his cognitive and aesthetic needs into one, the two pyramids are nearly congruent in the upper half.

Maslow's pyramid is a hierarchy of human needs, whereas the chakra pyramid is one of evolutionary potential. Maslow's pyramid in the lower half depicts basic needs of the individual human, whereas the evolutionary pyramid depicts the capabilities and potential of evolutionary classes (reptiles, mammals), orders (primates) and species (humans), that we traversed as we evolved.

Maslow received a fair share of criticism for his view that needs, lower down in the hierarchy, must be satisfied before individuals can attend to needs higher up. A typical example given by his critics was Vincent van Gogh who became self-actualized, i.e. manifested his higher purpose, yet remained poor and unacknowledged during his lifetime (his safety needs were not met). In the evolutionary map, van Gogh also is an important example. He has given humanity a new ability to see and in his days was one of the outstanding conductors for cosmic intelligence related to painting. While all of us today can relish van Gogh's paintings, I would like to hear what he himself would have had to say about the lack of material security, support for his work, his unsatisfying love-life, and lack of love for himself. Like Mozart, so Van Gogh clearly is a towering genius of his time. However, the evolutionary map states that chakric potentials need to be developed and activated in order, otherwise suffering and potentially mental illness, may be at hand. For example, you may be a genius like van Gogh, Janis Joplin or Jimi Hendrix, but you may still die young, alone and in a dark place. Those selling your artworks and writing your biographies may get wealthy on your work, while you may die in pain. What really is the value of genius for the individual. Here it is a value only for posterity and spectators.

In the evolutionary map, jumping ahead and activating higher chakras, while ignoring the upcoming ones, usually will lead to suffering and pathology. Activating for example, the throat, third-eye or crown chakra through psychedelic drugs, without prior attending to the navel- and heart chakras, will with great regularity lead to psychotic and schizophrenic tendencies. A similar constellation, with additionally blocking of the sacral chakra (i.e. blockage of empathy), could lead to a Charles Manson-like psychopath. If only the heart chakra is blocked, but all other chakras are activated, we would be met with the case of a cult-leader personality, who uses insights from the higher chakras to place them into the service of the navel/power chakra. Attending to levels in the right order in the evolutionary map demands even more rigid attention than in Maslow's hierarchy of needs.

Chapter 10.
HORIZONTAL YOGA AND THE MENORAH

The pyramid-map of evolutionary phases and mystical states is a metaphorical representation. Aldous Huxley's approach at identifying a perennial philosophy was simplistic, but in principle, still stands. The pyramid of mystical states explains the four levels of mystical states (heart- to crown chakra) and to which extent some levels have lesser and others greater diversity of experience and manifestation.

At the heart of the pyramid is the depiction of the chakras as evolutionary brain circuitry. However, the representation of the chakras in vertical order is only a functional representation. They are functionally aligned along the spine because the Kundalini (the divine creative force that acts as the evolutionary driver) in the human body acts as a counterforce to gravitation. Therefore to raise the Kundalini, we ideally sit bolt-upright in a yogic meditation position. This means that the vertical order of the chakras does not imply hierarchy but is only functional. A Buddha is not intrinsically higher than a microbe without microbes in his gut the Buddha could not digest and would therefore die, and his teaching would come to naught. The idea that at some point, history will end because all beings have entered nirvana, is faulty. Beings high in the pyramid will always depend on the evolutionary service of simpler organisms to literally carry the more complex organisms on their shoulders.

Thus there is no vertical hierarchy between evolutionary stages, but only a temporal order. Some are simply further down the track, but for the biosphere to function, there always needs to be harmonic distribution of organisms along all evolutionary stages. A biosphere consisting of Buddhas and Christs only, is not feasible. They need fungi and bacteria to create topsoil, plants to enrich the atmosphere with oxygen, and animals to create nitrogen to nourish the other organisms.

Again this view is not entirely new. Although he used completely different words, it was the Indian 20th-century mystic Sri Aurobindo who shifted yogic emphasis from an in-and-out approach (i.e. turning inside and rising through the chakras until dropping out of samsara into nirvana) to one of horizontal yoga, where interaction with the world and service becomes more important than a rat race to the top of the pyramid. Aurobindo was critical of the yogic tendency to sit somewhere in isolation, navel-gaze and only attend to our own levels of realization, our own shabby, little enlightenment (as is Krishna in the Gita). What is the point in that, we may ask, seeing that none of us can live in isolation. Each body is a community of life, consisting of trillions of cells, 40% of which are not even our own bodies but microbes, our microbiome, which devotedly serve us.

Then look at the macro-level how much energy was put into welding together the atomic nuclei, creating your body. Several generations of stars were born, lived and died, creating the carbon atoms in your body (which were welded together in supernovae), so it could exist, live and function. Our small, human bodies result from an incredible community effort, to which even stars and black holes have contributed. And how much energy has gone into our DNA and how many thousands of generations of life-forms existed, learned and perished, so today, we can be what we are.

Let's look at our situation today: Even if we are hermits, how many farm and agricultural workers are involved to produce our food, how many transportations workers to get it to us, civil servants, defence- and police-force personnel guaranteeing the basic functioning of our society, while merchants organize the distribution of goods, etc. No individual is truly individual, but we all are community on multiple levels.

While it may help to reduce one's extraversion and for some time to focus on one's spiritual needs and practices, mysticism ultimately is not done to benefit the individual but to introduce novelty into an encrusted and stuck society. Mysticism is an essential tool for the renewal of society. This is nowhere clearer than in the myth of the Hindu god Shiva, the king of yogis. At some point in his immortal life, the god had married Sati, the daughter of the lawmaker, supreme court judge and high priest Daksha. The haughty Daksha had always disliked his pot-smoking, tantric-sex practising, dreadlocked son-in-law, who for eons would sit motionless on mountaintops instead of holding down an orderly job, like he, Daksha. Sati, after her father yet again insulted her do-no-good husband, became so upset that her anger made her burst into flames, and she met her untimely end via self-immolation. There are several complex twists to the narrative that do not need to interest us. The important point is that Shiva, after his wife's death, ultimately turned his back on human society and, for a seeming eternity, sat motionless practising samadhi on the formless Absolute.

Soon the other gods and sages realized that novelty was withheld from society. Novelty and innovation result from mystical states, whether we realize this or not. Shiva being a metaphor for the community of mystics, their disconnect from society meant that any form of spiritual evolution could not be communicated back to society. A mystic, like an indigenous shaman, too, is somebody who goes to the other side, sees and understands, and then comes back and brings with them what she saw. The British poet William Blake said, "There are things that are known and there are things that are unknown. In between there are doors." A mystic is a person traversing these doors, entering the unknown and returning to society with vital information. For its evolution and harmonious function human society depends on mystics that step through these doors, come back and embody and import into the realm of the known what they saw in the unknown.

With the turning away of the king of the mystics, Shiva, this urgently needed innovation was withheld from society, which soon became too conservative and rigid. The gods hatched a plot. The safest way to get innovation back into society was for Shiva to fall in love, to have children and to be returned to the hearth of domestic life. Domestic life here is a metaphor for society and the community of life. The gods convinced the Great Goddess Shakti to take birth as the maiden ascetic Parvati, who strolled past the motionless Shiva, right when the god of love, Kama, struck Shiva with one of his feathered arrows. While Shiva burned Kama to ashes with the force of his third eye, the love-arrow nevertheless struck him as he glanced at Parvati, with the equilibrium of his meditation disturbed by desire for her. The king of mystics falls in love, leaves his icy mountaintop and thus returns to society.

While I have left out a lot of the details, the morale of the story is still visible and that is that mystical states are not isolated from all other aspects of life. Mystics have an important function in society and importantly also a responsibility towards it. The biological evolution of life on Earth results from spiritual evolution. Both processes are the combined result of the convergence of cosmic intelligence and infinite consciousness (the Mother and the Father), expressing themselves as matter and life, the divine child.

The problem with the vertical depiction of the chakras is that it gives rise to an in-and-out movement, where we become introverted, get trapped in the exclusive progressing of our spiritual evolution and in escaping the problems of life by rising above them. This follows the fact that religion usually depicts both matter and life (i.e. the body and physical existence) as an obstacle to spiritual evolution. We need to place a horizontal depiction of the chakras side-by-side with the vertical image.

We find this image in the Old Testament of the Bible, the Torah, as it is called in Judaism. Like the New Testament so also the Torah is a treasure chest for yogic truths and realizations. It is said of Moshe (Moses) that he raised the serpent in the desert and everybody who looked on became whole. This is a clear reference to the serpent power, the Kundalini. As already mentioned, the divine feminine, in Sanskrit called Shakti, in Hebrew is called Shekinah, with both terms sharing the same etymological root. The esoteric meaning of the frequently mentioned book of seven seals refers to the seven chakras. A visual representation we find in the Menorah, the seven-lamps produced by Moshe, which was revealed to him by Yahweh. Moshe is told (Exodus 25:31) to produce "seven flowerlike cups, buds and blossoms", which follows yogic texts where the chakras are called lotus flowers.

CHAKRAS, DRUGS AND EVOLUTION

Drawing 4: The Menorah

In this image, we recognize a horizontal representation of the chakras, and the related spiritual evolution of life on Earth. In Hebrew, reading is done from the right to the left, but the direction is not essential to understanding this image. The message is this: All beings enter the cycle by first developing their survival evolutionary circuitry. They then go through an evolutionary development spanning from the reptile, via the mammalian and primate brain circuitry to the humanoid level. The humanoid level is important because it represents the heart chakra, the axial chakra. As we can see, the fourth blossom/lotus is the one sprouting out of the central axis, or stalk. This central blossom represents the experience that all beings and life forms share one common self/atman, which is the infinite consciousness, the transcendental aspect of the

Divine. The yoga of this central blossom is called bhakti yoga, yoga of love, service and surrender. The service here consists not in performing rituals for a faraway god but realizing and recognizing the Divine in all of Her children. These are all beings we meet, and not just those who are part of our family, tribe, nation, faith, political party, caste or football club. Serving them does not just meant to not cause them further harm and suffering, but to foster their spiritual evolution so they, too, may realize themselves as divine love. Service also means we approach life from the desire to give, rather than the need to receive. The more we realize the abundance we carry within us, which overflow into the life of those around us, the more the dictum of the Bible, "To those who have, more shall be given, and to those who have not, the little they have, shall be taken away", applies. Abundance is not created by needing to receive, but by realizing our inherent fullness and desire to give, which is caused by our all carrying the transcendental aspect of the Divine, the infinite consciousness, in our hearts.

After the heart chakra, there are three more evolutionary stages. Firstly, the animistic realization that the entire cosmos is the crystallized body of the Divine, powered by the throat chakra. Secondly, experiencing how cosmic intelligence wants to embody itself through us and as us, represented by the third-eye chakra. Thirdly and finally, the realization of the immutable and eternal infinite consciousness, the God transcendent, as bestowed by the crown chakra. Important in all these higher chakra realizations is that we return from them, and centre ourselves again in the heart. Only then can we communicate to others what we have seen, and only then are our actions compassionate, and will contribute to the spiritual evolution of others.

The beauty of the Menorah image is that it does not show the goal of evolution as towering in an elusive crown chakra state of consciousness, rising above the toiling masses who produce our food and pay our taxes. Rather than as a static state, the Menorah shows evolution as a dynamic and natural process that all beings traverse through, and its purpose is not to reach a crowning state, but the purpose is service, to contribute to the life of others. The Menorah expresses that all life is bound together in a symbiotic process, in which all life forms support each other, to create more life. In this process, we all share one common self. The Menorah also expresses that in the current state of our evolution as humans, the heart chakra is the one most likely to alleviate our present problems.

In mysticism, there is a tendency of wanting to find methods and techniques, that deliver us to a state beyond fear and pain. This state is indeed possible. But would you want to have it, knowing that everybody else, who does share your same self (the *atman*), is still in pain and fear? And if your answer was to be yes, what value would this state really have?

Chapter 11.
THE SPIRITUAL CRISIS AND HOW WE WENT WRONG

We have come a long way together in this book. We examined the relationship between all major categories of mind-altering drugs and the yogic chakras. We then established an evolutionary map of transformative states and put it into context with Aldous Huxley's and Abraham Maslow's teachings, and related it to the Menorah. But there is still work to do. In this chapter I will first identify the nature of the current crisis of humanity and its relation to drug use. I will then trace the origin of this crisis to religion and science and identify what can be done. In the final chapter then we will look at a possible contribution that spiritual practice can make.

All drug use is a coming to terms with humanity's spiritual crisis. Either we use mind-contracting drugs to numb ourselves against our spiritual downfall, or we use mind-expanding drugs in a desperate attempt to find a solution. Drug use is ubiquitous in modern humanity. The WHO estimates that 50% of the global population have taken illicit drugs. Considering the efforts of the war on drugs, this number is astonishing. A major reason for young people to take drugs is self-initiation. Because our society lost its indigenous spirituality long ago, we cannot initiate our young people into something we ourselves have lost. So they must go and self-initiate. There is no point for us to complain about this. If we want to stop them from self-initiating, we must step up and offer them initiation ourselves. However, seeing the spiritual inertia of our culture, there is little chance of this happening anytime soon.

Another reason people today take to drugs is for self-medication. Levels of anxiety, depression, PTSD and other problems are constantly rising. The WHO predicts that soon a quarter of our entire health expenditure will be devoted to combating depression. At the same time the day draws closer when every second child born will present symptoms in line with autistic spectrum disorder. Humanity is in a crisis.

Do you remember a time, when it was promised that soon all diseases, crime, corruption, poverty and warfare would be extinguished? Where we would be working 3 hours a day, machines would perform all the hard and menial tasks, and people would be happy and fulfilled, living in a perfect society? What became of it? Pandemics are besieging us, many countries are incarcerating a greater and greater percentage of their citizenry, every year more wealth is concentrated in the hands of a handful of obscenely wealthy individuals, while politicians seem to have developed an ongoing agenda to serve their own interests and privilege. Increases in average age have halted and, in some countries, are already declining. But many of us just live longer to spend more time in decrepitude, simply being propped up by an ongoing cocktail of chemicals and medical procedures. Many of us work longer and harder hours than we ever did in history, but material security eludes many as wages are stagnating and job security is replaced with the gig economy. Global capitalism has morphed into a Godzilla-like monster that monetizes communities and nature and puts the spoils into the pockets of a handful. Meanwhile the driving of indigenous populations off their land continues, often under the disguise of ending poverty and enhancing education. In reality, however, this refers to a grabbing of their ancestral lands, turning it into mining leases for the already super-wealthy, and logging their ancient forests, which are so urgently needed as Earth's green lungs. Once the land is logged and mined it is then turned into denuded feedlots for livestock, held in atrocious conditions. The indigenous people, meanwhile, are massacred if they resist, and if not then pushed into reservations, where they descend into drug use, prostitution and domestic violence, due to continued traumatization and cultural genocide.

But it's not just indigenous populations. According to Freedom House, a US-based think tank, 2020 was the 15th year of globally shrinking liberties, and in 73 countries freedom was on the decline. Freedom House assesses parameters, such as electoral processes, freedom of speech and assembly, surveillance, etc., and stated that for 15 years in a row democracy is in global decline and tyranny on the forward march.

Improving or fixing our situation is firstly about admitting that at some time in the past we, as a global civilization, have taken a wrong turn. How can we fix a problem if we don't even admit that we have one? The belief that everything is just fine, and that with just a little bit more funding for science, technology, police and military, we can reject the invasion of uncertainty that besets us from all sides. While time is wasted by perpetuating this narrative, acidification of the ocean increases, and the corals die. In a few years for the first time, we will have more plastic in the oceans than biomass, i.e. organisms. Plastic often amasses in so-called gyres, plastic garbage patches several hundred kilometres long, and so wide, deep and thick that ships have to navigate around them. The pole caps are melting, and any of the next years could, for the first time, see an entire ice-free arctic during summer. The pole caps, however, work like giant mirrors that reflect heat back into space. Without those mirrors, the oceans will be left to absorb all this heat. The oceans, so far, have absorbed 95% of the excess heat created by greenhouse gasses. Their absorption capacity is now exhausted, they are pretty much full, and from now on, the atmosphere will cop it.

Meanwhile, the tundra is melting and releases giant deposits of methane, 100 times more toxic than CO^2. Will the biosphere be able to absorb and metabolize all this extra methane, a biosphere, which we daily decimate by making hundreds of species of plants and animals extinct? Since the 1960s we have killed two-thirds of all wild mammals, we have destroyed 80% of the wildernesses of the planet, depleted 80% of the fish stocks, killed 75% of insects, amongst them our vital pollinators.

But these are such abstract stories and they somehow do not seem to touch many people, who instead want to continue their slumber, akin to listening to the band on the Titanic, which continued to play while the doomed ship took water. So instead of giving numbers, I want to tell you about losing a small animal I have never met, but when I heard its story, I felt such an intense loss. This tale is symbolic for our massive destruction of nature's abundance and beauty. What I want to talk to you about is the Passenger Pigeon. The Passenger Pigeon was once the most numerous bird of North America, numbering up to 5 billion individuals. Some ornithologists believe it to have been the most numerous bird on Earth.

When Europeans arrived in North America, 25 to 40 percent of the continent's birds were passenger pigeons, traveling in flocks so massive as to block out the sun for hours or even

CHAPTER 11.

days. The downbeats of their wings would create a thundering roar that would drown out all other sound. Although a billion pigeons crossed the skies 80 miles from Toronto in May of 1860, little more than fifty years later, passenger pigeons were extinct. The last of the species, Martha, died in captivity at the Cincinnati Zoo on September 1, 1914. How could that happen?

As recently as 1880, the ornithologist Alexander Wilson observed that flocks of Passenger Pigeons darkened the skies for hours on end. It was estimated that an average flock, containing over a billion birds, would consume over eight million bushels of food per day. This was one of the many reasons that got them into the crosshairs of humanity. John James Audubon observed in 1813, "The air was literally filled with Pigeons; the light of noon-day was obscured as by an eclipse; []... I cannot describe to you the extreme beauty of their aerial evolutions, [], descended and swept close over the earth with inconceivable velocity, mounted perpendicularly so as to resemble a vast column, and, when high, were seen wheeling and twisting within their continued lines, which then resembled the coils of a gigantic serpent... []. The Pigeons were still passing in undiminished numbers and continued to do so for three days in succession" (Audubon J.J. *Ornithological Biography*, 1835). Three days in succession! How I would have loved to see such an abundant display of nature.

A single flock observed in 1866 in Ontario was estimated to have been 1.5km wide and 500km long. It took 14 hours to pass overhead and contained more than 3.5 billion birds. (Sullivan et al, *The Passenger Pigeon: Once There Were Billions*, 2004). Should the birds have flown in a row, the flock would have reached 22 times around the Earth. The nesting sites of the pigeons were of humongous proportions. One observed in Wisconsin in 1871 covered 2200km^2 (Fuller, *The Passenger Pigeon*, 2014).

The Passenger Pigeons had learned to fly, nest and roost together in vast numbers, which protected them from non-human predators. But exactly this made them vulnerable to merciless commercial and recreational hunting. Imagine a nesting site 2200km^2 in size? Native Americans had hunted the pigeons for centuries but had a rule that forbade them to enter the nesting sites. Not so white colonialists. Recreational hunters killed up to 60 birds with a single shot from a shotgun. A single ammunition seller in 1871 is thought to have provided three tons of powder and 16 tons of shots during a single nesting. In some hunting competitions, the winner had to kill up to 30,000 birds to claim first spot.

With constructing railroads and telegraph lines in the 19th century, locations of nesting sites were quickly telegraphed across the country and an army of up to 1200 "pigeoneers" descended quickly on the nestings, wherever they sprung up. Pigeoneer at some point become a profession and its exponents followed the flocks all year round. Often, they simply cut down nesting trees to dislodge the pigeons and collect them to sell them as meat. As many as 6 km^2 (1,500 acres) of large trees were cut down in a day to kill the pigeons they contained. Some of these hunters killed several million birds. By 1876, pigeons were shipped in such numbers that the price of pigeon meat fell so rapidly that the shipments failed to recoup the costs of the barrels and ice needed to ship them. The pigeons were then turned into fertilizer. Millions of birds were caught with spring-loaded nets.

The last large-scale nesting took place in 1874 and 1878 in Michigan and Pennsylvania. Here hunters killed 50,000 birds daily for nearly five months in a row. The survivors of these slaughters attempted a few more nesting sites, but each time they were disturbed and left before any young were raised. A few environmentalists campaigned for protecting the pigeons, but laws were implemented too slowly. Opponents of the naturalists claimed that they were exaggerating the situation, and that the pigeons could never be made extinct through human activities (note the similarity in argument by climate change deniers today). At that point there were probably only a few breeding pairs left in the wild. Hunters shot the last few wild individuals and destroyed the last individual nests during the 1890s. There were still a few scattered individuals left in captivity, of which the last one died in 1914. Even this last individual could not live and die in peace and had to be protected in its enclosure from people who threw objects and sand at it, enticing it to flap around.

Many people will respond to this harrowing tale by exclamations such as, "I cannot go there". This is exactly where we have to go. We have to feel the grief and desperation at our devastation of nature's beauty. I could repeat the sorry tale of the pigeons with many other species, biotopes and cultures we have destroyed in our worship of Thanatos, the urge to die, kill and destroy. Any solution cannot come from looking the other way, but only by honestly looking straight at the problem. The most sobering aspect of this story is that it took less than 50 years for a species that counted billions to completely disappear. We need to remember this when thinking about humanity. Our apparent prolific numbers are no protection whatsoever, actually, more to the contrary.

The quick disappearance of the pigeons was not only caused by the massive overhunting, but also by habitat loss. Between

1850 and 1910, 180 million acres of forest were cleared for agriculture. These numbers repeat themselves today in the clearing of the Amazon, Kongo and Indonesian rainforests. In Australia today, more bushland is cleared daily, than during the peak of colonialization. Habitat loss is also threatening humanity. If we do not convert our military, heavy industry, construction, freight and energy production to clean energies, climate change, rising oceans, salination and topsoil erosion will, in a few decades, destroy 80% or our arable lands and potable water reserves. The problem with all these numbers is that every time a team of scientists makes estimates, they choose the most conservative numbers they can come up with. They do so because if they should dare to shake the neoliberal and neoconservative tunnel-reality of our elite, they will lose their funding and academic careers. Inevitably then, a few years later, it is found that even worst-case scenarios, have been too conservative. They now need to be adjusted to new worst-case scenarios, which usually are not published by the media, because they are thought to cause the general populace too much anxiety. Meanwhile we are diddling our last chances away, as we did with the pigeons.

Another strategy to ignore our destructive ways is to say, "that was back then, but we have improved now, we have environmental laws". These laws are unfortunately only a token gesture. Today we are making 60 species extinct per day. That's much more than during the 19th century. Is that what is meant with improvement? Our rate of deforestation has increased, as has our rate of polluting the oceans. Governments are using the COVID pandemic to reduce "green tape", i.e. rolling back environmental protection laws to fuel further industrialisation. A recent declaration of the Australian government expressed lip service for saving the Great Barrier Reef (the only organism on Earth large enough to be seen from space), while expressing its commitment to "clean coal" (the burning of coal leads to acidification and heating of the oceans, which bleaches coral). Our so-called improvement, if it exists, mainly consists of improved spin-doctoring, paying lip service to protecting nature on one hand, while on the other continuing nature's ruthless exploitation and destruction.

WHAT WENT WRONG AND WHY ARE WE DOING THIS?

I'm assuming that everybody can see how similar our own situation is with that of the Passenger Pigeon. Why is it that neither the world's religions nor Western Science, by now our official state religion, seem to have so little to offer towards our current ecological and ecocidal crisis? Before he died, Stephen Hawking said that he was seriously worried that humanity might not survive the next 100 years. This he said because we are in the early stages of the sixth mass extinction of life. Because the bio-parameters guaranteeing homeostasis are kept in balance by biodiversity (I have explained this in great detail in *How to Find Your Life's Divine Purpose* and is beyond the scope of this book), the less life forms there are, the more the bio parameters (such as salinity and PH of oceans, oxygen-CO^2 balance, temperature of the atmosphere, etc.) will fluctuate. The more the bio parameters fluctuate, the more organisms will become extinct, with the more complex organism's scalps to be claimed early in the mass extinction. Who is the most complex organism on Earth? Right, it's us. So, who has the most to lose from making other organisms extinct? Humanity!

We could muse that humanity is committing a slow suicide, while other, less favourable similes compare us to a cancerous growth on the biosphere. Seeing that cancer consists of cells that go on a rampage, until they have killed the host's organism (which in this case would the biosphere), we probably have to look at some hard truths here. The strange thing is, that every time I sit down with non-environmentalists, and talk them slowly through the overwhelming evidence we are killing ourselves by destroying the biosphere, they resist until the last moment. When they ultimately accept the writing on the wall, they do not go to, "Okay, let's see what we can do about it then". No, in most cases they straight away flip over to the position of, "Well, it's anyway already too late". How can a fact be denied in one moment and in the next accepted as too far gone? The discussion seems to always go straight from denial to cynical stoicism, which shouldn't surprise us as they are both part of the same narrative, the one allowing us to not change our behaviour. It is crucial that we stay as long as we need at the point of honestly admitting our devastation and grief, even if it feels hopeless. Only from that space can resolve to tackle our problem grow. Both denial and cynical stoicism are coming from the same place, not wanting to feel what we have done and continue doing.

It is as if modern humanity is courting a death wish. Freud called this death wish Thanatos and considered it one of our two primary urges, with Eros (the will to live and to create more life) being the other. But where does this Thanatos come from? If you look at indigenous cultures around the Earth, they are motived by Eros, whereas Thanatos seems alien to them. Eros in Freudian psychology is a concept far larger than mere eroticism. Eros is the appreciation of beauty and life in all its forms. Eros is the keeper and guardian of the garden of life and creates a balance between all lifeforms, which again creates more life for all species. It also means to see the sacredness in nature and its perfection, free and independent from human domination, manipulation and coercion. It is in all aspects right the opposite to what human society does.

In *How to Find Your Life' Divine Purpose,* I have already shown that Western Science is the brainchild of religion, rather than its opponent. Western science is a method by which the biblical injunction "make the Earth thy dominion" is implemented. Dominion comes from *dominus,* a term for members of the Roman slaveholder caste. To make the Earth thy dominion means to enslave nature, which is what we have done. Religion has given the mandate, but the method was provided by science and technology. In that regard, science and technology are simply our method to achieve our religious aspirations, to become God on Earth. The belief that science and religion oppose each other is a smokescreen, installed to appear that we have two options to choose from.

In my previous title, I've also shown that most fathers of science came from a religious background. A good example is Occam's Razor, the scientific principle by which we cut away from our explanation all that is unnecessary. It is this principle that Richard Dawkins invokes when saying we don't need God to explain the world. Only that Mr. Occam was not actually an atheist, but a 14th-century Benedictine monk. As already quoted, René Descartes, another founder of science, received his calling when an angel appeared to him in a vision saying, "Control of nature is obtained by number and measure". This means that Descartes believed that God had sent him an angel, encouraging him onwards to construct the foundations of science. Sir Francis

Bacon, another architect of science, said that "nature must be strapped on a rack [a medieval torture instrument used to elicit confessions from witches] and tortured until she reveals all of her secrets". He closely tracks the mindset of the medieval Holy Inquisition. In all these examples, we see there is no conflict between religion and science, but that modern science is the creation of religion.

It is religion (or more precisely sky-based religions to differentiate them from Earth-based indigenous spirituality) that first stated that matter is dumb and dead, non-spiritual and non-sacred. By this declaration, religion created the precondition for us the loot, pillage, ransack and rape nature with science and technology. Now, I'm not opposed to the method of science (trial and error, don't assume that something is right until you can prove it, form a hypothesis and collect evidence, etc.), but the philosophy of science, which is the separation between subject and object, into an observing, detached scientific mind and an observed, empirical, material object. This hypothesis on which science is built is not science at all. Carl Popper defined science as that what cannot be falsified. That object and subject are interlinked has been proven repeatedly by quantum mechanics. The belief that observing subject and observed object are separate then is a religious dogma or at best, part of the philosophy of science, science's underlying, unproven assumptions and beliefs.

Another toxic aspect of the philosophy of science is the religious holding on to materialistic reductionism and empiricism. In the first few hundred years of science, it was held that science deals only with the empirical and material. In the 20th century, science then breached this levee and declared that only the empirical and material is of relevance. The logical conclusion of this newfound confidence became the new claim that the human is a skull-encased flesh-robot with a mind only a result of biochemical and bioelectrical occurrences in the brain. But we have here come to an infinite regress. Science is a system that researches only the empirical, that which can be measured and confirmed by sensory data. In the last 70 years Science claims that because the non-empirical cannot be measured, it does not exist. Now that is a metaphysical speculation.

So, how did we get to dominate the world with science and technology, based on a religious dogma, which is itself not scientific? And when exactly did that happen? It certainly happened a long time ago. The destruction of nature is not just as old as the 400 years of industrialisation. If we study the history of collapsed civilizations, which started at least as far back as Sumer, the early development of agriculture is already built onto the same tenets as late-stage industrialization. It is based on wholesale domination, coercion and manipulation of nature, by which we destroy all species and plants besides around one or two dozen domesticated species, which we define as being helpful. Thus we have come to where the vast majority of land-based animal biomass today does not consist of wild animals, but humans and their domestic livestock, such as chickens, cows, pigs, sheep and goats. There is little more left on Earth and that is due to a process that started thousands of years ago, and not just in 1584 when Columbus hit the Caribbean (one of the years quoted as the beginning of the so-called Age of Enlightenment).

We need to go all the way back to what in the Bible is called our expulsion from the Garden of Eden, and in the Indian Puranas called the myth of the four yugas to understand where we are today and why we are here. Adam, Eve and the Garden of Eden in the Bible, and the Satya Yuga (Golden Age) in the Puranas, are metaphors for the age when our ancestors still followed the indigenous mother culture of the planet. Both myths, the Biblical and the Puranic, show the beginning of our estrangement from nature and earth-based spirituality, and the subsequent rise of sky-based religions and ultimately their brainchild Western Science. In analysing the origin of our estrangement, I am not saying we should return to being club-wielding barbarians, but to understand what went wrong, we have to mercilessly and sometimes painfully analyse our history and assumptions.

Our exit from the Garden of Eden was said to be caused by our eating from one of the two trees therein, called the Tree of Knowledge of Good and Evil. Because we ate from that tree, we believed to have ingested the right to decide and judge what is good and what is evil. An example would be cow = good, and wolf = evil, or wheat = good and weeds = evil, agricultural sky-god = good and nomadic paganism = evil. The eating of the fruit of that tree is a metaphor for us assigning to ourselves the right to extinguish the vast majority of life forms, and foster and breed a handful of life forms, which were useful to us. We then destroyed nature and turned the planet into a giant farm and feedlot to harvest these "good" species. This means that the Tree stands for assigning to ourselves the right to "strap nature on a rack and torture her until she has revealed her secrets" or to "control nature through number and measure". Right here is the actual execution of the order to "make the Earth thy dominion [thy slave]".

Another dimension of understanding the Tree of Knowledge of Good and Evil is its implication that in the cosmos there is a conflict between two opposing forces, good and evil. Goodness, which previously was an inherent quality that every indigenous person on the planet knew to possess (and was to be cultivated), now became personified with an irate, bearded, white male, called God, who lived in the sky. Good was no longer inherent in us as a moral compass, but it was projected into the sky as God, a Zeus-like bearded, white, Aryan warlord, that we had to believe in and cow-tow to. Evil become identified with the opponent of the bearded, white guy, up on the clouds, the Devil, usually depicted black, and living in the bowels of the Earth.

Because we accepted this cosmic conflict between God and Devil, we also had to accept it within ourselves, as an ongoing inner conflict between Eros and Thanatos. We then projected this inner conflict onto the outer world, in constant warfare against ourselves, animals, plants and nature in its entirety. In many ways then, the Tree of Knowledge of Good and Evil actually stands for Thanatos, our death wish. Our hubris, our assigning to ourselves the right to dominate and outsmart nature by determining which plants and animals (and humans, too) are allowed to grow and flourish when and where, is our death wish. This assignment has led to our devastation of the planet and biosphere and now, thousands of years of agriculture, and hundreds of years of industrialisation later, we finally come to learn and understand that we should never have tried to become the masters of creation and the garden of life, but should have remained its humble servants, its guardians and protectors.

THE OTHER TREE, THE TREE OF ETERNAL LIFE

It is this, that the other tree stands for, the Tree of Eternal Life. This tree is a metaphor for our indigenous past, when we were still immersed in the indigenous mother-culture of the planet. The most grandiose excess of the Tree of Knowledge of Good and Evil (which is the metaphor for modern dominator-society, commencing with agriculture) was the quest for physical immortality through science. Currently, peak humanity is estimated at around 10 billion individuals. Imagine the greenhouse footprint of 10 billion people with an infinite lifespan? Within a single generation, we would double the population because death doesn't decimate it anymore. Did anybody think about that aspect of it?

But as in the Tree of Knowledge of Good and Evil, we all die (because we become extinct) so in the Tree of Eternal Life, we all live (paraphrasing Paul who said, "as in Adam we all die, so in Christ Jesus, we attain eternal life"). This eternal life already exists. It is the collective life of the biosphere, which is the true son begotten of the only God, Mother and Father, cosmic intelligence and infinite consciousness. The realizing that all matter, all beings, and everything that exists, are only the crystallized body of the Divine, means, in the symbolic language of the Bible, to eat from that other tree that grew in the Garden of Eden, the Tree of Eternal Life. We ejected ourselves from the Garden by eating from the Tree of Good and Evil, by accepting there is a force that effectively neutralizes the Divine. Admitting this was an error, there is only the Divine, re-admits us to the Garden.

Eating from the Tree of Eternal Life doesn't mean that the body of the individual becomes immortal. It does not need to because our consciousness and intelligence are already immortal. There is only one consciousness (the Father), and one intelligence (the Mother), of which we all partake. The Divine Child, which is all matter and all life forms, is in constant flux and in it all forms are constantly transformed. When we die, our bodies become reabsorbed into the atmosphere, the soil, the plants and animals around us. We will continue to live in them, in the same way as we can already see ourselves in them now. The Tree of Eternal Life means that in life as in death, I have an expanded sense of self that includes everything around me, all forms and all manifestation. It means that all humans, all plants, all animals, all microbes, are my brothers and sisters and that the mountains, rivers, oceans, stars and planets are my mothers and fathers. The indigenous people of the planet have always known this and that's why they served and protected all life, not just their own, and not just human life.

That we are separate from nature, that we are this body, that our self is discrete and estranged from the land and the Earth around us, is an error. The eating from the Tree of Knowledge of Good and Evil is a metaphor, representing our historical error to eject ourselves from the Garden of Eden, from nature. Eating from the Tree of Eternal Life means to rediscover via the mystical state, the original unity of all life and creation, which is only a crystallization of Universal Spirit. In it we "live, walk and have our being".

Chapter 12.
THE IMPORTANCE OF SPIRITUALITY, YOGA AND THE CHAKRAS FOR THE FUTURE OF HUMANITY

When the Dalai Lama was once asked whether he thought that drugs could offer a shortcut to enlightenment, his response was, "I sure hope so". My attitude is probably closer to "I doubt it" and I do so for the many reasons that I have outlined in chapters 1 to 6. What does work though, is yoga, and yoga and the vertical and horizontal map of transformative states (outlined in chapters 7 to 9) can be an answer to humanity's crises. The previous chapter showed that the biblical myth of our expulsion from the Garden of Eden and the two trees therein, give us a beginning for an understanding of what went wrong.

A parallel myth describing the expulsion, is the myth of the four yugas (world ages) mentioned in the Puranas (a series of Indian mythological texts) and also the Mahabharata (the largest Indian epic, containing the Bhagavad Gita). The interesting thing about the Puranic myth is that it is not a single incident such as the eating from Tree of Knowledge of Good and Evil, but a more complex four-step process, by which we descend into the confusion in which we still are today.

Satya Yuga: According to the Puranas our history began in the Satya Yuga, the Age of Truth or the Golden Age. The texts of this age are the Vedas and if we study the Vedas, we first notice that their language is so arcane that it is difficult to understand what they talk about. An extensive study reveals that the ancient Vedic seers offer hymns to nature, revealing that at the time of composition, humanity was still immersed in nature. This immersion was so complete that everything around us was integrated into our sense of self, including stars, sun, moon, mountains, rivers, oceans, etc. The mindset described in the Vedas is naturalistic or animistic, the understanding that the whole world is crystallized spirit. Offerings and rituals played a great role amongst Vedic people as they do in today's indigenous cultures. Like the Garden of Eden, the Puranic golden age is a description of our remote indigenous past, when we were one with nature. During that age, we had a quality of mind called suspended (*nirodha*). This means that whenever a task was fulfilled, our minds were automatically reabsorbed into the heart (a metaphor for consciousness). Resting in our true nature. This is how the minds of indigenous people still work today (if we have not yet destroyed their culture via colonialism). This does not mean that such a mind is simplistic, but rather it means that the person knows how to operate the off switch if the mind is not needed.

Through a process of entropy (breakdown of order), this original mind was disturbed, and we entered the next age, Treta Yuga (three-legged age). The exact reason for this name would lead to a lengthy excursion, so let's just remember that the number three plays a role. During this age, cities were built, and society assumed complexity. Some individuals became overwhelmed by the already commencing estrangement from nature and they regularly visited the jungles to get spiritual advice from sages, who were still living there. During this period, the Upanishads were composed. Upanishad means "sitting near [the mystic]" and these texts contain teachings that had become hidden to the many because they had become too busy and absorbed with the hustle and bustle of fast-paced city life. The quality of mind was called focussed or single-pointed (*ekagra*). This mind had lost the ability to expand to the point of including all of creation. But it was still single-pointed and focussed enough it could arrive at the truth, if it was given the time to focus on a single thing for long enough.

Dvapara Yuga: This period went again on for a long time and eventually again entropy (disorder) increased. This age is called two-legged age and again the only thing we need to remember for this explanation is that it contains the number two. During that age, the integrated function of the two brain hemispheres broke down, and people tended to either one extreme or the other. Two groups of texts were composed the Puranas and the Sutras, reflecting that people were mythological/intuitive or rational/philosophically inclined. The mind during that time was called oscillating (*vikshipta*) or confused because this mind constantly oscillates from one extreme to the other. During this period humanity lost its permanent sense of self, which lead the Armenian mystic George Gurdjieff to say that modern humans do not yet have a centre (but it can be created through practice). Similarly, the post-modernistic view of the self (that we are an amalgamation of constantly changing selves) and the psychological theory of situationism (that we do not perform actions from a constant sense of self but rather simply make up our minds based on particular situations and are therefore in constant flux), accurately describe this new phase of humanity.

Kali Yuga: Again, we stayed in this age for a long time until the progress of time further increased disorder (entropy). A good way to understand entropy is to think of the rusting process. Once the surface of metal is broken by rust, the process simply continues through time and moisture. Some scientists now propose that time itself is entropy.

This latest, our current age, is called the Kali Yuga, the age of darkness, recognizable by ubiquitous corruption and confusion. It is marked by permanent warfare and conflict amongst humans, self-serving officials which dip their fingers into the coffers of the electorate, and an abundance of false teachings. I know this all sounds sinister, but there is light at the end of the tunnel, so please bear with me.

The texts belonging to this age are the tantras (this term means technology or technique). This term is very misunderstood in the West. There are over 800 tantras and because people in this age lost their intuitive understanding of the truth, these technological and technical texts describe every activity in great detail. A handful of these tantras also describe in great detail explicit sexual techniques. For 18th and 19th century, puritan, sexually repressed Westerners this was such a sensation, that the term tantra, unfortunately, has not lost its association with the lurid and lewd.

The mind during that time is called materialistically infatuated (*mudha*). Instead of acknowledging all of nature as the crystallized body of the Divine, during that epoch, we became infatuated with our own physical bodies. Instead of realizing the incredible abundance of nature and community, we became infatuated with the wealth in our hip pocket. Forgetting that all children of all humans of all species, are meant to be our children, we became infatuated with our own progeny only. Instead of respecting wisdom in our elders and seers, we became infatuated with the cult of youth and celebrity.

The four yugas and Yogic technique: Yoga is a system to reverse the expulsion from the Garden of Eden by walking us backwards through the entropic events leading to the four ages. Although modern humanity is completely infatuated with physicality, in truth, we are infatuated with ideas we have about bodies. While on the one hand, consuming media that worships ideal, young bodies, high-performing athletes and pornography, on the other hand, we are profoundly disconnected from our own bodies. The first step then is to re-embody by practising the yogic limb of asana (posture). The purpose of asana is not to perform fancy postures, looking fantastic on Instagram. The purpose of asana instead is to completely anchor ourselves in our body, and to release the physical aspect of past conditioning and painful subconscious imprints. By becoming embodied beings (rather than being dissociated and hankering after ideals), and by releasing the physical component of conditioning, we are overcoming the tendencies associated with the materialistically infatuated mind and the Kali Yuga.

Once a certain proficiency in asana is achieved, we are now ready to tackle the problems associated with the third age, the Dvapara Yuga (two-legged age). Remember that during that age the integrated function of the two brain hemispheres broke down and we became identified with extremes such as fundamentalism and realism. We also lost our permanent sense-of self. The name of the age, two-legged age, insinuates that the practice to reintegrate our brain function and regain our permanent sense of self is associated with our two nostril and the techniques of pranayama. Pranayama also removes the pranic or subtle aspect of past conditioning and painful subconscious imprints.

Once we are established in this type of practice, we can then deal with the problems associated with the second age, the Treta Yuga (three-legged age). This means we are traveling back in time, back to the source and reversing the entropic movement our civilization has undergone. During the Treta Yuga, our Kundalini (divine creative force) slipped down to around our ankles, meaning our mental capacity for single-pointedness and concentration decreased. The name Treta (containing the number three) implies the method used to rectify this defect. By using the Kundalini-raising techniques of yogic meditation, we lift the Kundalini back up to the third-eye chakra. Yogic meditation also deletes the mental aspect of past conditioning and painful subconscious imprints. At this point, the process of reconditioning is complete, and we are now ready for samadhi (revelation).

Samadhi is the final layer of yogic techniques, rather than being just a state. It reverses the entropic movement that exited us from the Satya Yuga, and by extension the metaphorical Garden of Eden. There are two groups of samadhis, the objective (during which we learn to see the world without conditioning but rather as it truly is) and the objectless (during which we experience ourselves as pure consciousness and therefore eternal and infinite). With this fourth layer of yogic technique, the original suspended (*nirodha*) state of mind is re-established. This is a mind that is highly capable of understanding, realizing and problem-solving, but it simply suspends (i.e. is reabsorbed into consciousness) if no problem is to be solved. And it does so by itself, with no recreational drug use. This is what yoga is designed to do.

CHAPTER 12.

The suspended state of mind also implies our return into nature and the recognition that our Mother Earth, the biosphere, is a feeling, living being. The above description of practices associated with the four yugas is only a succinct summary of a complex process. I have described the practices in six previous volumes. The complexity of these practices may be surprising, and humanity always longs for simple solutions. But H. L. Mencken said, "for every complex problem there is an answer that is clear, simple and wrong".

Epilogue

The process of othering, the refusal to include somebody or something into our sense of self, is the source of many of our society's problems. Othering begins with the subject-object split, which we so prominently observe in the dichotomy of humans vs nature. Mystical experiences have the potential to heal this split. It is questionable whether this can be attained via drugs because drugs still follow the subject-object split via using a pharmaceutical approach, i.e. God in a pill.

As in the already quoted Puranic myth, the king of the mystics, Shiva, is again metaphorically sitting on the icy mountain top far removed from society, reflecting our society's abandoning of mysticism. The function of mysticism is the renewal of society, to integrate novelty, new views and ideas, without which society would stagnate in materialism, hedonism and empiricism.

Mystical states are there to expand our sense of self, to see all creatures and all matter as crystallizations of divine love. The integration of this realization makes us act responsibly in communal and ecological matters because it makes us see entities previously othered, such as ethnic groups, women, or the environment, now included in our sense of self. To be truly transformative, this is not something that can be taught as an intellectual exercise in our schools. It must be seen, experienced and integrated into one's psyche.

This becomes most consequential regarding our connection with nature. To see that all matter is the crystallized body of God, and that matter is crystallized divine love asks for a radical re-enchantment of the world. It asks for falling in love with the material world. It is because of matter we have a body, with which we can interact with other beings and can enjoy this life. Having a body is about falling in love with the material world, with nature. Notice that our society's current obsession with the body-beautiful is not a sign of being in love with one's body, but a sign of disembodiment.

Psychedelics could play a role for those who are not yet open to see the material world as the taking shape of spirit. However, psychedelics always entail risks and whether these can be mitigated enough by screening prospective candidates remains to be seen. Whether entheogens are employed or not, spiritual practice will always be the key. Spiritual practices can get us to exactly the same places where hallucinogens take us, but *sadhana* is wholistic and can be consciously accelerated and decelerated, depending on current needs.

When progressing in one's spiritual practice (whether this be yoga or any other), it is essential to understand there is no one-size-fits-all "enlightenment" or spiritual awakening. Rather, there is a variety of mystical states with differing functions. Pure consciousness states, states of devotional ecstasy, and shamanic sacred warrior states all have their intrinsic benefits, and, for the rapid spiritual evolution of humanity, are ideally all experienced side-by-side. The Menorah can teach us these states are not hierarchically ordered but spread out on a horizontal scale, more akin to the keys of a piano.

Mystical states can heal our confusion and end humanity's millennia-old fight against itself and against nature. To achieve that, we need to create a synthesis of science and spiritual practice. Science needs to be informed by mystical union with nature, achieved through spiritual practice. Our scientific, technological, and economic activities need to be informed

EPILOGUE

by mystical experiences, leading to an expanded sense of self. They teach us that our self does not end at our skin surface but encompasses all our surroundings and all other beings, too. A civilization based on bio-symbiosis and co-creation of all lifeforms can then use science to benefit all and the entire super-organism Gaia, rather than just for humans. For that to take place, the understanding must grow that divine love expresses itself as the cosmos, not only on one but on the four tiers of the map of transformative states (described in Chapter 8). We can then become the true guardians of this Garden of Eden.

Bibliography

Adams George C., *Badarayana's Brahma Sutras*

Attar, Farid-ud-din, *The Council of the Birds*

Bhagavad Gita

Bhagavata Purana

Blake, William – *Complete Works of William Blake*

Brhad Aranyaka Upanishad

Bucke, Richard Maurice - *Cosmic Consciousness*

Burroughs, William S. - *Naked Lunch*

Burroughs, William S. - *The Soft Machine*,

Burroughs, William S. - *The Yage Letters*

Burroughs, William S. – *Junkie*

Castaneda, Carlos - *The Teachings of Don Juan*

Chandogya Upanishad

Derrida, Jacques – *Of Grammatology*

Diamond, Jared - *Collapse*

Diamond, Jared – *Guns, Germs, and Steel*

Diamond, Jared – *The World Until Yesterday*

Dionysios, the Areopagite – *The Mystical Theology*

Eisenstein, Charles – *The Ascent of Humanity*

Eliade, Mircea - *Shamanism: Archaic Techniques of Ecstasy*

Fire, John - *Lame Deer Seeker of Wisdom*

Freud, Sigmund – *The Ego and the Id*

Freud, Sigmund – *The Psychopathology of Everyday Life*

Grof, Stanislav - *LSD Pathways to the Numinous*

Smith, Paul – *Diwan of Hafiz*

Hamill, Sam, *The Essential Chuang-tzu*

Hart, Dr. Carl, *Drug Use For Grown Ups- Chasing Liberty In The Land of Fear,*

Hoffman, Albert - *LSD: My Problem Child*

Huxley, Aldous - *The Perennial Philosophy*

Huxley, Aldous – *The Doors of Perception*

James, William - *Varieties of Religious Experience.*

Jung, Carl C., - *The Psychology of Kundalini Yoga*

Jung, Carl C., - *Transformation and Symbols of the Libido*

Tagore, R., *Songs of Kabir*

Kerouac, Jack - *On The Road*

Kesey, Ken – *One Flew Over the Cuckoo's Nest*

King James Bible

Krishna, Gopi - *Kundalini – Evolutionary Energy in Man*

Lao-tzu - *Tao Te King*

Leary, Timothy - *Politics of Ecstasy*

Lerner, Michael & Lyvers, Michael - *Values and beliefs of psychedelic drug users: a cross-cultural study*

Lévi, Éliphas - *Transcendental Magic, its Doctrine and Ritual*

Lilly, John C – *The Centre of the Cyclone*

MacLean, Paul D. - *The Triune Brain in Evolution*

Maehle, Gregor - *Pranayama: The Breath of Yoga*

Maehle, Gregor - *Yoga Meditation: Through Mantra, Chakras and Kundalini to Spiritual Freedom*

Maehle, Gregor – *Ashtanga Yoga Practice and Philosophy*

Maehle, Gregor – *Ashtanga Yoga The Intermediate Series*

Maehle, Gregor – *How To Find Your Life's Divine Purpose*

Maehle, Gregor – *Samadhi The Great Freedom*

Mahabharata

Maitri Upanishad

Marx, Karl - *Communist Manifesto*,

Maté, Gabor - *In the Realm of Hungry Ghosts*

McKenna, Terrence - *Food or the Gods*

McKenna, Terrence - *The Archaic Revival*

McKenna, Terrence - *The Invisible Landscape*

McKenna, Terrence - *True Hallucinations*

Meister Eckhart – *The Essential Sermons, Commentaries, Treatises and Defense*

Mohan, A.G. - *Yoga Yajnavalkya*

Murjani, Anita - *Dying To Be Me*

Narby, Jeremy - *The Cosmic Serpent.*

Ohler, Norman - *Blitzed: Drugs in Nazi Germany*

Padmasambhava - *Tibetan Book of the Dead*

Patanjali - *Yoga Sutra*

Pinchbeck, Daniel - *Breaking Open the Head- A Psychedelic Journey Into the Heart of Contemporary Shamanism*

Planck, Max - *Scientific Autobiography*

Plato - *Republic*

Plato - *The Last Days of Socrates*

Pollan, Michael - *How to Change Your Mind*

Prechtel, Martin - *Secrets of The Talking Jaguar*

R'abia of Basra – *Selected Poems*

Leary, T., Alpert, R. – *The Psychedelic Experience: A Manual Based on the Tibetan Book of the Dead*

Ram Dass, *Be Here Now*

Remarque, Erich Mari, - *All Quiet on the Western Front*

BIBLIOGRAPHY

Wilson, R. A., - *The New Inquisition: Irrational Rationalism and the Citadel of Science*

Barks, C., - *The Essential Rumi*

Sapolsky, Robert M - *Behave: The Biology of Humans at Our Best and Worst.*

Shankara – *Brahma Sutra Commentary*

Sri Aurobindo – *A Synthesis of Yoga*

Sri Aurobindo – *The Life Divine*

St. John of the Cross - *The Dark Night of the Soul*

Stevens, Jay - *Storming Heaven – LSD And The American Dream*

Strassman, Rick - *DMT The Spirit Molecule*

Strassman, Rick - *Inner Spaces*

Strassman, Rick MD, - *DMT and The Soul of Prophecy*

Strassman, Rick MD, - *DMT: The Spirit Molecule*

Swatmarama, *Hatha Yoga Pradipika*

Thompson, Hunter S., - *Fear and Loathing in Las Vegas*

Underhill, Evelyn - *Mysticism*

Vasishta Samhita

Wolfe, Tom – *The Cool Aid Acid Test*

Zerzan, John – *Future Primitive Revisited*

Author Information

Gregor started his yogic practices in the late 1970s. In the mid-80s he commenced yearly travels to India, where he learned from various yogic and tantric masters, traditional Indian *sadhus* and ascetics. He lived many years as a recluse, studying Sanskrit and yogic scripture and practicing yogic techniques.

Gregor's textbook series consisting of *Ashtanga Yoga: Practice and Philosophy, Ashtanga Yoga: The Intermediate Series, Pranayama: The Breath of Yoga, Yoga Meditation: Through Mantra, Chakras and Kundalini to Spiritual Freedom, Samadhi The Great Freedom, How to Find Your Life's Divine Purpose and Chakras, Drugs and Evolution* have sold over 100,000 copies worldwide and so far have been translated into eight languages. His blog articles can be found at www.chintamaniyoga.com.

Today Gregor integrates all aspects of yoga into his teaching in the spirit of Patanjali and T. Krishnamacharya. His zany sense of humour, manifold personal experiences, vast and in-depth knowledge of scripture, Indian philosophies, and yogic techniques combine to make Gregor's teachings easily applicable, relevant, and accessible to his students. He offers workshops, retreats and teacher trainings worldwide.

 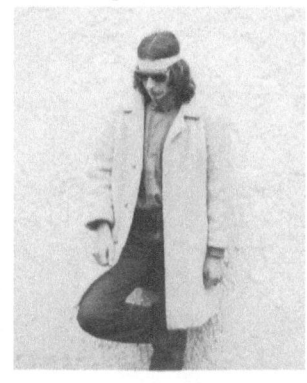

The author in 2020   The author in 1979

www.ingramcontent.com/pod-product-compliance
Lightning Source LLC
Chambersburg PA
CBHW020053200426
43197CB00050B/501